BODY SYMBOLISM IN THE BIBLE

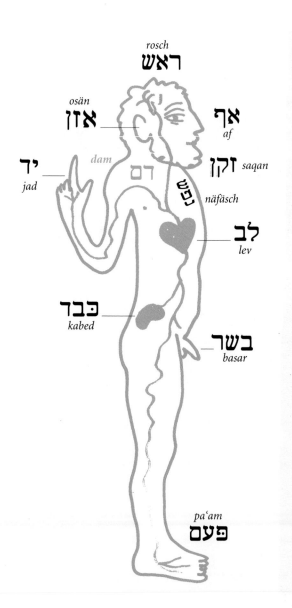

rosch
ראש

osän
אזן

af
אף

dam
דם

jad
יד

saqan
זקן

näfäsch
נפש

lev
לב

kabed
כבד

basar
בשר

pa'am
פעם

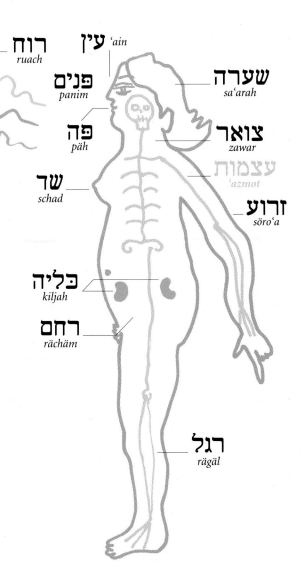

רוּחַ
ruach

עַיִן ʿain

פָּנִים
panim

שֵׂעָרָה
saʿarah

פֶּה
päh

צַוָּאר
zawar

עֲצָמוֹת
ʿazmot

שַׁד
schad

זְרוֹעַ
söroʿa

כִּלְיָה
kiljah

רֶחֶם
rächäm

רֶגֶל
rägäl

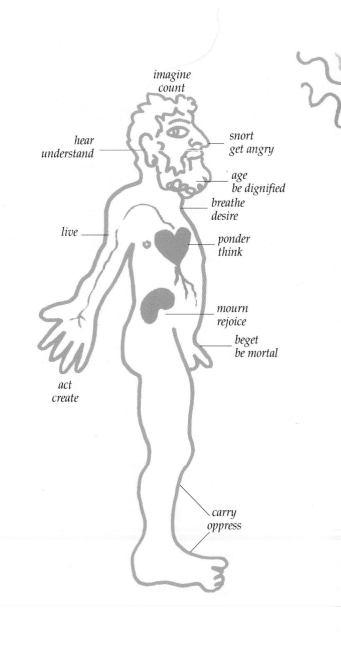

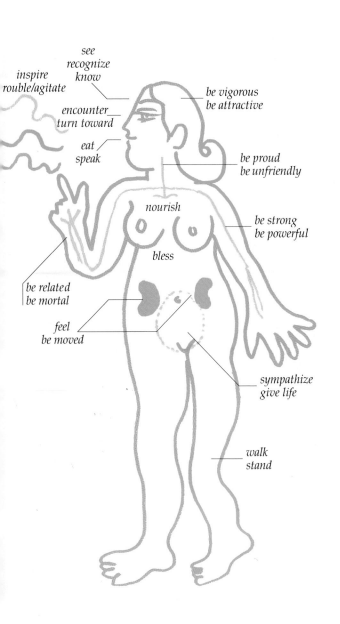

Body Symbolism in the Bible

Silvia Schroer
Thomas Staubli

TRANSLATED BY

Linda M. Maloney

A Michael Glazier Book

THE LITURGICAL PRESS
Collegeville, Minnesota

www.litpress.org

For Othmar Keel

A Michael Glazier Book Published by The Liturgical Press

Cover design by David Manahan, O.S.B. Illustration: *Adam and Eve,* manuscript detail from the Liebana Beatus Commentary, Guadalupe, Spain, 10th c., The Art Archive/Real biblioteca de lo Escorial.

Originally published as *Die Körpersymbolik der Bibel.* Darmstadt, Germany: Wissenschaftliche Buchgesellschaft, 1998.

Translations of biblical passages marked with an * are from the authors' German text. All other biblical passages are taken from the New Revised Standard Version Bible, Catholic edition, © 1989 by the Division of Christian Education of the National Council of Churches of Christ in the U.S.A. Used by permission. All rights reserved.

1	2	3	4	5	6	7	8

Library of Congress Cataloging-in-Publication Data
Schroer, Silvia, 1958–
    [Körpersymbolik der Bibel. English]
    Body symbolism in the Bible / Silvia Schroer, Thomas Staubli ; translated by Linda M. Maloney.
      p. cm.
    Includes bibliographical references (p.) and index.
    ISBN 0-8146-5954-3 (alk. paper)
    1. Body, Human—Biblical teaching. I. Staubli, Thomas, 1962–
II. Title.

BS680.B6 S37 2001
233'.5—dc21

                               2001029958

Contents

Foreword

While the old are artificially kept alive in the hospitals of the overdeveloped world, in the underdeveloped world people die young of malnutrition. We can read the situation of the world in the condition of its bodies. Hearts that suffer because of obesity, lungs clogged by nicotine, and livers marked by excessive alcohol consumption may from time to time send the feet of their owners to the bookstore, and the brain immerses itself in books on dieting, fitness training, yoga exercises, yin and yang, chakras and reincarnation.

Many people seek healing and meaning in religions and practices that are only weakly inculturated among us. Our understanding and use of this foreign wisdom is often correspondingly superficial, but it is easy to understand against the background of a centuries-long Christian history of interpreting the Bible in a way inimical to the body. Women in particular experience the deficiencies of our tradition with respect to bodily spirituality as a grave problem. Historical experiences are generalized, the concrete is allegorized, the material is spiritualized, the earthly is made heavenly. Thus, for example, the throat becomes the soul (see Chapter Two). We would like, for once, to move backward from soul to throat and attempt to show that the body is a temple of God and that regard for it leads to respect for human rights, the rights of women and men.

We do not claim to have given this topic an exhaustive treatment. We are also aware that the field of biblical anthropology is much broader than the little snippet we have chosen for our approach, the theme of body and bodiliness. More important to us than completeness was clarity and an impulse to readers to think further on their own. The book is based on ten half-hour Sunday meditations broadcast on DRS II radio, the second channel for German and Romansch Switzerland, in 1994–1996. The response to those broadcasts encouraged us to make some fundamental revisions of the texts, to give them an introduction and—most important of all—illustrations from the biblical environment, and to present them as a book.

Even this minor effort would not have been possible without the aid of people whom we wish to thank most sincerely at this point, above and before all our teacher and friend Othmar Keel. He taught us that theology is not an abstract science, but is rooted in miracles small and great, and also in the banalities of daily life. In his decades of investigation of ancient Near Eastern symbolic images he has repeatedly pointed out anthropological symbols. He was most generous in giving us access, for the illustrations in this book, to the collection he has built in the Biblical Institute in Fribourg. Hence the book is dedicated to him. In addition, Barbara Brunner, Dr. Katja Guth, Rolf Notter, Dr. Kurt Studhalter, and Prof. Dr. Christoph Uehlinger gave us advice or aided us in our search for material. Barbara Brunner also "relieved" the manuscript of many errors and made the index of biblical passages.

Abbreviations

ANET   *Ancient Near Eastern Texts Relating to the Old Testament,* ed. James B. Pritchard. Princeton 1950, 1955.

NHThG   *Neues Handbuch theologischer Grundbegriffe.* Munich.

TRE   *Theologische Realenzyklopädie.* Berlin and New York.

TUAT   Texte aus der Umwelt des Alten Testaments. Vols. 1–3. Gütersloh 1982–97.

Introduction

I. Aspects of Theological Anthropology: From the Human Being to the Male and Female Body

1. "And God made humankind in the divine image."
Human beings as images of God

The abbreviated Christian formula "image of God" (Latin *imago Dei*) as a theological description of the human being originates in the first creation story in Genesis, where we read:

> Then God said, "Let us make humankind in our image, according to our likeness; and let them have dominion over the fish of the sea, and over the birds of the air, and over the cattle, and over all the wild animals of the earth, and over every creeping thing that creeps upon the earth." So God created humankind in his image, in the image of God he created them; male and female he created them (Gen 1:26-27).

This text has provoked a great many questions: What do image (*ṣelem*) and likeness (*dəmut*) mean? How, exactly, should we understand the relationship between God and humankind? Why is God sometimes referred to in the plural, sometimes in the singular? And especially: how can we reconcile the human as image of God with the demand found elsewhere that no one should make an image of God? The discussion of these puzzles and paradoxes has filled entire libraries. Indeed, one can justly and rightly assert that Christian anthropology is to a great extent a speculative *imago Dei* theology in which one can perceive a number of different strands of tradition.[1]

1

- The Augustinian-Thomistic tradition uses the metaphor of the *imago Dei* to ground the graced likeness of the human being to God, which makes it possible for them to enter into a relationship with their Creator within a covenant offered to them by God.[2]
- The mystical tradition, as developed, for example, by Gregory of Nyssa, sees this as the basis of the co-creative freedom of the human being, which is inherent in its character as image but also calls it to a resemblance to God: that is, it is a path to divinity.[3]
- Through the inspiration of Karl Marx this tradition was appropriated in the modern period in a social sense, with emphasis on the aspect of human governance of creation (Gen 1:28).[4] According to this view human beings only realize their potential as image of God when they succeed in abolishing alienated relationships of production, when workers find meaning in their labor and are able to enjoy the fruits of their labor. This theology presupposes something never asserted before the Reformation: namely, the possibility that the human character as image of God could be lost.
- Currently, theology focuses on the knowledge that the image is divided by gender difference, and is only realized in the relationship of man and woman, that is, through a communicative process. This paradigm is also formulated in christological and trinitarian terms. Christ is the son of humanity who appeared in history. "Whoever has seen me has seen the Father" (John 14:9). By not making the differentness of the other the starting point for a violent conflict, but instead a beneficial communication, he opened up the future. In a trinitarian perspective we find revealed in Christ what was already true in God, namely a living *communio*, a unity differentiated within itself, which, for example, Karl Barth saw affirmed in the plural challenge "let *us* make humankind . . ." (Gen 1:26a).

Only timidly and, especially in Germany, only after World War II did Old Testament scholarship dare to withstand the pressure toward dogmatic speculation. (See Section 4, "What is the human being . . . ?" below).[5] The results[6] have been less generalized and elevated than those of the dogmatic theologians, but instead concrete and closer to real life. According to these scholars the word "image" *(ṣelem)* is to be understood as referring to freestanding or relief sculptures or small figures used to represent a power. The word "likeness" *(dəmut)*, used in parallel, describes the similarity of the figure to its model. Both words are found, in Aramaic, on a stele from the ninth century B.C.E., bearing a text in two languages, which was found at Tell el Fecherije (see Figure 1). The parallel Assyrian text has only the word *ṣalmu*. The statue shows the ruler of the city at prayer. It originally stood in the temple of the god Hadad of Guzana, to whom it was dedicated. According to the usual custom, the inscription, invoking curses on later generations, warns against replacing the name of this city ruler with those of others. This temptation was all the greater in that the statue not only expressed the gratitude and devotion of the ruler toward the god, but at the same time demanded of the people that they respect the ruler thus represented.

The observed impact of images had as its consequence that people saw

Figure 1:
Statue of Hadad-Ishi from Tell el Fecherije, formerly Guzana, in Syria, written in two languages (9th century B.C.E.). The beginning of the Aramaic inscription reads: "The *statue* of Hadad-Ishi, erected to Hadan of Sikani (= Guzana), the canal inspector of heaven and earth, who sends down wealth and gives pasture and drink to all lands, and who gives rest and sacrificial gifts to all the gods, his brothers, the canal inspector of all rivers, who provides a good life to all lands, the merciful god to whom it is good to pray, who dwells in Sikani, the great Lord, (his) lord."

them as effective real-symbols of what they depicted, and they worshiped the power of the image itself as an aspect of the deity. In Mesopotamia this god was called Ea, in Egypt he was Ptah. When, accordingly, Near Eastern kings saw themselves as representative images of god on earth they laid claim to a share of the active power of the deities who protected and blessed them (see Figure 2).

This interpretation of kingship was democratized in Israel and Judah, where the royal psalms were read as popular prayers. Every woman and man could, in fact must, see himself or herself as a representative image of God on earth, participated through the projection of her or his personality in the power of God, could claim her or his rights, but was also obligated to assume royal responsibility toward the neighbor and creation itself. The central significance of a biblical anthropology is obvious in the context of this biblical concept of the image of God in the living male-female human being; such an anthropology discovers in concrete bodies the symbolic, or better, the sacramental presence of God.

2. *"The human being has no advantage over the beast."* *The vulnerable creature*

The outstanding position of the human being in the two creation accounts in Genesis 1 and 2 is in some sense deceptive

Figure 2:
Underside of a scarab from Der el-Balah in Palestine (13th c. B.C.E.). The Egyptian god Ptah is usually depicted as a stiffly standing statue with a staff. Another motif frequently found in Palestine on seals in scarab form shows a somewhat smaller god alongside Ptah; this second god has a falcon's head with the sun's disk (Re-Harakhti) touching Ptah's staff, as a sign that he shares in the power of the great god. In Palestine Ptah was identified with El and the falcon-headed god with the king or with Baal. This constellation of sharing in the power of the god depicted as statue lived on, in altered form, in the Priestly document's concept of the male-female human being as image of God. Elohim takes the place of Ptah, and the human being replaces Re-Harakhti or the king.

as far as the biblical image of the human is concerned; however, it is not so much the texts themselves as the history of their interpretation that is at fault. For one thing, the book of Job (especially chs. 38–39) and Psalm 104 show that Israel's sages were not necessarily of the opinion that the human being was the crown or the center of the whole creation. They assigned humans a place *alongside* all the other creatures, each of which has its own reason for existence and all of whom know, according to Job 12:7-10, that God is their creator. Moreover, the high opinion of human beings that is expressed in the idea of the *imago Dei* (cf. also Gen 5:1) is not representative. The idea that the human being is only a little less than "the gods" or "God" is expressed in this pointed fashion only by Psalm 8:

> . . . what are human beings that you are mindful of them,
>   mortals that you care for them?
> Yet you have made them a little lower than God,
>   and crowned them with glory and honor.
> You have given them dominion over the works of your hands;
>   you have put all things under their feet,
> all sheep and oxen,
>   and also the beasts of the field,
> the birds of the air, and the fish of the sea,
>   whatever passes along the paths of the seas (Ps 8:4-8).

The overall tenor of the biblical texts is quite different: human life is short, threatened by all kinds of dangers, and especially marked by weakness, mortality, and sin. Human life is a breath (Job 7:7, 16; Pss 39:5; 62:9; 94:11; 144:4), a shadow (Ps 39:6); it is like grass that withers (Ps 103:15) or like spilled water (2 Sam 14:14). It comes from earth and dust (filth), and it inevitably returns there; in fact, the existence of the earth-creature "Adam" is that of dust (cf. Job 7:21; 10:9; 34:14-15; Pss 90:3; 104:29; Sir 33:10):

> As a father has compassion for his children,
>   so the LORD has compassion for those who fear him.
> For he knows how we were made;
>   he remembers that we are dust (Ps 103:13-14).

Death is the great human equalizer. Whatever their fate on earth may have been, in the end they return to dust (Job 21:23-26;

Psalm 49). In this common fate humans and animals are also closely related and bound to one another. Not only were both drawn from the same earth; the dark fate of death joins them together as well (cf. Ps 49:12, 20):

> For the fate of humans and the fate of animals is the same;
> as one dies, so dies the other.
> They all have the same breath,
> and humans have no advantage over the animals;
> for all is vanity.
> All go to one place; all are from the dust, and all turn to dust again.
> Who knows whether the human spirit goes upward and the spirit of animals goes downward to the earth? (Qoh 3:19-21).

The Israelites did not reject the inalterable fact of having to die. Death at a ripe age, when a person is sated with life, they could accept (Job 5:26, and elsewhere). Mortality is not simply abolished, even in the age of salvation to come (Isa 65:20-23). On the other hand, an untimely death is the greatest misfortune; it is seen as theft of the years of one's life, a breaking down of life's dwelling, and a senseless cutting of the fabric of life (Isa 38:10-13).

3. "Ecce homo." Philosophical and theological answers to the human question

In its approach to the "human mystery" the Bible has opened a huge spectrum, and the refinements attempted by philosophy and theology are correspondingly manifold. The following overview is by no means complete or balanced.[7] Instead, what we want to do is to draw attention to some aspects of a theological anthropology that are particularly questionable or worthy of consideration, and to attempt to show why we are more interested in the symbolism of the concrete male and female body than in abstract speculations about Adam, the man/human being.

JEWISH TEACHING ABOUT ADAM

The question of the human being as such is most concrete in Judaism in discussion of the significance of Adam. On the one hand he represents the primeval human being, the human in Paradise, and as such is not only prior to all other human beings but also superior to them. Thus at the end of a long listing of men who were important figures in salvation history in the book of Jesus Sirach we find: "Shem and Seth and Enosh were honored, but above every other created living being was Adam" (Sir 49:16).[8] On the other hand, Adam is seen as the author of sin. This has its historical explanation: Adam stands at the beginning of a fateful chain of human involvement in sin, the end of which is not in sight. This pessimistic view of history is expressed in apocalyptic literature, which hopes for an eschatological redeemer. But Adam can also be interpreted prototypically as the symbol of the sinful human being, newly actualized in every individual sinner. What is crucial for the Jewish understanding of humanity is that God planned for the possibility of sin in creating Adam, by giving the human being free will: "The Holy One, blessed be He, gave [Adam] a choice of two ways, that of life and that of death, but he chose the way of death" (*Mekh. Y* 112). But according to the rabbis God is prepared, even till the end of time, to share the consequences of what God dared in creating.[9]

CHRISTIAN DIALECTIC BETWEEN ADAM AND CHRIST

What is unique in the Christian view of humanity is that now the eschatological Christ is set over against the primeval Adam. For the evangelist Luke he is the last shoot of Adam's family tree (Luke 3:38) who withstood Satan's temptations; in this connection Mark describes him as master of the wild beasts and the angels (Mark 1:13; cf. Figure 4). Most significant for the future, as regards this Christian view of humanity, was undoubtedly Paul's interpretation of Christ as the new, or rather the last Adam: "'The first man, Adam, became a living being'; the last Adam [= Christ] became a life-giving spirit" (1 Cor 15:45). Adam is seen as the type of the future human being who was first revealed in Christ (Rom 5:14). Paul derives an extensive doctrine of redemption from this fundamental constellation: as Adam's sin put an end to the blessed primeval time, so with Jesus' cross and resurrection the blessed endtime begins.

Greek-educated Jews appear to have felt great pressure to harmonize the Platonic idea of the perfect human being with the real human being, revealed by Jewish Wisdom and prophecy as sinful. Philo of Alexandria (1st c. C.E.) distinguished a divine idea of the perfect, androgynous human being,[10] which according to him was presented in Genesis 1, from the image of God that was then created, according to Genesis 2–3. The latter derived, he said, from the creator Spirit (demiurge), and reflected in itself a microcosm of the world. Paul of Tarsus translated Genesis 1 into christology, while Genesis 2–3 remained reserved for Adam.

GNOSTIC SPECULATIONS ABOUT ADAM

Gnostic interpretations of Adam[11] also read Genesis 1–3 through Neoplatonic glasses, distinguishing the androgynously-conceived inner human supposedly represented in Genesis 1 from the external, body-soul human who appears in Genesis 2–3. The existence of the latter is explained as the work of a creator Spirit (demiurge). When God bent down from the world above, the divine body was reflected in the waters of chaos. The demiurge and his mother, divine Wisdom, constructed the human being according to that image, in a process that is differently described in Gnostic literature. Since the creative entities, in contrast to the perfect God, were imperfect spirits who only worked according to an imperfect reflection, the human was an imperfect being. By the introduction of these divine beings both God and the human being could be absolved of any guilt.

THE HUMAN IN ISLAM: BETWEEN GOD AND THE DEVIL

The key figure in Islamic doctrine of the human is Iblis (Satan), who, unlike the other angels, refused to pay homage to the divine image God had created: "And when We said to the angels: 'Prostrate yourselves before Adam,' they all prostrated themselves except [Iblis], who in his pride refused and became an unbeliever" (Sura 2:34).[12] As a consequence humanity was divided into the servants of Allah and the followers of Iblis, who will be called to account at the judgment. Adam and his successors, however, could also be regarded as God's caliphs (deputies) on earth, replacing the fallen angels (cf. Sura 2:30).

TRIUMPH OVER THE BODY IN WESTERN PHILOSOPHY

"When the Bible is read with a Platonic, Neoplatonic, or Aristotelian 'lens' the patriarchal interpretation of the biblical passages on women is reinforced, even though there were some exceptions, such as Renaissance Neoplatonism, that allowed for a positive image of women."[13] What Elisabeth Gössmann writes about women is true also of the body. Among the exceptions to which she alludes we should include Hildegard of Bingen, with her holistic thought in which the holy body has a place of honor. Certainly there are other exceptions, but none of them was accorded any regard by the theology and philosophy of the powerful. This last arrived, in the modern period, at an absolutely pessimistic view of the human according to which the human being is a wolf. Modern theories of the state and ethical systems are founded on that fundamental anthropological principle. For Kant the body was just adequate for the purpose of knowledge. The high point in this systematic repression of the body[14] was German Idealism, for which the spirit, the idea, and the state that propagated them were everything, while the bodies of others— proletarians in the European factories and plantation workers in the colonies—were of no significance. This contempt for the body led to its abuse, and thence to the exploitation of Nature— a merciless mechanism that even today, despite world wars and catastrophes (Three Mile Island, Bhopal, Chernobyl, Schweizerhalle, etc.), is taking on more and more drastic proportions.

THE STAR OF REDEMPTION IN THE FACE OF GOD

We think it was Franz Rosenzweig who decisively opened the windows of German philosophy and theology to the First Testament and its corporeal proclamation of God. His major work, *Der Stern der Erlösung [The Star of Redemption]*, written in the last hours of German-Jewish symbiosis and enjoying a broader reception than ever today among Jews, Christians, and Muslims, climaxes in an image for visible truth. That image is the face of God, which cannot be pictured otherwise than in the face of the neighbor, at the highest point of his or her bodiliness. In the human face Rosenzweig discovers the star of redemption, consisting of two superimposed triangles of the receptive and active points of life.

The basic level is ordered according to the receptive organs; they are the building blocks, as it were, which together compose the face, the mask, namely forehead and cheeks, to which belong respectively nose and ears. Nose and ears are the organs of pure receptivity. The nose belongs to the forehead; in the sacred [Hebrew] tongue it veritably stands for the face as a whole. The scent of offerings turns to it as the motion of the lips to the ears. This first triangle is thus formed by the midpoint of the forehead, as the dominant point of the entire face, and the midpoints of the cheeks. Over it is now imposed a second triangle, composed of the organs whose activity quickens the rigid mask of the first: eyes and mouth. . . . Just as the structure of the face is dominated by the forehead, so its life, all that surrounds the eyes and shines forth from the eyes, is gathered in the mouth. The mouth is the consummator and fulfiller of all expression of which the countenance is capable, both in speech as, at last, in the silence behind which speech retreats: in the kiss. It is in the eyes that the eternal countenance shines for [the human being]; it is the mouth by whose words [the human being] lives. . . .[15]

THE TRUTH IN THE OTHERNESS OF OTHERS

Emmanuel Lévinas took up the thread from Rosenzweig. Lévinas, the stump of a Jewish family murdered in the Holocaust, made the starting point of his philosophy the phenomenon of exteriority, the other in his or her otherness, which was brought to the point of extinction in the concentration camps. "[The human being] as Other comes to us from the outside, a separated—or holy—face. His exteriority, that is, his appeal, is his truth."[16] Exteriority is the key category in the philosophy of liberation, which is thereby radically distinguished from the bourgeois philosophy of *cogito ergo sum* ("I think, therefore I am"). It is experienced in its shocking concreteness in the address of the Other—How are you?—and most shockingly of all in his or her cry: Help me! I am hungry! Give me bread! Even the imprisoned, tortured body stripped of its dignity cries out: I am someone! I am a person! I have rights!

The very body, the corporeality, the flesh of the oppressed (their hungry, tortured, violated bodies), when exposed (as the hero is "exposed" before the firing squad) within the system, is a subversion of the law and order that alienates them. It is the revelation of the Absolute in history as an epiphany, not only a phenomenon, an epiphany through the poor. The face (*pnín* in Hebrew, *prosopon* in Greek), the person, the corporality, the flesh *(basar)* of the poor is itself the originating word *(dabar)* from which arises the philosophy of liberation. Philosophy of liberation does not think about words; it thinks about reality.[17]

THE SACRAMENTALITY OF THE BODY

In liberation theology the existential initiative just described is taken up and further developed in the praxis of liturgy, *diakonia,* and proclamation. The starting point for theology is listening to the people.[18] The people are not the anonymous mass, a manipulable crowd, but a living organism. Their powerlessness is shown in the fragility of their societies and organizations, their suffering in the relationships, biographies, and bodies of individuals. The bent back, the disordered menstruation, the scarred skin, the amputated leg, the dry breast: all these point urgently, as signs, to unhealthy working conditions, the distress of women in a society ruled by *machismo,* the merciless violence of the police apparatus in service of the ruling elites, the consequences of land mines buried since the last war, the dependence of the Two-Thirds World on the economic dictatorship of the First. It is no accident that the black doctor Frantz Fanon, in the wake of a savage confrontation with the broken bodies and souls of the victims of the war in Algiers, was driven to become the first to propose a comprehensive theory of liberation from colonial powers.[19]

The broken body is the *dia-bolus* of the distant God, the symbol of the diabolical, while the sound body is a symbol of divine presence: a sacrament. Leonardo Boff[20] has vividly shown that everything that fills the universe can become a sacrament, that is, contains the possibility of being transparent to the divine. The traditional seven sacraments of the Catholic Church (baptism, confirmation, Eucharist, marriage, anointing of the sick, reconciliation, and orders) are only some particularly thick density points of divine grace, nodal points of life. However, the human body is also a central sacrament because we dwell within it and it is constantly present to us in others.

Therefore the body of Christ is the most prominent image for meditation in Christianity. In the Eucharist, the good gift, the bread of life (of which Jesus said "this is my body") it is the symbol of the fullness of divine blessing; in the figure of the Crucified it is the *dia-bolus* of the godforsaken damned of this earth; in the glorified body of the Risen One it is the revolutionary symbol of the victor over the powers and mighty forces of destruction.

PHYSICAL COMMUNITY AS COMMITTED CHURCH

Liturgical contemplation of the body of Christ corresponds to attention to the bodies of our neighbors. In particular, the Church in Latin America has for that very reason, in recent decades, been in the forefront of the struggle for human rights. This work brings the broken, marginalized body of the other, condemned to silence, into the center; it makes a record of the acts of the criminals in charge of the state; it places them before the consciences of the world public and thus gives the silent a voice. In this way it has given testimony to the faith, and in many lands it has accepted severe persecution as a consequence, often ending in martyrdom, the destruction of bodies. Not seldom the Church offices of human rights were and are the only organizations that represent the interests of the people against a corrupt state. This work is by no means a matter of course, because human rights are a fruit of the Enlightenment, which, because of its anticlerical ideology, was regarded by the Church for a very long time as a hostile movement.

At the same time liberation-theological anthropology[21] insists unmistakably that it is the Church's duty to forge a courageous path between the collectivism absolutized in Communism and the individualism idolized in the form of the market economy in capitalism, a path that mediates between person and society and advances the cause of both. The starting point for the realization of the Pauline promise of a new creation (2 Cor 5:17) is, within the Church as well, the Others, the weak. Only then can the Church become an organism that need not feel ashamed of being compared with the body of Christ. What is called for is a Church that is a "community of communities" departing from authoritarianism (authoritarian structures and authoritarian attitudes), and what are needed are responsible persons who show themselves to be "masters of spiritual direction."

WOMEN'S LIVES AS THE MEASURE OF LIBERATION

For the Brazilian religious Ivone Gebara, liberation begins with the resurrection of women, their entry into places that for so long have been inaccessible to them: politics, jobs and professions, theology. Her subjects are women who understand that their life means more than obeying their husbands, going about with swollen bellies and delivering another generation of daughters to misery and daily humiliation. In her "humanocentric" anthropology, which centers not on "man," but on the differentiated existence of men and women, their mutual direction to one another, and their historical variety, the starting point is not the spirit, but the body.[22] For a theology on those premises the traditional categories are no longer adequate, since even today theological scholarship in large measure remains under the spell of a patriarchal triumphalism in which the human spirit is more human and therefore more divine than the human body. This is connected to a gender hierarchy according to which the man is A, the woman B (so Karl Barth: see pp. 18–20 below). Old Testament exegesis, whose task should be the interpretation of texts, is caught in the wake of this male-centered theology with its skeptical attitude toward the body. It has seen the *imago Dei* as self-command (Franz Delitzsch), the sense of the eternal, the true, and the good (August Dillmann), self-knowledge, the ability to think, and immortality (Eduard König), reason (Paul Heinisch), personhood (Otto Proksch, Ernst Sellin), spiritual superiority (Walter Eichrodt), spiritual capacities and the infused nobility of a ruler (Benno Jacob), divine viziership (Johannes Hempel), but almost never the body (Hermann Gunkel) or the flesh (Gerhard von Rad).[23]

When today especially Latin American theologians like Ivone Gebara make women's bodies the starting point of their theology, we are faced with a manifestation of a deep-seated conversion to a new way of thinking that finds its finest bases in the biblical tradition. The sound and undamaged, or the raped and dishonored female body is the focal point for many feminist theologies.[24] The palette of feminist theology in Europe has also been colored for years by confrontation with the widest variety of forms of violence against women. The priority thus announced corresponds, at the deepest level, to the convictions retained in the biblical tradition. If woman is the image of God, if her body is a temple of the Holy Spirit, every injury to her integrity is blasphemy against God and desecration of a temple.

4. "What is the human being . . . ?"
In search of a body-oriented biblical anthropology

The question of the human—this much, at least, our sketch of philosophical and theological concepts of anthropology must have made clear—must be posed more concretely, as a question of human bodies, indeed, as a question of individual parts of the human body: hand, heart, head. Hans Walter Wolff made an important stride in that direction in 1973 in his anthropology of the Old Testament. However, certain filters and accents in his treatment provoke resistance on our part. James Barr has raised a massive objection against the semantic reconstruction of a biblical anthropology, and we cannot let that objection stand unchallenged either. But the urgent appeals of feminist theologians for the overcoming of androcentric anthropology show us clearly what kind of contribution we hope to make with this book.

HANS WALTER WOLFF'S OLD TESTAMENT ANTHROPOLOGY[25]

In his search for an answer to the question "how, in the Old Testament, the human being is brought to self-knowledge," Wolff employed an anthropological theory of language to help him unpack "the being of the human." He thus set up a clear signal against the long tradition of anti-body interpretation, and that signal attracted considerable attention.[26] An investigation of the Hebrew word complexes applying to parts of the body reveals a complete psycho-somatic system, not derived from esoteric principles, but resting on observation of the body and life experience, and indebted to a linguistic system that, in contrast to the Greek, had developed scarcely any abstract concepts; rather, its origins in concrete physicality were still clearly visible.

Despite this inductive initiative, however, at crucial points Wolff remained the prisoner of systematic prejudices. His male and Protestant-professorial view of human reality led him not only to insights, but also to distortions. We may illustrate with three examples:

1. Although the eye (mentioned 868 times) is, among body parts, the third most frequently mentioned in the Hebrew Bible (after the face, 2040 times and the hand, 1617 times), Wolff, limited by his word-centered theology of hearing, did not examine the eye's symbolism. It is true that he could not avoid observing that the eye often appears together with the ear (Prov 20:12), and that seeing, together with hearing, is necessary for observing the deeds of YHWH (Exod 14:13, 31; Deut 29:1-3; Isa 43:8). "But the opening of the eyes happens through the word: Exod 14:13-14, 30-31; Isa 43:8-13 [12!]; 30:20-21. Thus the superior value of the ear and language for genuine human understanding is unmistakable."[27] In Chapter Five we will show that the Bible is unaware of such superiority of the ear, and in fact developed its own theology of the eyes that is worth knowing.

2. That Wolff, despite his claim to a linguistic foundation of *human* existence, really had only *male* existence in view is shown by the fact that he completely overlooked an organ that is central to biblical metaphors for God: the womb. This is an especially striking example of the blank spots in a science dominated by men. In Chapter Three the rich symbolism of the womb in Near Eastern thought will be more fully explored.

3. In a chapter entitled "Distortions of Love" prostitution, fornication, promiscuity, rape, divorce, celibacy, homosexuality, sodomy, and transvestism are lumped together. It is symptomatic that in this very chapter the Old Testament scholar Wolff twice applies Karl Barth's church dogmatics to emphasize biblical value judgments. When he assigns morality to Israel and immorality to Canaan, Wolff perpetuates a very common anti-Canaanite cliché that is no more historically tenable than the anti-Jewish prejudices of Christian literature.[28] And when he cites only the standard legal texts on homosexuality (Lev 18:22;

20:13), but makes no mention of David's love for Jonathan,[29] his work tends to foster an attitude that is unprepared to respect the difference of the Other, at least in regard to sexuality.

We have no desire in saying this to belittle Wolff's achievement; we only want to warn against systematic narrowing and exclusivity. This is evident when Wolff, in responding to the reviews of his book in the Afterword to the third edition, did not feel compelled to address the themes just mentioned, but did find it necessary to defend himself against those who deplored the absence of the "sinful" human being in his anthropology. It is also evident from the fact that a Festschrift for Wolff, appearing just twenty years after the publication of his *Anthropology,* contained no contribution by a woman, nor were pictorial materials yet addressed as possible sources.[30]

JAMES BARR'S OBJECTIONS TO A BIBLICAL ANTHROPOLOGY

We find some fundamental challenges to Wolff's project and his method in James Barr's book, *The Semantics of Biblical Language,* which appeared in English in 1961 and was translated into German in 1965.[31] Wolff cited Barr's work in a footnote but did not enter at all into the debate. Barr's sharp criticism was directed, as far as biblical scholarship was concerned, primarily at Thorleif Bomann's *Das hebräische Denken im Vergleich mit dem griechischen* (Göttingen: Vandenhoeck & Ruprecht, 1952; 6th ed. 1977) and at the *Theological Dictionary of the New Testament,* edited by Gerhard Kittel and Gerhard Friedrich (whose publication began in German in 1933). Barr questioned whether a people's language can provide evidence of its thought structures. He accused Bomann and others of setting up a psychological opposition between Hebrew and Greek thought by comparing text groups and genres, as well as epochs, that were not at all comparable in that way. Barr considered it impossible to derive the meaning of words in a foreign language by discerning a field of meaning from a group of perhaps ten examples in order, then, to apply the meaning to the eleventh instance. For him the concrete context in which a concept appears, not a comparative statistic, is the only semantic evidence for its meaning. In saying this, Barr in fact called into question the presuppositions and methods of all the dictionaries of the exegetical guild.

Barr would have to repeat his criticisms against Wolff and also against this book, for we also presume that a concept like *nephesh* gives us a clue for unlocking the thinking and the image of the human in Israel or in particular writings. Barr's book, as far as we can tell, despite its rapid translation, was scarcely noticed in the German-speaking world, and its theses were never fully discussed. That was probably not solely because of the provocative nature of the book, but also because of a certain complacency in German exegesis, which only reluctantly gave (and gives) ear to scholarly developments in other languages. We cannot present a comprehensive dialogue with Barr at this point, but some arguments that encourage us to hold to the approach we have chosen must be mentioned here.

1. It seems very questionable to us that the structure, grammar, and semantics of a language offer no insights into the thought structures of its speakers. Of course not too much can be derived from a single phenomenon, but the absence of concepts or an especially broad differentiation within a semantic field has—reciprocally—a great deal to do with the thinking and ideas of the people who speak the language. A very current example of this is the feminist challenge to the androcentric pattern of a great many languages spoken today, but also to ancient languages. Only in a culture that thinks androcentrically and is patriarchally ordered could languages arise that use grammatically masculine forms as generic, so that women or the feminine for the most part—but not consistently—are included without explicitly appearing. Feminist exegesis has also demonstrated that the grammatical gender of a word, particularly in Hebrew, is not irrelevant, but that femaleness or femininity is frequently and consciously included in the concept, for example in the case of the word *rūaḥ*.[32]

We find evidence of the connection between thought, world-images, and language also in ancient Near Eastern art. Pictures are less artificial than semantic constructions, yet the art of ancient cultures is certainly comparable to language in its structures, grammar, and "vocabulary" (iconeme, motifs). The world of pictures thus offers us a corrective factor for our assessment of linguistic phenomena. The unique features of the art of ancient Egypt and western Asia have been described by Heinrich Schäfer, Emma Brunner-Traut, Othmar Keel, and others. They undoubtedly offer us insights into the thought of people of the ancient Near East, and numerous parallels to the linguistic phenomena of those times and places can be discerned.[33]

2. We agree with Barr when he says that it is not appropriate to do theology (and certainly not to preach) purely through a system of concepts. Theologically it is the texts and their context, not a semantic field, that are relevant. We attend to this objection—as have Wolff and many others—by quoting and situating the biblical texts as frequently as possible.

3. The contrasting of Hebrew and Greek thought, as attempted, for example, by Macmurray[34] and Bomann, certainly requires some revision and a good deal of refinement. Frequently the extreme contrasts were brought about by scholastic fixing of Greek philosophical systems (see below, Chapters One, Three, and Ten). Still, it seems to us impossible to avoid a confrontation with conceptual systems, including the images of human beings and of God connected with them, especially in the Greek philosophical tradition that has so fundamentally shaped the West. Here again it is feminist scholars, this time the philosophers, who for a long time have put their finger on the sore point, namely an absolutely androcentric, dualist thought expressed in conceptual systems (see more on this below). The purpose of this critique is not confrontation with an ancient culture, but the healthy recollection of very different possibilities for ordering the world, in thought and in reality. Here we find a search through history for utopia, a utopia in which, for example, women have their own place in the world, something they *a priori* cannot have in the Greek and Western traditions of thought, because they are always located as the wholly Other and of lesser value in comparison to the masculine standard.

FEMINIST PERSPECTIVES IN BIBLICAL ANTHROPOLOGY

The theologian Ina Praetorius has defined the concept of "androcentrism," which has acquired special significance for feminist scholarship, as follows: "By androcentrism we mean a structure of prejudices characteristic of patriarchally-organized societies, through which—naïvely or prescriptively—the *conditio humana* is equated with the life conditions of adult men. Statements about 'the human being' derived from male contexts of life and experience are presumed to be universally valid: the man is the measure of everything human."[35] It is indisputable that this is true also of biblical scholarship. Dominant Christian theological scholarship has done everything possible, in its interpretation of Genesis 2–3, to give biblical foundation to the concept of the man as the measure of everything human.[36] But historical-critical exegesis, even before feminist scholarship existed, quickly recognized that this narrative of origins does not speak of the man as the first created and the woman as the first led astray. Adam is the human being, the earth-creature, before it is sexually diversified. It is only with the creation of the *ʾishshah* that the *ʾish* arrives at his sexual identity. However, such insights do not protect respectable exegetes from androcentrism. Thus Franz Josef Stendebach could still write in 1972 of Genesis 2–3: "The human being is here anything but independent. His environment, his world, his wife as his personal counterpart, food and clothing, all are God's gifts to him; in every aspect of his life he is entirely dependent on this God."[37] Thus Stendebach really thinks of the human being as a male human being to whom the woman is secondarily attached. In this unhappily formulated sentence he unintentionally gives himself away. Women, or the female, do not appear in the androcentric world view, or only as "the Other," defined by and subordinated to the human being/male. This symbol system shapes men as well as women to a degree that makes it almost impossible to think or speak in a woman-centered way. Skepticism is therefore appropriate when biblical scholars speak of "the human being." The androcentric, and hence reductionist reconstruction of reality they offer has as a consequence, among other things, that the concept of work is defined one-sidedly as wage work, or the idea of sin is conceived in terms of typically male failings such as overvaluation of the self, the will to power, etc. Androcentric prejudice makes female life invisible and locates women on the margins of "anthropology." (See Figure 3.) It is thus no accident that Hans Walter Wolff overlooked the *reḥem* as an important element in the image of the human (see above, p. 15). The androcentrism of the Western philosophical and theological tradition has also made itself at home in conceptual systems. Feminist philosophy has demonstrated that the fundamental dualism of Western philosophy corresponds to gender differences. In the following paired concepts femininity is explicitly or implicitly identified with the lower in rank, masculinity with the higher in rank or the better: soul and body, spirit or matter, intellect and will, reason and emotion, culture and nature, transcendence and immanence, public and private, activity and passivity, acting and suffering, sublimity and beauty, substance and accident.[38]

Figure 3:
"Cleaning Woman," sculpture by Duane Hanson (1925). One of the most important tasks of scholarship and art is to make visible what is invisible, suppressed, or marginalized. This figure confronts us with a woman weary with her labor, her empty gaze, her varicose veins. Her concretely depicted body provokes questions where it is placed, on the parquet floor of the museum, where patrons usually look at art by men, frequently depicting idealized female bodies, and where the cleaning women ordinarily do not appear until after the doors are closed.

It seems almost impossible to put an end to, or even to see through such conceptual systems, because the words of our language are twisted; we can no longer even use them without continuing to spread the ancient lies about masculinity and femininity or the traditional impoverishment of the rich variety of the world's reality.

The biblical image of the human offers us an opportunity to break through the androcentrism of our Western tradition at several points. This is not to say that Israelite society was not patriarchal, but the stereometric way of thinking in that culture, with its interest in the dynamic, as manifested in its language and imagery, conceals a potential for resistance against our fixed conceptual systems and internalized images, a potential that can be activated. In the first place it is the strangeness and alien nature of the biblical way of thinking and imagining that encourages us to enter into dialogue with it. In addition, the concepts themselves—as is often the case in English or German as well—may contain wisdom going back to times when patriarchal cultures had not yet gained a firm foothold.

This situation poses some challenges to a new biblical anthropology. For example, texts rich in tradition that supposedly have to do with human sinfulness or hubris, such as the story of Cain and Abel or the one about the Tower of Babel (cf. Chapter Seven below) must be read anew as texts about the sin and hubris of *male* human beings. Statements about "the human" with claims to universality must be treated much more carefully and skeptically than has been the case in previous research. Texts and images heretofore unnoticed, that confront us with a non-anthropocentric theology of creation, must be made the focus of our attention (see Figure 4). And probably an anthropology that is more just toward women will not try to conceive all-encompassing systems, but will work in a highly fragmented manner. The fragmentary character of women's lives, women's work, etc. may correspond very well to the Near Eastern and biblical way of thought, which assembles aspects into a whole. Biblical tradition and women's ways of being are alike, interestingly enough, in a certain immunity to the construction of systems according to Greek/Western logic. Our otherness and alienation with respect to Semitic thought

Figure 4:
Neoassyrian agate cylinder seal (ca. 720 B.C.E.). A "Lord of the Wilderness" tames two wild steer-demons. To the right, on the mountain, we see a worshiper with a kid; two other kids play near the "Lord of the Wilderness." A deity who rules the wild creatures is one of the oldest pictorial motifs in the Ancient Near East. In the book of Job (ch. 39) Israel's God Yʜwʜ appears as lord of the animals; in Mark 1:13 this is attributed to Jesus Christ. It is not so much a question of the subduing of the animal world as of the idea that a principle of reason governs even in a creation that contains chaotic and dangerous powers. The human being is part of that cosmos, alongside other creatures, and assumes the position of an astonished observer.

and the Hebrew language can be thought of as analogous to the otherness of women in a traditional, androcentrically-organized world of symbols.³⁹

II. Aspects of Biblical Body Spirituality: From Sinful Flesh to the Temple of God

1. "This . . . is bone of my bones and flesh of my flesh."
Aspective apprehension and description of the body

The primary determinants for the images of divine and human in the First Testament are the special ways in which people of the Ancient Near East observed and thought, ways that are sharply different from our habits of observation and thinking. Semitic thought as expressed in images and language is stereometric. It collects various aspects of reality and combines them synthetically instead of organizing them artificially as examples in dualistic systems. In Hebrew sentences we seldom find formulations of clearly causal or temporal relationships between one subject or event and another. Much more frequently short sentences stand in a loosely connected sequence, so that there is a certain amount of leeway within which the internal relationships can be created by the hearers or readers. The well-known *parallelismus membrorum*, the common phenomenon of verses with several parallel lines, especially in sayings collections, functions in much the same way. Such verses are fond of setting up contrasts, but often the individual parts of the verse add to and complement the statement of the others. Typical of this, Laban in his joy at meeting a relative says to Jacob: "Surely you are my bone and my flesh!" (Gen 29:14). This of course means "you are my relative," but "bone and flesh" express the whole in terms of certain aspects. In this way aspects of reality are collected and placed alongside each other in a status of equality. This is also the case with the so-called merisms. The two-part merism "heaven and earth" or the three-part "heaven, earth, and sea" describe a whole in terms of a number of essential, often polar parts. Characteristically, two- and three-part formulae can alternate; the whole can be expressed through the mention of various aspects and different numbers of aspects.

In principle the same features can be found in art as well. Heinrich Schäfer (1918) and Emma Brunner-Traut (1990) accurately described the characteristics of ancient Egyptian pictorial art. These pictures resemble drawings and paintings by children who have not yet been taught how to draw with perspective, as well as the "crude art" of people our society calls psychically sick. Different from our artistic tradition, shaped by Hellenism, these pictures are not ordered by a perspective within which a particular object appears (subjectively) in different ways. The picture shows not how something looks from different angles, but what is important. What we are to see, then, is what is particularly typical. In terms of the conceptual system of drawing theory we could also say that the Greek method of observation[40] concentrates more on the body, which is only possible by a constant shifting of perspective. The Egyptian and Ancient Near Eastern observers were more interested in the body as—to simplify somewhat—a vehicle of meaning, that is, in its socially constructed aspects.

Thus a person in a typical Egyptian picture is presented to us in a way that today most often recalls Picasso: face in profile, eyes and shoulders viewed from the front, torso and legs in profile. The organization of persons and objects in the picture is scarcely determined by spatial perspective either, although it is not entirely arbitrary and the distribution of figures in the space is certainly clear. Thus Egyptian pictures often present us with strange mixtures of side view and front view. On the whole, pictures in the art of Egypt and western Asia appear flat because various aspects are simply added together. Unlike our understanding of what art is, this art is not shaped by subjective artistic impulses, but is completely conventional, a kind of artisan work. Many motifs, themes, and constellations of themes remain stable, and even almost canonical, for centuries. Comparing an Egyptian and a Greek picture, each showing an archer in action, illustrates the differences here described. (See Figures 5a and 5b.)

2. *"Your eyes are like doves." Beauty as expressive rather than perfected form*

Semitic thought, as shown both in its language and its plastic arts, is never oriented to forms, appearances, and perspectives, but always to the *dynamis,* the activity of something. When the lovers say to one another in the Song of Songs "your eyes are doves," this is not about the shape of the eyes but about the quality of the beloved, loving glance. The doves, as vehicles of the metaphor, say nothing about the appearance of the eyes, but express the content, the message of the glance, because doves were known to be messengers and companion birds of the goddess of love (cf. Figure 44). So also in the case of hand, foot, nose, etc., Israelites did not think primarily of their external form, but of their activity, the power exercised

Figure 5a:

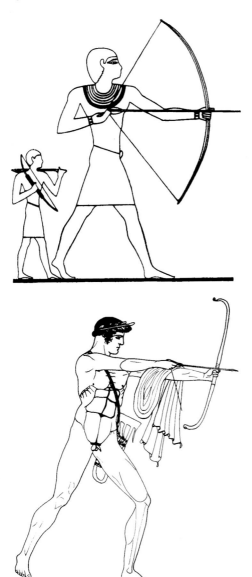

Egyptian and Greek depictions of an archer. The Egyptian picture adds the idealized aspects of individual parts of the body together to make a harmonious whole. The man is the sum of his parts, his appearance the canonized combination of individual aspects. The Greek archer, in contrast, is shown from an idealized perspective. On the one hand this gives the impression of spatial depth on the flat surface of the picture, and on the other hand parts of the body are concealed by the optical perspective selected. The individually chosen perspective is only one of many possibilities. It sees the man as a whole at an instant of action, rather than his parts.

Figure 5b:

by a strong hand, the foot standing on the neck of the enemy as a gesture of subjugation, the wrathful snorting of the nose. This is true of all bodily organs and parts, and accordingly also of anthropomorphic images of God. Since it is the dynamic, the activity that counts, and not the form, Semitic thought developed a structure of the concrete and the abstract that is completely different from the Greek. Every concrete thing, for example the hand, that is, points beyond itself. On the other hand it is simply impossible to think of or name an abstract concept like power or strength without a concrete expression. This close interweaving makes it linguistically almost impossible to construct any overly abstract symbolic and conceptual worlds. In this lies a great challenge to us from the cultures of the Ancient Near East as a whole and from the biblical idea of the human in particular.

The Near Eastern ideal of beauty also differs markedly from the Greek/Western notion. A beauty contest among goddesses who, according to Homer, choose a mortal, Paris, to decide by selecting the most beautiful among them by the form and appearance of her body would be unthinkable in the Ancient Near East. Egyptian, Akkadian, and Hebrew descriptive songs do not concentrate on the body and its form, but on the expression and dynamic of the person described. The eyes are beautiful because they send messages of love, the hair because it floats and is full of strength, the teeth because they are perfect and contrast sharply with the red lips, the throat because of its proud bearing, expressing self-confidence, the woman's breasts because of their refreshing movement . . . . For all these qualities the poets of the biblical love songs find appropriate comparisons, especially from the world of animals and plants, evoking a world overflowing with life:

> How beautiful you are, my love,
>   how very beautiful!
> Your eyes are doves
>   behind your veil.
> Your hair is like a flock of goats,
>   moving down the slopes of Gilead.
> Your teeth are like a flock of shorn ewes
>   that have come up from the washing,

all of which bear twins,
    and not one among them is bereaved.
Your lips are like a crimson thread,
    and your mouth is lovely.
Your cheeks are like halves of a pomegranate
    behind your veil.
Your neck is like the tower of David,
    built in courses;
on it hang a thousand bucklers,
    all of them shields of warriors.
Your two breasts are like two fawns,
    twins of a gazelle,
    that feed among the lilies.
Until the day breathes
    and the shadows flee,
I will hasten to the mountain of myrrh
    and the hill of frankincense.
You are altogether beautiful, my love;
    there is no flaw in you (Song of Songs 4:1-7).

Ultimately it is not the individual person who is beautiful, but the relationship between two or more people. The ideal of beauty is not physical, but an ideal of relationship. Instead of the word "ideal" we could also speak, in the framework of biblical anthropology, of God: "where two or three are gathered in my name, I am there among them" (Matt 18:20). God happens where human relationships allow God to be at work. God reveals Godself precisely there: in peaceful, that is, respectful community, where every individual is honored and sees the image of God in the neighbor. The sages of Israel employ their own model of the body to make concrete the conditions for such a community, for example in the following numerical saying:

There are six things that the LORD hates,
    seven that are an abomination to him:
haughty eyes, a lying tongue,
    and hands that shed innocent blood,
a heart that devises wicked plans,
    feet that hurry to run to evil,
a lying witness who testifies falsely,
    and one who sows discord in a family (Prov 6:16-19).

Only where we do not misuse our bodies in that way can the opposite come to be: a community that is mutually advantageous and solidary, understood as the highest gift of divine blessing and compared to the anointed body of the High Priest and Mount Hermon blessed with dew:

> How very good and pleasant it is
> > when kindred live together in unity!
> It is like the precious oil on the head,
> > running down upon the beard,
> on the beard of Aaron,
> > running down over the collar of his robes.
> It is like the dew of Hermon,
> > which falls on the mountains of Zion.
> For there the LORD ordained his blessing,
> > life forevermore (Psalm 133).

3. "My body dwells securely." Physical prayers of physical people

Against the background of the ideal of beauty just described it is easy to understand why the isolated human being incapable of relationship is a horror to the biblical sages. This horror is also pictured in the image of an idol, which appears to have a body but is incapable of using it:

> Their idols are silver and gold,
> > the work of human hands.
> They have mouths, but do not speak;
> > eyes, but do not see.
> They have ears, but do not hear;
> > noses, but do not smell.
> They have hands, but do not feel;
> > feet, but do not walk;
> > they make no sound in their throats (Ps 115:4-6).

The sevenfold (!) inability of the idols shows that they are completely useless. In contrast, the psalmists never tire of assessing their own living bodies, which are the measures of the degree of life one has. In a great many psalms we find an astonishing accumulation of bodily organs and parts: thus the pitiable condition of the body in Psalm 22, which Jesus prays on the cross, shows how desperate the one crying out this lament is:

I am poured out like water,
    and all my bones are out of joint;
my heart is like wax;
    it is melted within my breast;
my mouth is dried up like a potsherd,
    and my tongue sticks to my jaws . . . (Ps 22:14-15).

Thus those who pray the psalms present themselves before God in their concrete corporeality; their prayer is an expression of longing for integral, whole humanity before YHWH:

I bless YHWH who gives me counsel [contemplation; experience];
    in the night also my heart [lit: kidneys] instructs me [intuition].
I keep YHWH always before me [confidence];
    because he is at my right hand, I shall not be moved [self-confidence].
Therefore my heart is glad [reason],
    and my soul [lit: liver] rejoices [emotion];
my body also rests secure.
For you do not give me [lit: my throat = soul] up to Sheol,
    or let your faithful one see the Pit (Ps 16:7-10).

Translated into our much more abstract language, this prayer would sound something like this:

"I bless the power of God that grows in me out of prayer and experience.
It instructs me at night through dreams and in the daytime through intuition.
It gives me confidence and self-awareness.
It sharpens my reason and gives me good emotions.
My body feels altogether well,
    and I am no longer afraid of death."

4. "This is my body." The celebration of the body in the celebration of the bread

Not only prayer, but liturgy as well focuses attention on the body in the form of bread, of which the priest says in the words of Christ at his last meal with his disciples: "This is my body" (Matt 26:26; Mark 14:22; cf. Luke 22:19; 1 Cor 11:23). For most of the faithful *Hoc est corpus meum* has always been a mysterious formula, as is most drastically shown by "Hocus pocus," a form of ridicule derived from it. In fact it is not at all obvious how Jesus could say of a piece of bread "this is my body" and of a cup of wine "this is my blood." We are well aware that the debate over this problem has filled libraries and led to divisions in the Church. There is no way we can even sketch it here, but we do not want to neglect to point to the special sensitivity of the Christianized peoples of Latin America to this problem, a sensitivity that is closely associated with their centuries of experience of physical degradation and martyrdom.

The primeval date of the beginning of Latin American theology of liberation is often seen in the conversion of the Spanish Dominican Bartolomeo de las Casas in 1514. As he was preparing a sermon, he came across the following passage in Jesus Sirach:

> If one sacrifices ill-gotten goods, the offering is blemished;
> > the gifts of the lawless are not acceptable.
> The Most High is not pleased with the offerings of the ungodly,
> > nor for a multitude of sacrifices does he forgive sins.
> Like one who kills a son before his father's eyes
> > is the person who offers a sacrifice from the property of the
> > > poor.
> The bread of the needy is the life of the poor;
> > whoever deprives them of it is a murderer.
> To take away a neighbor's living is to commit murder;
> > to deprive an employee of wages is to shed blood
> > > (Sir 34:21-27).

In contemplating this text, Las Casas came to the conclusion that the exploitation of the Indians and their lands, in which he had heretofore participated, could not be God's will. It was impossible for him to celebrate the holy Mass centered on the bread of life, which according to Jesus Sirach is the life of the poor.

Against the background of this story of conversion the Argentinian Catholic theologian Enrique Düssel has provided a lucid description of the physical dimensions of the Eucharist.[41] The needy human being tills the earth and produces bread, "fruit of the ground and work of human hands," as it says in the Roman Canon. The body is consumed in its work: blood and sweat are offered so that bread may be produced, to be eaten by the hungry. The consumption of the bread compensates for the consumption of the body in work: the person is restored. Therefore we speak of the bread of life or the "good gift" (eu-charist). This is the circle of life that is celebrated in the Eucharist. But it is destroyed by human sin, namely when the powerful gather to themselves the fruits of their labor and of that of others. They become rich while those betrayed become poor. The injustice and violence of this circle causes the bodies of the poor to be destroyed. The exploited people's life expectancy declines while retirement homes fill with the wealthy. When the rich, celebrating Mass, take the bread they have stolen from the poor and say to God "we bring you this bread," they blaspheme God. Their worship is idolatry. The bread thus brought is the sweat and blood of the poor made objective. Jesus Christ, the Son of God, sacrificed his life for the restoration of a just circle of life. His death was the quintessence of his practice of healing the poor and his culture of resistance to the rich. His martyrdom made his body in the sacramental (real-symbolic) sense the bread of the poor. Jesus anticipated this self-surrender in the celebration of the Passover when he broke bread in the midst of his disciples and thus added a new dimension to the ancient festival of liberation, "because the death of the just man, the poor, the Son, is the passage from death to life; passage through the desert of the slavery in Egypt to the promised land, the land of this earth and the eschatological land of the kingdom, which has already begun when the poor eat, satisfy their hunger, in history."[42]

5. *"And the Word was made flesh." God becomes a real body*

The First Testament sets up a broad field of tension between the status of the humans as *imago Dei* on the one hand and their close relationship to the animals, their vulnerability and mortality on the other hand. Humans exist within that field of tension. Only through God's breath, Spirit, and word does the earth-creature become a living being, but then, as a being always laden with guilt, it is continually in need of God's forgiveness and mercy in order to live. Being the image of God is, in fact, a permanent and excessive demand on human beings, as Job in particular formulates (Job 7:17-18); he finds the special honor of the human to be a burden because he feels himself pursued, controlled, and invaded by God. The Second Testament seeks a theological escape from this almost unbearable tension by focusing on God's becoming human. All its writings hold with the utmost conviction to the truth that God became a human being—and that means *embodied*—in Jesus Christ. The prologue to the Fourth Gospel (John 1:14) formulates this belief in the incarnation in a succinct statement: "the Word [*Logos*] became flesh and lived among us." "*Logos*" is not an originally biblical concept; it achieved importance in the context of Jewish and Hellenistic thought, and in the prologue, the overture to the gospel, it is explained as well. It is really too simplistic to translate "*Logos*" as "Word." It is true that in the idea that at the beginning the "*Logos*" was, was with God, and *was* God there is a reference to the creation of the world when "God said . . ." in Genesis 1. But the *Logos* is more than the creative Word; it appears here as the heir of personified Wisdom, who according to Prov 8:22-31 and other texts is in the beginning with God, joins God in calling creation into being, is happy to be with human beings, and who, in the conception of the Wisdom teachers, could also act with divine authority in place of Israel's God. Wisdom in Israel already had a strongly mediating function between the divine and human spheres. She was Israel's God, and was so in the image of a creative, publicly active, prophetically accusing, counseling Israelite woman who invites to her banquet. The Fourth Gospel uses that tradition for its programmatic formulation of the complete entry of God into human bodiliness. The *Logos,* the wholly creative, world-ordering power and wisdom of God, becomes flesh in a concrete, mortal human being. Here the boundary between the divine and the human is drastically ruptured, for if there was anything with which the divinities of the Ancient Near East, including YHWH, had nothing at all to do and from which they were sharply distinguished, it was human "flesh," the very essence of vulnerability and mortality (see pp. 212–14 below).

The prologue to the Fourth Gospel operates at a high level of abstraction. It is only through the whole gospel that follows, the stories of Jesus' words and deeds, that it unfolds the content of the introductory formula. In general it is especially the gospels that attempt to make utterly concrete and visible what it means to say that God has become human, has become flesh. God enters into physical human reality, into bodily and other kinds of suffering, through Jesus' miracles of healing and resuscitation. On the other hand, Paul carries on a reflection against this background on the significance of the human body itself.

6. "Speak but a word." Healing of body and spirit

"Lord, I am not worthy that you should enter under my roof; speak but a word and my soul will be healed." Catholic Christians repeat this statement before receiving the Eucharist. It is a slightly altered quotation from a healing story found in Matthew's gospel (Matt 8:5-13) and in Luke's (Luke 7:1-10). A Gentile centurion from the Roman occupation forces in Capernaum begs Jesus to heal his mortally ill servant. When Jesus asks to be taken into the house to the sick person the centurion, trusting utterly in Jesus' power to heal, says:

> "Lord, I am not worthy to have you come under my roof; but only speak the word, and my servant will be healed" (Matt 8:8).

Thus the quotation originally stands in the context of the holistic, physical healing of a human being. In its liturgical use it has experienced a crucial alteration. It expresses the faith of the one who prays it that Christ, who comes and indeed enters into human persons in the form of bread and wine, thereby makes the soul healthy. Very few who say this prayer imagine Christ as a psychotherapist, and yet the fullness of what was meant by this sentence in the gospels, namely healing, and even resurrection from death, is no longer evident. Unfortunately this is a typical example: the Christian tradition is inclined to spiritualize the bodiliness of human beings and to subordinate or even postpone care for the body in favor of care for the soul.

Most of the biblical writings are very far from such spiritualizations, from a number of points of view. The separation of soul and body is utterly alien to the Hebrew Bible, so that the soul can never be considered as an entity to be treated in and for itself. At death the breath and spirit God has given it leave the body. There is no continued life of a soul, and thus there remains only the hope that the name will continue in posterity and in their memory. Strong influences from the Greek image of the human and the idea of a continuing life of the soul after death are found first in the book of Wisdom, which originated in Alexandria shortly before the Christian era and made an effort to accommodate Jewish traditions and Hellenism.

Just as the worshipers of YHWH could hope for forgiveness of sins from their God, they expected YHWH also to give them very concrete healing of their physical infirmities, illnesses of all kinds, and distresses that we would classify as "physical." It is terrible to realize that illnesses and evil spirits could come from God, and yet it is from that very realization that arises the trust that one can approach the same tribunal and ask for healing. YHWH is counselor, support, physician, and therapist; YHWH gives comprehensive restoration of health and welfare (cf. also the rehabilitation of Job). Indeed, those who pray can even expect that God will rescue from the grave a life already condemned to death—will awaken to new life people who, in the view of that time, were already regarded as dead. Throughout the Ancient Near East illness was often experienced as the consequence of conscious or unconscious failings with respect to a deity, and even as the result of the misdeeds of an entire group, a people, or as the consequence of the sins of earlier generations. Behind this is no simple dogma of retaliation, no image of a directly intervening, punishing God. Instead, the whole world order has been so arranged by the deity (or deities) that right action in the long run brings good consequences and wrong action in the long run brings bad consequences. The divinity has no need to apply this order personally in every individual case, because it is self-fulfilling. But the gods are the guarantors of that order; they can support it, intervene to accelerate it, or delay its action and, when there is repentance, even set it aside.

7. "Faith, love, hope." Jesus' praxis of eyes, hands, and feet

The First Testament's picture of humans and God was not fundamentally changed in the first and second centuries C.E., when the New Testament writings were composed. Thus the reign-of-God proclamation of the Jesus movement was inextricably bound up with healings, expulsion of demons, and raising the dead, in all of which no distinction between the human body and soul was presumed. In the Roman period the colonial pressure was especially severe in the Near East. This era is the background for the healer and exorcist Jesus of Nazareth, who is described in the gospels. For his followers, he concentrated in his own person the hopes and dreams of the oppressed. He became the image of the redeemed human being, the one on whom the oil of joy was poured out, the Anointed One. His life was an encouragement, indeed an appeal to all who listened to him to free themselves and others and be healed of the effects of colonial power. Healing is the basis of the reign of God he preached:

> Then Jesus called the twelve together and gave them power and authority over all demons and to cure diseases, and he sent them out to proclaim the kingdom of God and to heal (Luke 9:1-2).

The healing of the possessed and the sick and the raising of the dead had the greatest value in Jesus' activity alongside his teaching. Many people had their first contact with Jesus as a miraculous healer. The evangelist Mark deliberately selected and combined the various healing stories in such a way that the entire human body appears in the pictures of illness presented by these stories. Jesus heals a possessed man in Capernaum, Peter's mother-in-law, who has a fever, a leper, a lame man, a man with a withered hand, the possessed man in Gerasa, a woman suffering from a hemorrhage, the dead daughter of Jairus and the possessed daughter of the Syro-Phoenician woman, a person with a hearing and speech impairment, a blind man in Bethsaida, an epileptic boy, and blind Bartimaeus. We thus find ailments of the eyes, mouth, ears, feet, and hands, illness of the internal organs and the skin, fever, and finally various forms of mental disease.

Men and women in their physicality, the need for healing and forgiveness are thus at the center of the proclamation of the reign of God. And for Mark, as far as work for the reign of God is concerned, what counts is the praxis of the hands, the feet, and the eyes, so that the Markan Jesus makes the drastic recommendation that one should rather cut off one's hand or foot or tear out one's eye if they lead one to sin rather than land in hell (Mark 9:42-48).

The Portuguese theologian Fernando Belo has derived from this, among other passages, a praxis of Jesus that he calls the practice of hands, feet, and eyes.[43] Within his structuralist reading of the Gospel of Mark he sets the *practice of hands* in relationship with the action level of the text. Jesus' action has a healing effect because he overcomes the debt economy through a praxis of giving. Among Christians this is called love of neighbor. The *practice of feet* he connects with the strategic level of the text, that is, with conversion, which makes one a disciple of Jesus and thus leads one toward the royal reign of God, where the first become last and the servants are the models. The utopian dimension of this praxis, which also achieves a geographic dimension as the Church spreads, is the kernel of Christian hope. Finally, Belo associates the *practice of eyes* with the analytic level of the text. Whoever has eyes to see penetrates the machinations of the powerful and recognizes the structures of death in society; such a one reads reality like a book. And whoever reads the gospel with such eyes recognizes that Jesus' praxis is messianic and rich in blessing: it is what Christians call faith. Accordingly, the God of Jesus is a God who hears people's cries and, as so vividly described in Revelation, personally dries the tears on their faces (Rev 21:4). "The hairs of your head are all counted" (Matt 10:30), says Jesus, and he means that this God gazes on the children of humanity tenderly and with gentle care.

8. "She has performed a good service for me."
Bodily wellness and the erotic

Some of that tenderness and attention to bodily wellness—beyond his healing activity—was exuded by Jesus himself. In this respect he was a genuine Israelite and Near Easterner who could enjoy life in all its dimensions. He loved to eat and drink in company with other people. He took care that people who came to him from afar had something to eat. Ultimately he left his disciples the community at table, joyful and festive eating together, as the sign of his presence. He was not ashamed to wash his disciples' feet, but he also enjoyed having a woman anoint his feet with oil. In Mark's gospel we read how Jesus even blissfully allowed a sympathetic woman to pour expensive perfume on his head:

> While he was at Bethany in the house of Simon the leper, as he sat at the table, a woman came with an alabaster jar of very costly ointment of nard, and she broke open the jar and poured the ointment on his head. But some were there who said to one another in anger, "Why was the ointment wasted in this way? For this ointment could have been sold for more than three hundred denarii, and the money given to the poor." And they scolded her. But Jesus said, "Let her alone; why do you trouble her? She has performed a good service for me. For you always have the poor with you, and you can show kindness to them whenever you wish; but you will not always have me. She has done what she could; she has anointed my body beforehand for its burial. Truly I tell you, wherever the good news is proclaimed in the whole world, what she has done will be told in remembrance of her" (Mark 14:3-9).

These words of Jesus have not been fulfilled—at least not yet, for very seldom is anything said in the churches about the effusive loving attention of this woman. The writings of the Second Testament have a harder time with tenderness, eroticism, and sexuality than those of the First. The love poetry of the Song of Songs, although its reception into the canon is not owed to its primary meaning, has preserved for us an insight into the world of lovers at that time. Beyond social conventions, a man and woman rejoice in their beauty, their glow, the glances of love; they break forth in jubilant song about the body of the beloved and thus achieve the utopia of the man and woman together, as envisioned in God's original plan of creation. Of course, the Song of Songs is not representative of Israel's attitude to eroticism and sexuality in general. Thus extramarital sexuality is always problematic, whether in legal texts, Wisdom writings, or the works of the prophets. In addition, the prophetic and deuteronomistic traditions defamed female sexuality in particular, and all forms of sexuality associated with the cult. The story of the transfer of the Ark of the Covenant to Jerusalem (2 Samuel 6) shows that the conflict over the relationship between cult and eroticism goes far back in Israel's history. David dances an erotic dance before YHWH, very much in the life-loving tradition of Canaanite cultic festivals. In the story in 2 Samuel it is Michal, Saul's daughter, who takes offense at this behavior. In reality it was probably groups of people in Jerusalem at a later period who pushed for reserve in this area in particular, and who in time—despite the resistant memory of David's dancing—prevailed. Within marriage sexuality was no problem, either in ancient Israel or in Judaism. It needed a Paul to take that step; in face of the approaching reign of God he regarded celibacy as the truly better way of life for a Christian man or woman. The biblical traditions of both testaments, as the foregoing shows, are somewhat divided as regards the erotic in particular. Sexuality is not an unbroken part of the self-evident physicality of the human; it again and again becomes a problem. Theology has, even today, done too little to pursue the reasons for these developments; some memory work needs to be done, and things formerly suppressed be brought to light, so that man and woman, in this dimension of their lives also, may be whole and healthy before God.

9. "Glorify God in your body." The body as temple of the Holy Spirit

In very many fundamental and theologically profound discourses on the bodiliness of being Christian, Paul expressed and made concrete his conviction that God has become human. Thus, in dependence on ancient traditions, he compares the community of Christians, the body of Christ, to an organism in which each organ has a function and is indispensable (1 Cor 12:12-31). Especially exciting, however, is the initiative toward a body-centered christology, theology, and pneumatology that Paul suggests in the sixth chapter of 1 Corinthians:

> Or do you not know that your body is a temple of the Holy Spirit within you, which you have from God, and that you are not your own? For you were bought with a price; therefore glorify God in your body (1 Cor 6:19-20).

Paul is addressing himself to the men in the community and warning them against intercourse with prostitutes. Corinth, a port city, was a dangerous place, a kind of metropolis of bordellos, frequented by foreigners as well as the local citizenry. Paul gives a theological reason for his warning; that is, he connects the theme of prostitution with God, Christ, and the Holy Spirit. The human body does not belong to the individual man or woman, but to God and the Holy Spirit. It is no accident that Paul develops this theology of the body through the example of sexual morality (see above). However, the explosive material here is not so much in the exemplary case as in the fundamental character of the enormously expansive idea that the human body is a temple of God, Christ, and the Holy Spirit. This idea is based on the image of the human in the First Testament and the character of man and woman as image of god. In the Ancient Near East and in Israel the temple is the place where the deity is present on earth in a very special way. Gardens, wells, or pools, splendor, good odors, and many other things made temples little oases of holiness, gardens of paradise. Here it was possible for people to meet the deity, to receive a share in the fullness of life. As holy places, the temples were also places of purity. Here the filth of life and the dirt of daily existence could not exercise their dominion; all worshipers came washed and purified before the god in order to petition, to thank, and to offer praise with prayers, music, and dance. Taking the Pauline metaphor of the human body as the temple of the Holy Spirit seriously in all these aspects means also taking seriously the perfect presence of God in the bodiliness of the human body, and with it the resulting inviolability of the dignity of that body. There is also an imperative in this image. The temple of God on earth must be protected, sheltered from profanation and violation. Every part of our bodies is holy to our God, and according to Paul we glorify God when we keep the body holy in all its dimensions.

An Understanding Heart

In our culture the heart is regarded as the center of the life force, and also as the seat of conscience, the center of the self, the seat of the soul and the emotions, as attested by any number of expressions:

- to be close to someone's heart
- to give one's heart to someone
- to take something to heart
- to be unable to find it in one's heart to . . .
- to take one's heart (courage) in one's hands
- to take heart
- to have one's heart in the right place
- to pour out one's heart
- to take someone to one's heart
- to be one in heart and soul
- to lose one's heart

When we speak in a transferred sense of the heart of the city, the heart represents the "middle" and "center." German still makes a distinction, even in its grammar, between the physical organ, the heart *(Herz)* and the symbol *(Herzen)*. It is not the same thing to have a heart attack *(Herzinfarkt)* as to be pained to the heart *(Herzenskummer)*. One can have a "sick heart" or be "sick at heart."

Undoubtedly the great symbolic value of the heart is connected to the fact that the heart is the only one of our internal organs that we can constantly feel, more or less. We thus have an anatomical feeling for our internal self where, in its mysterious way, half of our life takes place. Thus it is no surprise that in the Bible, where the relationship between the inner and the outer person is the constant subject of reflection and discussion, the heart is a central idea.

Symbol of the Inner Person

The Hebrew word for "heart" is *lēb* or *lēbāb*. It is amazing that in many places where the Hebrew text speaks of the *lēb* the translations do not use the word "heart." This is by no means to be attributed to a lack of care on the part of the translators; on the contrary, it shows that "heart" in Hebrew does not mean the same thing as "heart" in English or German. For the ancient Israelites the images, associations, and functions attached to this organ were sometimes the same as ours, but sometimes they were very different.

In the First Book of Samuel (1 Samuel 25) we read how Nabal, a rich Israelite farmer, refuses to pay David and his men for protecting his flocks. Boiling with rage, David sets out to take revenge on Nabal's whole household. Only the timely intervention of the clever Abigail, Nabal's wife, prevents a bloodbath. It is not until the next morning, when he is sober, that Abigail tells Nabal that she personally brought David the tribute he demanded. Nabal hears the news, and then the text says:

> . . . his heart died within him; he became like a stone. About ten days later the LORD struck Nabal, and he died (1 Sam 25:37-38).

This sounds at first like a heart attack, but it cannot be, because Nabal lives another ten days. Instead, the writer presumes that the heart, as the central organ, makes the movement of the limbs possible. When the heart dies the body is immobilized, like a stone. Our medical knowledge leads us to attribute such symptoms to a stroke, but in Israel the brain was no more acknowledged as an organ than were the lungs.[1]

On the other hand, the Israelites described the connection between the heart in the breast and a variety of unpleasant states of agitation up to and including illnesses in much the same way as we describe such sensations. When the prophet Jeremiah heard the shouts of warring men coming near, he suffered a heart attack and groaned:

> "My anguish, my anguish! I writhe in pain!
>   Oh, the walls of my heart!

My heart is beating wildly;
I cannot keep silent . . ." (Jer 4:19).

A seriously ill person complains in prayer that his heart is throbbing and his strength is failing (Ps 38:10). Here the heart represents the center, the innermost part of the human body, as we speak of the heart of the sea, the heaven, or a tree to describe its midpoint or the most inaccessible part, much as when we call the center of a city its "heart."

God knows the inmost part of a person very well. The hearts of the children of humanity lie open to YHWH, who knows the secrets of their hearts. One's heart can be full of fear or calm, fearful or proud. It can powerfully desire something and it can rejoice. The sayings in the Wisdom books teach us that hope deferred can make one's heart sick, and that a glad heart promotes good health (Prov 13:12; 15:13; 17:22, and frequently elsewhere).

Heart and Heartlessness: Intelligence and Stupidity

However, in Israel the heart was not primarily the seat of emotions, and certainly not of love. In the Song of Songs, significantly enough, the word "heart" appears only three times. This is very different from the Egyptian love songs, which describe in a multitude of images how the heart races and leaps when a person has really fallen in love.

In the Bible the heart is primarily the locus of reason and intelligence, of secret planning, deliberation, and decision. According to Deut 29:4 the human being has eyes to see, ears to hear, and a heart (NRSV "mind") to understand. The heart processes and orders the impressions that come from without.[2] Solomon, the patron of Wisdom, asks God for a listening heart (NRSV "understanding mind"), that is, an alert and attentive mind and spirit (1 Kings 3:9). His prayer is answered:

God gave Solomon very great wisdom, discernment, and breadth of understanding [heart] as vast as the sand on the seashore, so that Solomon's wisdom surpassed the wisdom of all the people of the east, and all the wisdom of Egypt. He was wiser than anyone else . . . . He composed three thousand proverbs, and his songs numbered a thousand and five. He would speak of trees, from the cedar that is in the Lebanon to the hyssop that grows in the wall; he would speak of animals, and birds, and reptiles, and fish (1 Kings 4:29-33; cf. 3:12).

The breadth of heart that is described here is, in fact, a vast education.

As much as the heart's wisdom was admired, heartless people were feared as much or more. In Proverbs, for example, we read:

> On the lips of one who has understanding wisdom is found,
>   but a rod is for the back of one who lacks sense [heart]
>   (Prov 10:13).

In Israel a lack of heart did not mean a coldness of affect, but thoughtlessness, irrationality, or simply stupidity. The prophet Hosea complains of Ephraim, that is, the northern kingdom of Israel:

> Ephraim has become like a dove, silly and without sense
>   [heart];
>   they call upon Egypt, they go to Assyria (Hos 7:11).

The context here makes it obvious what "heartlessness" means: Israel has lost its mind, has become as irrational and silly as a dove. This irrationality is drastically depicted in an Egyptian relief in which an enemy holds his own heart in his hand (Figure 6).[3]

The Place of Spiritual Treasures and Secrets

Those who are intelligent, on the other hand, take to heart the words of God, the prophets, or the teachers of Wisdom; that is, they internalize them and take them fully into themselves, into their hearts. Deuteronomy commands:

> Keep these words that I am commanding you today in your heart. . . . Bind them as a sign on your hand . . . (Deut 6:6, 8).

The heart is pictured as a blank tablet to begin with; it will be inscribed with instructions that are of enduring importance and hence should be indelible.[4]

Memory and recollection are also located in the human heart, along with one's secrets. In the famous story of Samson (Judges 16) Delilah uses all the means in her power to tease the secret of

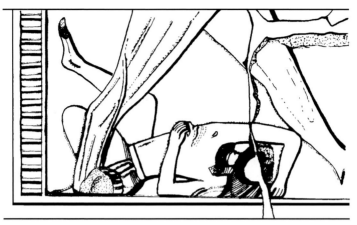

Figure 6:
For fear of the powerful royal sphinx that is approaching, an enemy falls to the ground and loses his heart, which he holds in his left hand. It has been removed from its place. It was common in Egypt to say of enemies that "their heart is no longer in their body."

the hero's superhuman strength out of him. In her disappointment she asks him:

> "How can you say, 'I love you,' when your heart is not with me? You have mocked me three times now and have not told me what makes your strength so great" (Judg 16:15).

Samson's heart is not with Delilah. Spontaneously we understand her to be saying that he does not love her enough; but what she means is that he has not entrusted her with his knowledge and his secrets.

In the Gospel of Luke we have a famous passage that makes it immediately obvious that the heart is the secret inner place of thought. After his parents have vainly sought him, the twelve-year-old Jesus astonishes them with the question whether they did not know that he had to be in the Temple, with his Father. Then Luke 2:51 concludes that his mother kept all these words in her heart, which in biblical language means simply that she considered and reflected on them.

A human being conducts his or her most secret reflections and plans in the heart, "speaks" to or in her or his heart. What

Figure 7:
Illustration from the Book of the Dead, from the papyrus of Chonsu-mes (1085–950 B.C.E.). The dead person appears before the judgment of the dead with Maat-feathers and a heart amulet for protection. The jackal-headed god of the dead, Anubis, weighs his heart against a symbol of Maat, justice. The weight indicator on the scale is also a heart symbol hanging from a Maat-feather. The ibis-headed scribe-god, Thot, reports to Osiris, the judge of the dead, on the results of the weighing. The crocodile-headed goddess who devours the dead waits for hearts that are found to be too light. This "second death" was what the Egyptians feared.

someone says need not correspond to what he or she thinks in his or her heart. There are people "who speak peace with their neighbors, while mischief is in their hearts" (Ps 28:3). It may be that people are deceived by such behavior, but God sees behind the facades and knows what is happening inside them.

Human Conscience

The heart is also something like conscience. It strikes David after he has secretly cut a corner off Saul's cloak (1 Sam 24:5). The one who prays Psalm 51 asks God for a clean heart, that is, a clear conscience (Ps 51:10). However, the association of heart and conscience was not as marked in Israel as in Egypt, where the heart played an incredibly large part in the conception of the underworld. The dead person had to withstand a severe test before the gods on entering into the kingdom of the dead: the weighing of the heart. The heart was weighed in one side of the scale's balance against Maat, the goddess of good order, on the other side (Figure 7). This notion lives on in the medieval European

Figure 8:
Section from the Last Judgment scene above the central door of the cathedral in Berne, Switzerland (second half of the 15th c.). In the medieval Christian judgment of the dead the archangel Michael weighs not hearts, but souls, represented as tiny human figures. Christ has replaced Osiris. Here, too, the souls that are found to be too light are cast into the maw of hell.

image of the weighing of souls (Figure 8). According to a fixed formula (Book of the Dead saying 125) the dead person makes a kind of negative confession of sins in which all sins are denied, one after another,[5] somewhat as follows:

> I have not killed,
> I have not commanded to kill,
> I have not made suffering for anyone,
> I have not lessened the food-offerings in the temples . . .
> I have not laid anything upon the weights of the hand-balance
>   . . .

The heart of the dead person knows very well the deeds of its master or mistress. It appears before the judgment seat as an omniscient witness and in some circumstances must testify against its master or mistress. In contrast to the other internal organs, which were buried in special vessels called canopic jars, the heart was left in the mummy when it was prepared for burial. The Egyptians tried to counter their great fear that the heart could desert one at the judgment by means of amulets (see Figures 9-11) and spells. In the papyrus of Ani from the fifteenth century B.C.E. the person being tested prays:[6]

> O ye gods who seize upon Hearts, and who pluck out the Whole Heart; and whose hands can fashion anew the heart of a person according to what he hath done; lo now, let that be forgiven to him by you. . . . Let not my Heart be torn from me by your fingers. Let not my heart be fashioned anew according to all the evil things that are said against me. . . . Ho to me! Heart of mine; I am in possession of thee, I am thy master, and thou art by me; fall not away from me; I am the dictator to whom thou shalt obey in the Netherworld.
>   . . .
> Let not this Whole Heart of mine be torn from me. . . .
> This Whole Heart of mine remaineth weeping over itself in presence of Osiris. And this Whole Heart of mine is laid upon the tablets of Tmu, who guideth me to the caverns of Sutu and who giveth me back my Whole Heart which hath accomplished its desire in presence of the divine Circle which is in the Netherworld.

The Israelites were never as interested in the world of the dead as were the people in Egypt. YHWH, Israel's God, was not responsible for the underworld, for this God was a God of life and the living. According to Israel's faith and the words of the prophet Ezekiel the new heart that is lacking to human beings will therefore not be given after death, but before God during one's lifetime:

> "I will give them one heart [or: a new heart], and put a new spirit within them; I will remove the heart of stone from their flesh and give them a heart of flesh" (Ezek 11:19).

As this tour of the Hebrew texts has shown, there is a large spectrum of meanings connected with the word *lēb*, heart. Since the Israelites had no hesitation about imagining God in human imagery, they thought that YHWH also a heart, like a human being. God's heart can be in pain in face of human wickedness, it can feel affection, and it can truly recoil when seized by feelings of regret or rage (Hos 11:8).

When we keep all these connections in our hearts, that is, when we have become deeply aware of them, we may have new ears for the well-known verse in the Song of Songs where the lover implores his beloved:

> "Set me as a seal upon your heart, as a seal upon your arm" (Song 8:6).

Heart and Hurt: A Contrast with the Western Tradition of the Heart

In our Western culture we have a kind of heart-symbolism that is very different from the biblical one, for example when an aria from Johann Sebastian Bach's *St. Matthew Passion* shows how it is a gift accepted, misunderstood, or refused:

> I will give you my heart,
> My happiness, sink down therein.
> I will immerse myself in you,
> If the world is too small for you,
> Ah, you shall to me alone
> More than world and heaven be.

How does it happen that the heart, as the place of sense and aspiration, intelligence and understanding, becomes a gift that has not the least thing to do with intelligence, but is regarded as all the more pure, the less it is fettered by reason?

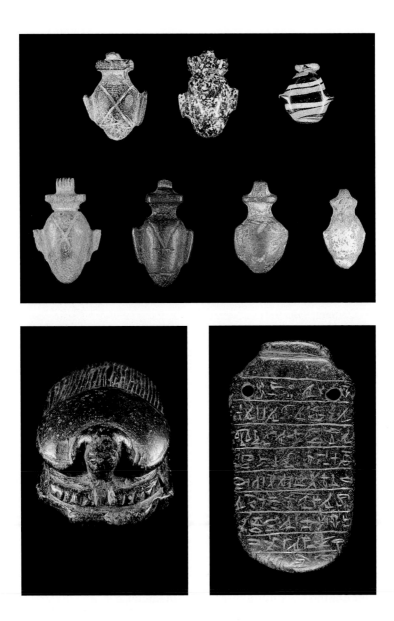

Figure 9:
Heart amulets. We can clearly see the arterial opening at the top of the heart and the muscles at the sides, the so-called auriculae. Coronary vessels and decorations were etched into the hearts. This amulet, extremely popular from the end of the Middle Kingdom onward, was worn on a loop or ring. It was meant to put the heart in a favorable condition in face of the judgment of the dead. The green color preferred for such amulets indicates regeneration and life.

Figures 10a and 10b:
Heart scarab. In Book of the Dead saying 30b we read: "My heart of my mother, my heart of my mother, my heart of my changing forms—do not stand up against me as a witness, do not oppose me in the court of judgment, do not bow down against me before the weigh-master!" The instruction for the saying reads: "To be spoken over a small beetle of green stone, bound with white gold, its ring of silver. It is placed around the throat of the dead person."

Figure 11:
Wall painting from the tomb of Sennefer in west Thebes (ca. 1400 B.C.E.). The scene illustrates the important role of amulets for the dead in Egypt. The man to whom the tomb belongs wears a double heart amulet. His spouse hands him two more neck chains: on the left one hang a snake staff, a stylized pole bearing sheaves of grain, and an Isis knot, on the right a scarab.

The search for an answer to that question leads us to the ancient Greeks. As is frequently the case, our culture does not follow the Near Eastern tradition of the Bible, but that of Greco-Roman antiquity. Plato, in his *Timaeus,* distinguishes various realms of the soul within the human body, with a hierarchical order from higher to lower. According to this order the immortal part of the soul is in the head, the mortal below the neck. The mortal part of the soul is divided into an upper part, which Plato calls male, and a lower, which he calls female, separated by the diaphragm. It is the duty of the male part of the soul to mediate between divine reason and feminine desire, and the heart is at its service for that purpose.[7]

> And the heart, which is the junction of the veins and the fount of the blood which circulates vigorously through all the limbs, they [the gods] appointed to be the chamber of the bodyguard, to the end that when . . . reason passes the word round that some unjust action is being done which affects them, either from without or possibly even from the interior desires, every organ of sense in the body might quickly perceive through all the channels both the injunctions and the threats and in all ways obey and follow them, allowing their best part to be the leader over them all.

Despite many changes in detail, the idea of the heart as the connecting link between the often warring powers within the person has remained; indeed, it has become a matter of popular wisdom, so that we hear in a song:

> Dear angels, stand by me,
> to keep my body and soul together,
> so that my heart may not break.

The broken, or at least sorely tried heart was the basic theme of the poetry of courtly love and its romantic imitators. Behind almost all the despairing efforts of the poets to give expression to their feelings stands the lapidary rhyme "heart/hurt" (German *Herz/Schmerz*). The heart represents the identity of the human being over which he or she worries anxiously or desires to share fully and utterly with the beloved. Thus in the famous strophe of the woman in "Minnesangs Frühling":

Thou art mine; I am thine;
That must thou know for certain.
Thou art enclosed within my heart:
    I have lost the key:
So must thou forever rest therein.

The heart-symbolism of the courtly lovers enjoyed a continuing religious life, especially in German mysticism and its late medieval and Baroque variants, the Sacred Heart piety that arose in Germany in the fifteenth century, and the veneration of the Mother of Sorrows (*mater dolorosa:* see Figure 12).

Meister Eckhart taught as a central element of wisdom that what the human being can know is the direct outflow of the heart of God and can only be received by the soul that lives in the solitude of the heart.[8] In the encounter between God and the human, the divine and human hearts can no longer be distinguished. Giving and receiving become one. This religious language opened secret places that made it possible to compensate spiritually for the increasing mastery of the body that was a consequence of the Enlightenment. The fact that, throughout all the ages, people still remembered the Song of Songs and had no problem in adopting those highly erotic love songs as part of their Jesus-mysticism impressively shows how timelessly and boundlessly the logic of the heart functions.

While the secular and spiritual literature of the Middle Ages reveals a broad spectrum of heart symbolism, quite often referring to the whole of the inner person, the top-heavy worldview of the Enlightenment condemned the heart to the sector of mysterious, irrational powers and forces that can dominate us and of which we really know that they are more part of us than anything we can acquire intellectually. Thus Goethe's Werther in one of his letters complains of the prince, with tempestuous honesty: "He also esteems my intellect and my talents more than this heart that in truth is my only pride . . . . Ah, what I know anyone can know—my heart belongs to me alone."

The human being and the environment suffer from the soulless dissection of the inner person in the name of reason or rationalization. Thus heart disease, the most common cause of death in our civilization, becomes a symbol of a false system of values. But all over the world people, especially mothers,

Figure 12:
Statue in the parish church of Euthal, Switzerland (1791). The heart of the royal Pietá is pierced by a sword: an illustrated metaphor whose drastic expression surpasses even Egyptian art (cf. Figure 6). A visionary who was praying to the Mother of Sorrows in 1972 heard Mary speak the following words: "You know not what it means to be the mother of souls! My heart, too, is split in two! I have suffered the full depths, and so I have become your queen. I will again show you the love that streams from my heart. All grace flows to me from the Son. On the cross his wound broke open and poured itself forth into my heart." (Quoted from Jutta Ströter-Bender, *Die Muttergottes. Das Marienbild in der christlichen Kunst. Symbolik und Spiritualität* [Cologne: DuMont Buchverlag, 1992] 120).

know their life-creating inner strength; they know the force
that joins the pulse of the earth to the heart's beating. A poem
by Dorothee Sölle reminds us of this:

> The Plains Indians pray
> for a moist heart
> In Argentina I listen to the mothers of the disappeared
> but my heart is dried up
>> haven't I already heard that
>> doesn't that woman have a shrill voice
>> should the absent really go on living
>
> Out of a moist heart
> the mothers of the Plaza de Mayo speak
>> the stories are old and worn
>> because the disappearing stops time
>> so that they cannot heal
>> the woman's voice is shrill and empty
>> because the disappearing destroys not those who have
>>> disappeared
>> probably they are all dead
>> I think, and do not see
>> how their disappearing also drags me
>> out from my country
> so that I stop being a mother
> and start thinking like a general
>
> I pray God
> for a moist heart.[9]

From Throat to Soul

The sacramental roots of abstract significance in the concrete and physical are obvious, even more than in the case of the heart, in what we customarily call the "soul" in Western culture, though we cannot articulate any particular concept or idea of it.

The Breathing Throat: Crux of Life and Symbol of the Person

It can really give you goosebumps when Near Easterners at a festival, for example when the company gathered for a wedding greets the bride, break out in joyful noise. They emit shrill tones while striking their hands against their throats (see Figure 13), which results in a remarkable, penetrating warble. There is an onomatopoetic word for this warbling in Hebrew: *hallēl* (imitating the sound, like our words "gurgle" or "yodel"). The call to *hallēl* is *hallelū*, and when the warbling yodel is to be made for the God Yhwh one cries: *hallelū-jā!*

In yodeling and hallelujah-warbling a primitive sound breaks forth out of the internal parts of the person by way of the throat. Therefore at the end of Psalms 103 and 104 we find:

Bless the Lord, O my throat! Hallelujah!

However, this verse is usually translated: "Bless the Lord, O my soul!" Why have the translators given the Hebrew word *nephesh*, which in the first place means "throat," as "soul"? What does the throat have to do with the soul?

Basic to understanding the image of the human in the Ancient Near East is the way of thinking in that time and place, characterized by a synthetic combination of aspects of a thing and by an emphasis on its dynamism rather than its purely external appearance (see pp. 22–29 above). That means: when one thought of an organ, one thought automatically of its abilities and activities at the same time.

Concretely, with reference to the throat, *nephesh* therefore does not mean merely the *visible* part of the body, but also the *audible* calling, croaking, or warbling throat and the *greedy,* never satisfied, hungry and thirsty, devouring and air-breathing throat. In short: what goes into a person and what comes out of him or her—air, water, food, sounds, language—are concentrated in the narrow passage of the gullet (see Figure 14). The *nephesh* becomes the symbol of the needy, greedy human being, of the *élan vital,* the power that makes the human being a creature that pants for and craves life. After all, that is how God made the human being:

> Then the LORD God formed the human being from the dust of the ground, and breathed into its nostrils the breath of life; and the human being became a living *nephesh* (Gen 2:7).

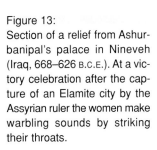

Figure 13:
Section of a relief from Ashurbanipal's palace in Nineveh (Iraq, 668–626 B.C.E.). At a victory celebration after the capture of an Elamite city by the Assyrian ruler the women make warbling sounds by striking their throats.

This *nephesh*-ness of the human being means that we are entirely oriented to relationship, from the very beginning. Everywhere and at all times we have needs that can only be satisfied by other things or other persons. These life-sustaining encounters with the Other are ultimately what we call experiences of God. "Thank God" means: thanks be to all that satisfies my needs. In the language of the Psalms:

> Let them thank Yʜᴡʜ for his steadfast love,
>   for his wonderful works to humankind.
> For he satisfies the thirsty *nephesh*,
>   and the hungry *nephesh* he fills with good things (Ps 107:8-9).

Although *nephesh* can easily be translated "throat" here, behind the organ we can discern the all-encompassing—including spiritual—neediness of the human being. Some of the biblical proverbs play on the material and spiritual sides of the *nephesh;* for example:

> Like cold water to a thirsty soul *[nephesh]*,
>   so is good news from a far country (Prov 25:25).

We could freely translate: what fresh water is to the throat, good news is to the soul.

Figure 14:
Egyptian Sema amulet (664–525 B.C.E.). It represents the two lungs, the trachea, and, in the expansion at the top, the heavily emphasized throat. This symbol can also mean "to join in one." The amulet was supposed to guarantee the ingress of life-sustaining air, necessary even for the dead.

Still more existential, closer to home than nourishment, is breath, which the *nephesh* needs. "Save me, O God, for the waters have come up to my neck," cries the petitioner in Ps 69:1. We would describe the feeling of urgent peril in much the same way: "I'm in hot water up to my neck." Throat and breath run together in Hebrew into a single word. In 1 Kings we read of the impressive raising of the dead son of the widow of Zarephath by the prophet Elijah:

> Then he stretched himself upon the child three times, and cried out to the LORD, "O LORD my God, let this child's life [*nephesh*] come into him again." The LORD listened to the voice of Elijah; the life [*nephesh*] of the child came into him again, and he revived (1 Kings 17:21-22).

Just as the *nephesh,* as the fundamental life force, comes in with the breath, so at death it disappears in the departing breath, for example in the case of Rachel, who did not survive the birth of her second son, Benjamin (Gen 35:18).

Thus the *nephesh* represents life itself. Where there is no *nephesh* there is no life. This is clear in a self-lauding speech of Lady Wisdom in which life and *nephesh* are parallel:

> . . . whoever finds me finds life
>   and obtains favor from YHWH;
> but those who miss me injure themselves [do violence to their
>   *nephesh*];
> all who hate me love death (Prov 8:35).

In the legal corpus of the First Testament *nephesh* is used as a technical juridical term for the life of an individual creature. The well-known law of talion, used to regulate the taking of revenge in the oldest part of the Law, the Book of the Covenant, says:

> . . . life [*nephesh*] for life [*nephesh*],
> eye for eye,
> tooth for tooth,
> hand for hand,
> foot for foot . . . (Exod 21:23-24).

This general formulation can be applied to human or animal, to every being with *nephesh,* that is, every living thing. When a creature is slaughtered, its life is sacrificed. The life of human and animal belongs to God. Indeed, it was supposed that the locus of the *nephesh,* the life, was the blood. So that the life of animals might not be confused with that of human beings the Bible placed an extraordinarily powerful taboo on the consumption of blood. For that reason, even today, Jews and Muslims slaughter by slitting the animal's throat. When the Law says that the blood is the *nephesh* (Deut 12:23) it is clear that at this point the meaning "throat" has completely vanished in favor of "life."

Nephesh was used especially as a technical juridical term in the so-called anathemas, where the word is best translated "person." The anathema formulae protected Israel's most sacred institutions—male circumcision, Passover, the Day of Atonement, and the Sabbath (cf. Lev 17:10; 20:3-6):

> . . . anyone [any *nephesh*] who does any work during that entire day, such a one [*nephesh*] I will destroy from the midst of the people (Lev 23:30).

The anathema formula also served, however, as a massive warning against crimes that evaded social control. These included especially sexual behaviors, the consumption of the fat and blood of animals and of certain meat sacrificed to idols, and performing priestly services in a condition of uncleanness. All these actions could be done secretly and must therefore be subjected to a punishment that would probably never be carried out in fact because it was reserved to God, but that, like a curse, would apply to everyone who did such acts. To put it another way: while in most cases the sinful *nephesh* could be absolved through the sacrifice of the *nephesh* of animals, there were cases in which this was not possible because a taboo had been violated. In such cases the *nephesh* was subject to death. These are the kinds of cases traditional Catholic moral doctrine calls "mortal" sins.

That the *nephesh* is a gift of life that is either protected or rejected by God is illustrated with particular clarity in something Abigail says to David. She is trying to prevent this guerilla chieftain from destroying her village. She flatters his magnanimity and says to the future king of Judah:

> . . . the life *[nephesh]* of my lord shall be bound in the bundle of the living under the care of YHWH your God; but the lives *[nephesh]* of your enemies he shall sling out as from the hollow of a sling (1 Sam 25:29).

The Desirous Throat: Driving Power and Spark of the Soul

We have moved from the throat by way of breath and life to the person itself. A second line of meaning of the word *nephesh* leads by way of desire to the soul. Every desire, not only hunger and thirst, is connected to the craving of the *nephesh*—for example, the instinct for survival expressed in the human eagerness to work:

> The appetite *[nephesh]* of workers works for them;
>   their hunger [mouth] urges them on (Prov 16:26).

Then there is the sex drive that caused the Canaanite prince Shechem to rape Dinah:

> When Shechem son of Hamor the Hivite, prince of the region, saw her, he seized her and lay with her by force. And his soul *[nephesh]* was drawn to Dinah daughter of Jacob; he loved the girl, and spoke tenderly to her (Gen 34:2-3).

Thus the *nephesh* is the force of driving lust or tender longing, and thus also the most crucial component of the human in relation to God. According to the Shema, the appeal of God to believers from Deuteronomy that is recited daily by Jews even today, one should love God with the whole heart, *the whole soul,* and with all one's strength. The word almost universally translated "soul" is again *nephesh,* used here in the sense of an all-encompassing inner desire. The spectrum of the soul's sensations in the First Testament is a broad one, extending from joy, love, hate, sorrow, bitterness, and despair by way of sympathy to the manifold forms of fear, including the fear of the foreigner before the despotic power of the native. The First Testament repeatedly warns against such arbitrary behavior:

> You shall not oppress a resident alien; you know the heart [*nephesh*] of an alien, for you were aliens in the land of Egypt (Exod 23:9).

Thus in the biblical view of humanity the *nephesh* represents the center of vitality, the life force, and the lust for life. It can suffer, rejoice, be carried away, or be rescued from death; it thirsts for God's presence and ultimately can only be utterly at rest with God (cf. Jer 6:16; Pss 62:1; 131:2).

The spectrum of meanings of *nephesh* from "throat" to "soul" left its traces in the Second Testament, though the latter was written in Greek. When the old man Simeon says to Mary, in Luke 2:35: "a sword will pierce your own soul," the evangelist would have been thinking of the throat; the prophecy would originally have meant: "they will put the knife to your throat." However, in line with the Western location of the soul in the heart, the Mother of Sorrows was much later depicted with a sword, or even seven swords piercing her heart (see Figure 12).

The road from throat to soul was not as long as it first appeared, and the way back was just as short, for the many fears and longings stored up in the soul press for an expression through the throat. If it is not cinched shut, as it were, it lends its voice to the mood of the soul, in warbling and singing, in sobbing and weeping, in chattering and whispering, in shouting and shrieking, in giggling and laughing, in grumbling and complaining, in roaring, murmuring, or humming.

The Soul Amputated from the Body

The Hebrew word *nephesh* reveals a very broad spectrum of meaning. Astonishingly enough, the Greek translation made in the third century B.C.E. rendered six hundred of a total of seven hundred fifty-five occurrences of *nephesh* as *psychē*, and thus promoted a good many misunderstandings and reductionistic readings, because Greek philosophy's concept of the soul is in no way comparable to the Hebrew idea of the *nephesh*. It is true that many think that the Septuagint does not presume the complicated doctrine of the soul found in the philosophers, but thinks instead of the popular Greek understanding of *psychē*,[1] but this cannot be demonstrated. Originally *psychē*, like *nephesh*,

was an onomatopoetic concept for exhalation, the audible and
visible breath, much like the Indian word *atman*, related to German "Atem" (breath) [English: atmosphere, etc.], and referred
to the soul. For earlier Greeks *psychē* was primarily the shadowy
image of the ensouled body, an airy, winged being (Figure 15)
that came forth from the mouth or the bleeding wounds of the
dying. In Egypt we have images as early as the Middle Kingdom in which a "soul" arose from the corpse, out of the emis-
sions of the flesh, and was pictured with wings. This Ba-bird
could leave the tomb and provide the dead with the necessities
of life (Figure 16). The Greek shadow souls, on the contrary, led
an altogether miserable, unconscious and spiritless existence in
Hades. When, in Homer's *Iliad*, Patroclus's soul visits the sleeping Achilles and begs him for a proper burial for his dead body,
Achilles holds out his hands longingly to him:

> In the same breath he stretched his loving arms
> but could not seize him, no, the ghost slipped underground
> like a wisp of smoke . . . with a high thin cry.

Figure 15:
Scene from a white-background Lecythos from Athens (Greece, 5th c.
B.C.E.). Hermes, the messenger of the gods, leads a dead woman to
Charon, the ferryman, who will bring her across the Styx. The souls of the
dead in the form of tiny winged people are flying about in the background.

Figure 16:
Vignette from the Book of the Dead, from the Neferubeneph papyrus (Egypt, 13th c. B.C.E.). The dead person can be seen, in front of the entrance to a tomb, in two forms, as shadow and as Ba-bird. The Ba-bird looks at the sun and thus provides the dead person with light. Sometimes special statues were set up in the precincts of the tomb into which the Ba-bird could enter to "fill up" with sun.

> And Achilles sprang up with a start and staring wide,
> drove his fists together and cried in desolation, "Ah god!
> So even in Death's strong house there is something left,
> a ghost, a phantom—true, but no real breath of life.
> All night long the ghost of stricken Patroclus
> hovered over me, grieving, sharing warm tears,
> telling me, point by point, what I must do.
> Marvelous—like the man to the life!"[2]

Diverging from the Homeric and popular ideas about the soul, Greek philosophy, beginning in the seventh century B.C.E., developed the concept of the soul that has decisively influenced our entire Western conception from that day to this. The *psychē* now became the quintessence of the individual, an essence almost divine in nature, existing before a person's

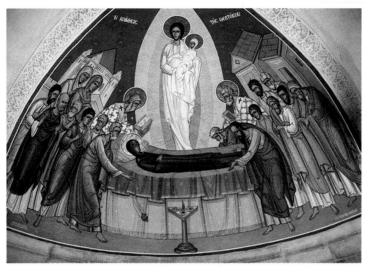

Figure 17:
Icon of the Assumption in Eastern style in the crypt of the Abbey of the Dormition of Mary in Jerusalem (Israel, 20th c.). The soul of Mary, who has died surrounded by the disciples, is shown as a child in heaven, held in the arms of Christ.

birth and also after his or her death, therefore independently of the body (Figure 17). Even in the teaching of the earliest Presocratics, the so-called Orphic philosophers, the transmigration of souls played a central role. It was believed that the soul had been torn away, through strife and discord, from an original primeval spiritual union of all souls, and as punishment for earlier misdeeds was buried in a body as in a grave. It is reported of the mystic Empedocles:

> He regards the weary paths of the souls as including their repeated entry into different bodies . . . . For the souls change from one body to another, since Strife displaces and punishes them and does not permit them to remain in their original unity. Instead, the souls are afflicted by Strife with every kind of punishment, and must shift from body to body . . . .[3]

Preferred souls had a chance to escape. After enduring a process of purification through several lives they could ascend to the gods. But others entered into the forms of animals and plants, so that Pythagoras and Empedocles, who followed him, strictly forbade the mistreatment or killing of any ensouled creature.[4]

The Incarnation, God's becoming flesh, becoming human as the consequence of sin, a fall into the world! Greek anthropology left us as its inheritance not only the division of soul and body, but also contempt for the body, which can only be a prison, a grave for the immortal and much more valuable soul, and therefore must at all costs be ruled by the soul in every respect. Later Greek philosophy did not alter this basic attitude. The doctrine of souls was further refined by Plato, Aristotle, and—with portentous consequences even today—especially by the Scholastics.

Rejoining What Has Been Severed

Our Western image of the human has sickened on the disastrous division of soul and body initiated by Greek philosophy. It is probably no coincidence that notions of the migration of souls and reincarnation are offering strong competition again today. The Greek soul cannot do anything else, to put it bluntly, than wander about, while the Hebrew *nephesh,* by its very nature, cannot be reborn since it vanishes with death. That is why the Jewish and Christian traditions, until recently, remained generally immune to doctrines of reincarnation or the migration of souls, and why the Christian belief in resurrection has emphasized the resurrection of the body, not only of the human soul.

Why is the belief in rebirth and the wandering of souls so attractive to many of our contemporaries? Wherever this body of ideas is borrowed nowadays, from Hinduism or Buddhism, no religion sees reincarnation as something positive and desirable, but always as a fate, indeed a curse, that one attempts to escape if possible. For many wealthy Europeans and Americans, however, reincarnation seems a refuge, because they cannot bear the thought that our earthly life, with all the goods we collect, is so short, that death is a definitive, radical limit. It is a consolation to them in view of the imperfection and fragmentariness of our life to hope for another chance or the securing of what they have already acquired.

Such consolations are foreign to Hebrew thought. Old Testament faith was directed to concrete, earthly life, life before death. A living *nephesh,* a *nephesh* always hungry for life: that is the human being as long as he or she lives, but only that long.

It may be that the more unified Israelite image of the human, which knows no division between soul and body, can help us to overcome the consequences of the Greek dichotomies. If we take this image of the human as our basis, the Church's pastoral service must concern itself more radically than heretofore with bodiliness, with the concrete neediness, longings, and desire for life of people today. If we take this image of the human as our basis, contemporary psychology must deal with the question posed to it by Eugen Rosenstock-Huessy at the beginning of the twentieth century, namely whether it can really offer a doctrine of the soul.[5] For beyond all the evidence, everything that can be explained, everything that can be deduced and derived from comparison, beyond the conscious and the unconscious, the normal, sick, or insane, beyond everything that can be therapeutically treated, influenced, dealt with, analyzed, the soul of a human being constitutes itself between fear and courage, disappointment and hope, intelligence and passion, apathy and the hunger for truth and justice, love and death. It is inextricably bound up with the one, unique life and all its joys and sorrows, the spiritual goods of trust, poverty, possession, and enmity. It is a mystery that we must protect and to which only loving persons with a knowledge of souls can have access.

God in the Belly

It is one of the basic human experiences that a bad feeling can be sensed as a cramping in the *abdominal region*. And who today would dispute that a great many illnesses connected with the stomach and bowels can be traced to ongoing stress? Nowadays in groups that are knowledgeable about the body and its working, the belly has become practically synonymous with the region of feeling or the irrational. In this our current usage is strikingly close to that of the First Testament.

The Entrails: Seismographs of Feeling

Israel's sages and priests were precise observers of psychosomatic connections. For example, they knew that stomach cramps could be caused by emotional irritation:

> The words of a whisperer are like delicious morsels;
> they go down into the inner parts of the body (Prov 18:8).

YHWH is even described as a psychoanalyst who is breathed in with the air and illuminates the dark corners of the person:

> The human spirit is the lamp of the LORD,
> searching every innermost part (Prov 20:27).

However, they were not content with such general statements about the abdomen as a whole. They attempted to make connections between particular feelings and individual organs, much like the familiar practice of examining the entrails of animals. As early as the third millennium before Christ a Sumerian king boasted that he could see "counsels for everything in the world in a single sheep."[1] The *liver* was especially important for this purpose, as it is the largest gland in mammals and is very heavy. Therefore it was called in Hebrew "the weighty" *(kābēd)*. In the Israelite city of Megiddo excavations uncovered a model liver for candidates for the priesthood, inscribed in Akkadian (Figure 18). However, in Israel the liver never achieved the same significance as in comparable texts from Mesopotamia, where it was second only to the heart in importance. It is possible that the examination of the liver (see Figure 19) was not practiced in the cult at Jerusalem. The prophet Ezekiel, who came from the priestly clans, only mentions it negatively as an oracular practice of the king of Babylon (Ezek 21:21). But it was also known in Israel that the liver is an especially delicate organ, and that it was not a good idea to tangle with someone if "a louse had crawled over his liver" (that is, if something was "biting" him or her). The similarity between the words "liver" and "live/life" that we sense in English is present in Hebrew as well, for example when a mourner refers to her liver when she sings of her pain at the fall of Jerusalem, the daughter of the people:

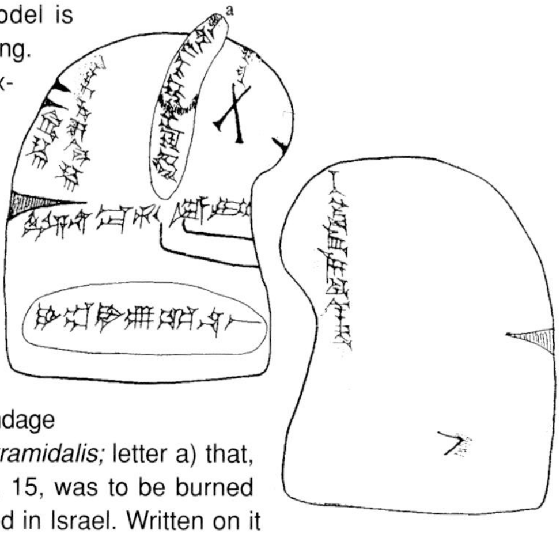

Figure 18:
Clay model of a liver, 15th c. B.C.E., from Hazor (Galilee). The model is about eight centimeters long. It was used as a study example for those preparing to perform sacrificial rites, to instruct them in the examination of the liver that was part of every sacrifice. The individual parts of the liver are carefully inscribed in Akkadian cuneiform. Clearly visible is the appendage of the liver *(processus pyramidalis;* letter a) that, according to Lev 3:4, 10, 15, was to be burned when sacrifice was offered in Israel. Written on it is: "God's pardon for human beings."

> My eyes are spent with weeping;
>   my stomach churns;
> my bile [liver] is poured out on the ground
>   because of the destruction of my people (Lam 2:11).

However, the liver is also associated with positive feelings in the Psalms, much as German talks of frank speaking or "getting something off one's chest" in terms of speaking "out of the liver":

> Therefore my heart is glad,
>   and my soul [liver] rejoices;
> my body also rests secure (Ps 16:9).

For the most part those who prayed the Psalms associated the *kidneys* with the heart, also regarded as the locus of intelligence:

> When my soul [heart] was embittered,
>   when I was pricked in heart [kidneys] . . . (Ps 73:21).

What was felt in the kidneys, then, was some kind of prickling feeling, or even a deliberate stab, a wound that touched the realm of feeling. The integrity of a person was preserved by the heart and kidneys, that is, thought and feeling. Even God tests character by shoving both organs, like gold or silver bars, into an oven to test whether they have been mixed with worthless slag in order to deceive. This image from the language of metallurgists appears fairly often in the Psalms; frequently it is those praying who, confident of their innocence, challenge YHWH to test them:

Figure 19:
Roman shard of *terra sigillata* (no precise dating). It shows a sacrificing priest examining a liver.

> Prove me, O LORD, and try me;
>> test my heart [kidneys] and mind [heart]! (Ps 26:2).

Different still from the sensitive liver and the vulnerable kidneys is the irritable *gall* or *bile:* it is important to prevent this from rising or spilling out. Its name in Hebrew is "the bitter," and according to Matthew the Romans mixed it with wine at Jesus' crucifixion and offer it to the tortured man, spitefully, to make his life bitter at the last (Matt 27:34). During his missionary activity in Samaria, Peter describes Simon Magus as a man filled with gall and wickedness because he tries to buy the power to heal with the Holy Spirit (Acts 8:23). Here "the gall of bitterness" appears to represent the envy that overcame Simon in view of the apostles' miraculous deeds.

Thus biblical thought locates different emotions in the individual organs within the abdomen. At the same time, however, the belly with all its entrails is closely related to other organs. Together with the heart, indeed, they fill the entire space within the torso, the central part of the body. Heart and entrails, thinking and feeling compose a common space of human inwardness out of which we react and make decisions. Our language has no expression for this reality. However, a Japanese biblical scholar[2] has pointed out the analogy to the Japanese word *hara,* which may be familiar from the expression *hara-kiri* (literally "cutting the abdomen"). Japanese rest with upright calm in the *hara* as the center of the human being. This center, borne by the pelvis as by a bowl, is thought to be the basis of human well-being and psychic impulses.

There is also a complex relationship in the Psalms to the throat as seat of the soul by way of the breath, speaking and singing, the ideal cooperation of lungs, diaphragm, and larynx:

> Bless the LORD, O my soul [throat],
>> and all that is within me [my whole belly], bless his holy name
>>> (Ps 103:1).

The Womb: Compassionate Giver of Life

"In the name of Allah, the Compassionate, the Merciful"— with this *bismallah* formula all the Suras of the Quran save one begin. The Arabic word *rahman* is one of the most common descriptions for God: God is merciful and gracious. In Hebrew there is a group of words with the same root as Arabic *rahman* or *rahmat*, "compassion." Hebrew *raḥēm* means "to have compassion" or "to have mercy," and *raḥamim* is "compassion" or "sympathy." All these words contain a still simpler and earlier word, namely *reḥem*, the female lap, uterus, or womb. Together with the heart the *reḥem* is the internal organ most commonly mentioned in the First Testament. But although the concept had such a central place in the biblical image of the human, many male biblical scholars and theologians have completely ignored it.[3] It was only with the advent of feminist biblical exegesis that this gap in patriarchal education was partially filled.[4] The search for the biblical meaning of the womb promises to be an exciting voyage of discovery through texts in the Bible that lead us from a female organ to a metaphor for particular human emotions, and from there to an aspect of the Israelite image of God.

In Israel's imagination and belief the female womb, the uterus, belongs to God. God not only created it, but also has the power to close or open it. The childless Hannah, in her despair, turns to YHWH at the sanctuary in Shiloh and pleads earnestly for a child (1 Sam 1:10-13). Only God can give pregnancy (see Figures 20 and 21). Jacob is justly angry when his beloved wife Rachel, who has not conceived a child, begs him: "Give me children, or I shall die!" "Am I in the place of God, who has withheld from you the fruit of your womb?" he replies (Gen 30:1-2).

It is YHWH who gives children; indeed, they are formed, shaped, or woven by God in the womb. Thus YHWH can say:

> "Before I formed you in the womb I knew you,
>   and before you were born I consecrated you . . ." (Jer 1:5).

For those praying the Psalms this mysterious creation of human beings in their mothers' wombs is a miracle that evokes amazement and gratitude (Ps 139:13-16). Ultimately it is God himself or herself who receives the human being at birth, as a midwife receives the child from its mother's womb:

> Yet it was you who took me from the womb;
>   you kept me safe on my mother's breast.

Figure 20:
Detail from a monumental painting in the tomb of Pharaoh Ramses VI in western Thebes (1145–1137 B.C.E.). It shows the goddess Nut, who is giving birth to her son Horus with the aid of the midwives Isis and Nephtys. The disk within which Re is depicted as a child symbolizes both the mother's uterus and the sun, which represents the royal child in the heavens.

> On you I was cast from my birth,
>> and since my mother bore me you have been my God
>> (Ps 22:9-10).

In Israel a woman's fruitful womb and the breasts with their milk were an image of blessing not produced by human effort, but to be received solely as a gift from God (see Figure 22; compare Figure 103). Tiny figures of goddesses with prominent breasts were placed in the grave with the dead to provide them with a final blessing. In Israel a woman's full breasts were an image of abundance and salvation pure and simple (cf. Isa 66:10-11). Thus in Jacob's blessing God's favor is invoked on Joseph:

> . . . by the Almighty who will bless you
> with blessings of heaven above,

blessings of the deep that lies beneath,
blessings of the breasts and of the womb (Gen 49:25).

The child nursing at its mother's breast is an image of contentment (Ps 131:2), while dry breasts represent the greatest suffering and the most dreadful misery (Hos 9:14).

In a transferred sense people spoke of the womb of the ocean, the dawn, or the earth. Tiny amulets bearing the shape of an omega, symbolizing the woman's uterus, were placed in the graves of miscarried fetuses, infants, and small children (see Figures 23 and 24). Occasionally when the corpse was laid on a stone bench the head would be placed in a large relief in the form of an omega. Thus the human being returns at the end of life to the protection of the earth's womb, as Job says:

Figure 21:
From the Armenian Echmiadian book of the gospels, 6th c. C.E. From the Egyptian goddess of heaven, Nut, who bears the sun god Re, Christianity developed the Marian figure of the Madonna Platytera. The picture shows the enthroned Madonna with the Christ child in a spherical halo that at the same time symbolizes Mary's womb. This early example is part of an Epiphany picture, for the feast celebrated by the Eastern Church as its Christmas. Appearing within a church building, Mary is simultaneously interpreted as the *ekklēsia*, in which Christ has taken up his abode.

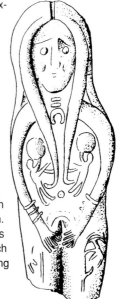

Figure 22:
Pressed terracotta figurine from Revadim in Israel (1500–1300 B.C.E.). The figure shows a long-haired woman opening her vulva. Wild goats on palm trees are depicted on her thighs. An infant is sucking at each breast. At her throat she wears an amulet in the form of an omega. This is a goddess personifying the fruitful forces of the earth that enable people, animals, and plants to flourish. In the Syrian port city of Ugarit this goddess was called Aṯirat (Hebrew Asherah). She bore titles such as "womb," "nourisher of the gods," and "nursing mother of the gods."

Figure 23:
Faience scarab from Tell Fara, north, in Palestine (ca. 1700 B.C.E.). In Palestine, Syria, and Anatolia tiny stamp seals bearing an omega are found especially in the graves of children. This is a uterus-symbol, which on Mesopotamian boundary markers and steles represents the mistress of birth, Ninchursanga. This goddess, like Aṭirat in Ugarit, could be addressed as "womb." Omega-shaped head niches in Jerusalem tombs from the 7th c. B.C.E. could express the hope of the dead that they would return, at death, to the womb of all living things, an idea also found in the Bible (Sir 40:1; cf. Job 1:21): "Hard work was created for everyone, and a heavy yoke is laid on the children of Adam, from the day they come forth from their mother's womb until the day they return to the mother of all the living."

> "Naked I came from my mother's womb, and naked shall I return there . . ." (Job 1:21a).

The *reḥem*, the womb, is also the locus of powerful emotional impulses. In 1 Kings we find the famous story of the two prostitutes who lived together and each bore a child at the same time. One of them suffocates her child in her sleep, and it dies. When she sees it, she exchanges the dead child for the living one. The rightful mother tries to obtain justice at the royal court. It is a difficult case because there are no witnesses. Then King Solomon makes a wise judgment. He orders that the infant be cut in two because both women claim it. The different reactions of the two women to this decision bring the truth to light:

> . . . the woman whose son was alive said to the king—because compassion (*raḥamim*) for her son burned within her—"Please, my lord, give her the living boy; certainly do not kill him!" The other said, "It shall be neither mine nor yours; divide it" (1 Kings 3:26).

Here *raḥamim* is motherly love, for the sake of which this woman is even prepared to relinquish justice. Compassion wells up in the womb, sympathy for a living being. *Raḥamim*, the capacity for sympathy, for empathy, for sharing the feelings

Figure 24:
Early Babylonian terracotta relief of Ninchursanga, "mistress of birth," "mother of the gods," and "mother of all children" (ca. 1800 B.C.E.). The goddess, in a pleated dress, is walking to the left while nursing an infant. In her right hand she holds an unidentifiable object, perhaps a piece of bread that she is giving to the two children looking out over her shoulders, as if she had them bound on her back in a carrying shawl. At her feet, in fetal position, sit two emaciated figures, probably representing miscarriages.

Above each of them is a lengthened omega, the symbol of the motherly, solicitous, and life-restoring aspects of the goddess.

of another, is in the first place something of which women are especially capable. However, men can also be overcome by *rahamim,* for example Joseph when he sees his brother Benjamin for the first time and is so moved that he cannot hold back his tears (Gen 45:2). Sympathy is regarded as important, even in relationships between related tribes. The prophet Amos curses the Edomites because they had stifled pity, brotherhood, in fraternal wars (Amos 1:11). Even much later, in the living tradition of the African-American spirituals, there is confident recollection of Abraham's bosom (see Figure 25), to which, according to Luke 16:22, poor Lazarus was borne by angels after his death: "Rock my soul in the bosom of Abraham."

God's Wombliness

Far more remarkable than the application of an experience specific to women to masculine emotional life is the fact that Israel's God is repeatedly visited by *rahamim,* powerful impulses of sympathy and compassion. It is true that these emotional impulses on the part of God are not associated only with motherliness, but with fatherliness as well, but the Israelites remained

Figure 25:
Stone carving from the south portal of Chartres cathedral (13th c.). In the parable of poor Lazarus the evangelist Luke tells how, after his death, Lazarus is carried by angels to Abraham's bosom, while the rich man suffers tortures in the underworld. In the Christian Middle Ages the souls in Abraham's bosom were a very popular image for Paradise.

conscious of the source of the metaphor of God's *raḥamim*. Thus in Deutero-Isaiah Yʜᴡʜ says to the people of Israel:

> "Can a woman forget her nursing child,
>> or show no compassion for the child of her womb?
> Even these may forget,
>> yet I will not forget you" (Isa 49:15).

God's attitude toward Israel, that rebellious and yet beloved people, is compared to the attitude of a mother to her child. Often different spirits war in Yʜᴡʜ's breast. Wrath and a sense of justice urge divine punishment on Israel, but then sympathy burns in Yʜᴡʜ's belly, and so the people are once again spared. This picture of God's motherly emotions was most fully developed by the prophet Hosea. In Hosea 11 God complains of Israel:

> "When Israel was young, I loved him;
>> out of Egypt I called my son.
> But when I called them, they ran from me . . .
> But it was I who nursed Ephraim (Israel),
>> taking him in my arms . . .
> And I was for them like those who take a nursling to the breast,
>> and I bowed down to him in order to give him suck . . .
> How can I give you up, O Ephraim?
>> How can I hand you over, O Israel? . . .
> My heart recoils against me,
>> my womb is utterly inflamed within me.
> I cannot execute my burning wrath,
>> nor can I utterly change (what is within me), so as to destroy
>> Ephraim (Israel)!
> For I am God and not a man,
>> holy in your midst, and I do not come to destroy."[5]

Thus according to Hosea what sustains God's relationship to Israel and gives it solidity is not a set of typical masculine traits, but rather Yʜᴡʜ's motherly characteristics, for Yʜᴡʜ is God and not a man. In cases of conflict, Israel's God allows grace to supercede law. Even the oldest version of the biblical story of the Flood traces the rescue of humanity to the fact that Yʜᴡʜ is suddenly seized with pity on the creatures Yʜᴡʜ was about to destroy. God's oath never again to destroy humankind

arises out of the same impulses by which the mother goddesses were overcome in the older Near Eastern models for
the Flood story, when they had to watch their human children
being killed. For example, a Sumerian flood story tells how the
mother goddess Nindu reacts to the decision of the father god
Enlil to destroy humankind with a flood because they disturbed his sleep:

> Then Nindu wept for her creatures,
>   the pure Inanna was full of sighs over her humans.[6]

In times of crisis and danger the Israelites did not hesitate to remind God of the divine capacity for sympathy and
compassion:

> "Where are your zeal and your might?
>   The yearning of your heart and your compassion?
>   Do not hold back, for you are our father . . ." (Isa 63:15*).

Such are the prayers from the time of Trito-Isaiah, after the exile,
but there are similar ideas in the Psalms (cf. Ps 77:9). Israel con-
soles itself again and again that God is merciful, that divine
mercy is greater than all human stupidities and provocations:

> In overflowing wrath for a moment I hid my face from you,
>   but with everlasting love I will have compassion on you,
>   says the LORD, your Redeemer (Isa 54:8).

In countless phrases the whole First Testament recalls that Israel's God is a God of mercy and compassion:

> Gracious is the LORD, and righteous;
>   our God is merciful (Ps 116:5).

We began with the womb, the seat of sympathy and empathy, and finally, perhaps unexpectedly, we have arrived at a
biblical image of God. According to the first creation account
the man and woman are the image of God, and thus it is really
nothing more than consistent that a female organ can reveal
not only a good deal about the biblical image of the human,
but also about the nature of God. On the other hand it is not
surprising that Christianity has transferred all the merciful

and intercessory aspects of God found in the tradition of the
Egyptian icons of mother goddesses to Mary (see Figure 26).

Despising the Menstruating Woman

Through these associations the woman's uterus acquired a
value that is no longer a matter of course today, because for our
culture a quite different text from the First Testament, from the
book of Leviticus, became normative:

> When a woman has a discharge of blood
> that is her regular discharge from her body,
> she shall be in her impurity for seven days,
> and whoever touches her shall be unclean
> until the evening. Everything upon which
> she lies during her impurity shall be unclean;
> everything also upon which she sits shall be
> unclean. Whoever touches her bed shall wash
> his clothes, and bathe in water, and be unclean
> until the evening . . . (Lev 15:19-21).

Israel's prophets expanded this law, which tends
toward discrimination against women, into an
image of uncleanness. The organization of the
world into "pure" and "impure" is, of course,
not to be confused with moral valuation, but
later developments show that the step from
"unclean" to "disgusting" was pretty short.
Ezekiel does not even hesitate to compare
the sinfulness of the

Figure 26:
Ptolemaic cast bronze figure of Isis nursing, in Ethiopian
style. The image of the mother goddess nurs-
ing the infant Horus suppressed all other icons
of compassionate goddesses in the late Egyptian period. Isis took over the sun's disk and cow
horns from the love goddess Hathor. For Egyptian observers the image evoked the story of the divine mother
who, in flight from the wicked accusations of her son Seth,
who sought to murder his brother, hides herself in a papyrus thicket at Chemmis and there brings up Horus.

house of Israel, which led to their exile, with a woman's menstruation (Ezek 36:16-17). The Jew Jesus of Nazareth, through his unconditional acceptance and healing of a woman who suffered a flow of blood for twelve years, pointed in the opposite direction (Mark 5:25-34). Nevertheless, this enmity toward the body and women in the prophetic and priestly tradition has a history of almost unbroken influence from then until now. Among its consequences are an alienation of women from this part of themselves, their center. This is impressively confirmed by the recollections of a Nootka Indian woman from the West coast of America. She tells how the life of the women of her tribe was changed by the arrival of the white priests:

> Instead of being raised and educated by women who told them the truth about their bodies, the girls were taken from their villages [by priests] and put in schools where they were taught to keep their breasts bound, to hide their arms and legs, to never look a brother openly in the eye but to look down at the ground as if ashamed of something. Instead of learning that once a month their bodies would become sacred, they were taught they would become filthy. Instead of going to the waiting house to meditate, pray, and celebrate the fullness of the moon and their own bodies, they were taught they were sick, and must bandage themselves and act as if they were sick.[7]

Menstruation is still a taboo theme in our supposedly progressive civilization. The particular sensitivity of a menstruating woman to all kinds of perceptions is discredited as hysteria or moodiness, pills are prescribed for cramps, and advertising suggests to women that they should make the phenomenon of menstruation disappear by the use of "feminine hygiene" products. But beyond that there are some much more crucial developments at work. Medicine and genetic technologies are assuming more and more influence over women's wombs. Artificial insemination, surrogate motherhood, prenatal diagnosis—all these are now shorthand phrases in the press. What remains of the Old Testament conviction that the womb belongs to God alone, God who gives and takes life? If we take the Bible seriously a technological seizure of the woman's uterus is not only an attack on the dignity of women but an insult to God.

"The Very Hairs of Your Head Are Numbered"

Our language has any number of expressions that testify to the importance of the head and parts of the head in human interaction. A face-to-face confrontation or face-off is more dangerous than a hostile exchange of letters. Fear of losing face suggests care in dealing with an opponent. Shaking one's head expresses amazement or rejection. Being pigheaded, stiff-necked, or going head to head with someone—all these denote resistance of one sort or another. Having one's nose in the air is a sign of pride and arrogance. Besides the many metaphorical images associated with the eyes, ears, and mouth, another large set relating to the head, the face, the forehead, the neck, the nose, and the hair contains special meanings. In fact, a good deal of our body language concentrates entirely on the head. It was very much the same in the cultures of the Ancient Near East and in Israel.

The Head: Crown of the Human Person

The human head has always been regarded as the top of the hierarchy of body parts, and therefore represents, as *pars pro toto*, the whole person. When a crowd of people has to be counted, one counts heads. In the Late Stone Age in Palestine the skull was carefully buried by itself, and frequently it was sumptuously decorated and placed in the living quarters. In Egypt the dead were given head amulets meant to guarantee the functioning of that part of the body beyond death. Such gestures were attempts to make the dead ancestors present. In the Ancient Near East beheading was a common form of execution, giving an especially drastic emphasis to the destruction of the opponent's whole being. The reliefs produced by the bellicose Assyrians frequently show whole mounds of severed heads of enemies near the battlefields; indeed, the head as war trophy has a long tradition in western Asia (see Figure 27). No wonder the bodyguards in Israel were called "head guards!"

Thus the head is especially vulnerable, but also especially honorable. The heads of prophets and kings were anointed or crowned (1 Sam 10:1; Mark 14:3), and at the time of Jesus one would swear by one's own head (Matt 5:36). On the other hand, a humble person at prayer bowed the head in an act of self-abasement, and in great sorrow and despair an Israelite would strew ashes on her or his head. The prophet Amos (2:7) accuses the exploiters of the people of treading the heads of the little people, that is, the poor, in the dust. The Song of Songs tells how precious the head is when the woman describes the head of her beloved as if it were that of a golden idol (see Figure 28):

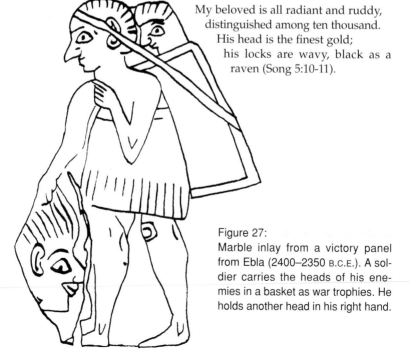

> My beloved is all radiant and ruddy,
> distinguished among ten thousand.
> His head is the finest gold;
>   his locks are wavy, black as a
>   raven (Song 5:10-11).

Figure 27:
Marble inlay from a victory panel from Ebla (2400–2350 B.C.E.). A soldier carries the heads of his enemies in a basket as war trophies. He holds another head in his right hand.

Figure 28: Gold head of Hathor (3.5 x 2.7 cm) from the tomb of the high priest and prince Sheshonk in Memphis (ca. 850 B.C.E.). Hathor was, among other things, the goddess of eroticism and beauty, and was called "the golden."

The Face: Focus of the Person

According to biblical conceptions the face turned toward someone is the expression of contact and relationship, while turning the back signifies breaking of relationship and lack of interest. The whole spectrum of human moods is reflected in the face and its expressions.[1] In sorrow one covers one's face (2 Sam 19:5; see Figure 29). When kings are depressed and resigned they go to bed and turn their faces to the wall, that is, they refuse to look at reality; thus, for example, when Ahab is disappointed at his unsuccessful negotiations with Naboth over the latter's vineyard:

> Ahab went home resentful and sullen because of what Naboth the Jezreelite had said to him . . . . He lay down on his bed, turned away his face, and would not eat (1 Kings 21:4; cf. 2 Kings 20:1-2 and Isa 38:2).

A free countenance is characteristic of an open-hearted, honest person, but anyone who has something to hide, is angry, or is contemplating a crime casts down his or her gaze and looks dark. YHWH speaks to Cain openly about this before he goes into the field with Abel to kill him:

> . . . YHWH had regard for Abel and his offering, but for Cain and his offering he had no regard. So Cain was very angry, and his countenance fell. YHWH said to Cain, "Why are you angry, and why has your countenance fallen?" (Gen 4:4-6).

Figure 29:
Painted wood figure of the Egyptian goddess Isis (ca. 1000 B.C.E.). Mourning for her dead son Osiris, the mother goddess holds a hand before her face. In sorrow the mourner makes herself like the one mourned: she causes her face to disappear.

The appropriate reaction to the appearance of God or an angel—really a very instinctive fearful response—is to throw oneself worshipfully to the ground, that is, in Hebrew "to fall on one's nose" or frequently "on one's face" (cf. Judg 13:20; 1 Sam 28:20; 1 Kings 18:39; see Figure 30):

> When Abram was ninety-nine years old, Yhwh appeared to Abram, and said to him, "I am God Almighty; walk before me, and be blameless. And I will make my covenant between me and you, and will make you exceedingly numerous." Then Abram fell on his face, and God said to him . . . (Gen 17:1-3).

Shame shows on one's face (Pss 44:15; 69:7, and frequently elsewhere), and to spit in a person's face is an expression of the most extreme contempt (Num 12:14; Deut 25:9; Job 30:10). Life or death can depend on a pleasant expression, as the book of Proverbs is well aware:

> A king's wrath is a messenger of death,
>   and whoever is wise will appease it.
> In the light of a king's face there is life,
>   and his favor is like the clouds that bring the spring rain
>   (Prov 16:14-15).

The forehead or brow is considered the center of the face; even today many peoples like to place tattoos or a colored dot there. The forehead is something like a person's public bulletin board. Here a cross as the sign of belonging to a divinity could be cut (see Figure 31), or a jewel affixed. The forehead is especially adept at defiance and resistance, and so Yhwh sends the prophet Ezekiel with a specially hardened brow to the defiant people Israel:

> . . . the house of Israel will not listen to you, for they are not willing to listen to me; because all the house of Israel have a hard forehead and a stubborn heart. See, I have made your face hard against their faces, and your forehead hard against their foreheads. Like the hardest stone, harder than flint, I have made your forehead; do not fear them or be dismayed at their looks, for they are a rebellious house (Ezek 3:7-9).

Figure 30:
Relief from the tomb of the civil official Haremhab in Sakkarah, Egypt (copy *in situ;* ca. 1300 B.C.E.). The attitudes of the group of foreign princes who are begging Pharaoh Tut-ankh-Amon for asylum comically illustrate the process of falling down *(proskynesis)* before the king. Their raised hands express petition. They not only humble themselves by falling on their faces; they also lie on their stomachs and even on their backs. (Details and reconstruction of the motif in Thomas Staubli, *Das Image der Nomaden im Alten Israel und in der Ikonographie seiner seßhaften Nachbarn* [Fribourg: Universitätsverlag; Göttingen: Vandenhoeck & Ruprecht, 1991] 44–46, Figures 30a–c.)

Face to Face with God

As the human face can be hard (Ezek 3:8-9), that is, repellent, or friendly and inviting, so also the face of the Godhead reveals its moods and intentions. Even before there was a political state of Israel men and women in Palestine wore seals or plates on throat or wrist (see Figure 32) on which the smiling face of a goddess was engraved. Women in Judah later liked to set up a statue of a goddess in their houses or had one placed in their graves; the large breasts and smiling faces of these figures promised blessing and compassion (cf. Figure 103).

Figure 31:
Ivory inlay from Arslan Tash (northern Syria; 9th c. B.C.E.) with the motif of the "woman at the window." The cross on her forehead decoration shows that she is dedicated to the goddess and legitimates her act of showing her inviting, friendly face in the window, which ordinarily would be regarded as indecent.

Not infrequently at the beginning YHWH, Israel's God, was self-revealed to worshipers face to face. After the night battle with the river demon at the Jabbok (Gen 32:22-32), Jacob realizes that he has been fighting with YHWH, and he calls the place of the struggle Pniel, "face of God," because he had seen God face to face and lived. Before the renewal of the tablets of the Law, Moses goes into the tent of encounter with God:

> Thus YHWH used to speak to Moses face to face, as one speaks to a friend (Exod 33:11).

Later, a direct encounter with God was more and more frequently regarded as dangerous. Therefore, immediately after the just-quoted episode in the book of Exodus, YHWH personally instructs Moses in exactly the opposite fashion:

> . . . you cannot see my face; for no one shall see me and live." And YHWH continued, "See, there is a place by me where you shall stand on the rock; and while my glory passes by I will put you in a cleft of the rock, and I will cover you with my hand until I have passed by; then I will take away my hand, and you shall see my back; but my face shall not be seen" (Exod 33:20-23).

Only in the Temple could the Israelites "behold the face of God" (2 Sam 21:1; Ps 41:12; cf. Ps 17:15). Recently there has been renewed discussion of the question whether this was a purely metaphorical expression, or whether there may have been a statue of YHWH in the Temple at Jerusalem.[2]

It is dreadful when God's face is turned away because of Israel's sin, when God's back is turned (Deut 31:17; Job 13:24; Ps 51:11-12; Ezek 7:22), for all creatures live from the face of God turned toward them, signaling compassion and care, affection and loving companionship (Pss 31:16; 104:29, and frequently elsewhere). Probably the most beautiful form of this knowledge of our dependence on God's care in the First Testament is the so-called blessing of Aaron in the book of Numbers:

> Thus you shall bless the Israelites: You shall say to them,
> YHWH bless you and keep you;
> YHWH make his face to shine upon you, and be gracious to you;
> YHWH lift up his countenance upon you, and give you peace (Num 6:22-27).

The text speaks twice of YHWH's face or countenance. The shining countenance indicates the divine presence in the stars (Figure 33), which were understood to be visible and life-sustaining signs, God's first works in creation. The face turned toward one is more indicative of God's kindness in the neighbor, which culminates in peace among humanity. In a necropolis near Jerusalem the Aaronic blessing has been found on silver amulets from the sixth century B.C.E.; these were placed in the graves of the dead. The shining countenance of God evoked in it ap-

Figure 32:
Engraved gold plate from the Levant (1500–1300 B.C.E.). The Hathor hairstyle (cf. Figure 28) of the goddess with the friendly face indicates Egyptian influence. The additional schematic engraving of a pubic triangle, navel, and nipples emphasizes the erotic aspect of the goddess and her fertility.

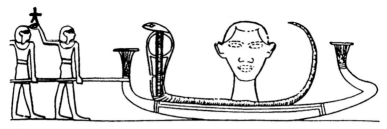

Figure 33:
Section from the seventy-third scene in the Book of the Gates in the tomb of Rameses VI (Egypt 1142–1135 B.C.E.). The face of the sun is drawn forward in the sun's bark by gods. The star in the god's hand is the sign for "giving praise." Viewing the face of the sun is equivalent to a rejuvenation cure (or "face lift") for the dead. The text of the Book of the Gates reads at this point: "This is the face of Re, who voyages to earth. Those who are in the underworld praise it."

parently replaced the friendly face of the goddess, otherwise frequently placed in graves in the form of terracotta figures (cf. Figure 35) to accompany the dead into her dark realm.

The "light of the countenance" is a source of happiness (Ps 31:16-20). When Jesus ascends a mountain with Peter, James, and John (Matt 17:1-9) he is transfigured before their eyes and his face begins to shine like the sun (Figure 34). The shining countenance and transfiguration make Jesus at that moment transparent to the presence and loving care of God for human beings, things ordinarily manifest in the divine words and works.

The Neck: Bastion of Pride

The neck or throat fundamentally expresses pride and self-confidence. In the Near East, from ancient times, a self-confident bearing was part of the ideal of female beauty. Goddesses were often depicted completely naked, or without ornament except for their throats, which were emphasized by a chain (see Figure 35). In the Song of Songs the man several times describes the throat of his beloved as like a watchtower or a precious tower of ivory (Song 7:4; cf. 1:10), because she seems to him proud and unconquerable:

Figure 34:

Transfiguration of Christ in the apse mosaic of the Monastery of St. Catherine on Mount Sinai (565/66 C.E.). Seven rays of light shine from the luminous body of Christ over the apostles Peter, James, and John. The fourth ode of the canon for the feast in the Greek liturgy says: "Out of your body went forth the rays of your divinity upon the prophets and apostles."

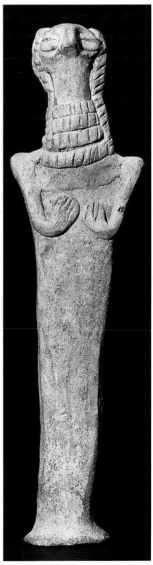

> Your neck is like the tower of David,
> > built in courses;
> > on it hang a thousand bucklers,
> > > all of them shields of warriors (Song 4:4).

While the pride of the woman here still has something fascinating about it, Isaiah presents the high-held necks of the upper-class women of Jerusalem as purely a sign of haughtiness (Isa 3:16-24; cf. Ps 73:6). According to numerous biblical statements stubbornness (stiff-neckedness) was a common vice of individual Israelites, or even of the entire people, and led to outbreaks of YHWH's wrath (Exod 32:9; Deut 9:27; Judg 2:19; Prov 29:1; Isa 48:4; Jer 7:26; Zech 7:11, and frequently elsewhere). The neck could be stiff, powerful, and iron-like, but it could also be put in a noose; the enemy could set his foot on the opponent's neck or lay a yoke on him (Josh 10:24; Jer 27:8-12, and frequently). As a sign of the threatened conquest of Judah by the king of Babylon, and in the sense of an appeal to accept the yoke of subservience in order to survive, Jeremiah laid a wooden yoke on his neck while proclaiming his message (Jeremiah 27–28).

Figure 35:
Terracotta figure from northern Syria (2200–1500 B.C.E.). Simple figures of goddesses of this type were made in great numbers, and frequently there was no detailing; however, the jewelry at the throat was never omitted.

The Nose: Wrath and Patience

The nose is the organ of smelling, which rejoices in a pleasant odor such as that of an apple or of the beloved (Song 7:9), and can be offended by a stench such as that of excrement or corpses (Amos 4:10). God breathed life into the human being in the form of the breath that goes in and out through the nostrils as long as the person is a living throat (Gen 2:7; see chapter 2 above). Isaac does honor to his future wife, Rebecca, through the hands of his servant, by giving her a heavy gold nose ring. The Assyrian kings placed nose rings of a very different kind in the noses of disobedient vassal kings (cf. Figure 90), or in their lower lips, and led them by these rings, like animals, through the streets to be taunted by their people. The Assyrian king Assarhaddon (680–669 B.C.E.) had huge stone steles bearing this motif set up to prevent rebellions in the provinces of his kingdom.[3] YHWH's prophet Isaiah, in helpless rage, threatens the king of Assyria with the same fate as he stands before the gates of Jerusalem:[4]

> "Because you have raged against me
>   and your arrogance has come to my ears,
> I will put my hook in your nose
>   and my bit in your mouth;
> I will turn you back on the way by which you came"
>   (2 Kings 19:28).

In an analogous sense a "strong nose" can mean decision and a "high nose" arrogance. Much more frequently in the First Testament, however, we read of an enflamed nose. This metaphor is based on the idea of angry snorting. One example is Elihu, one of Job's friends, who first allows his older friends to speak, but finally cannot control his own rage:

> Then Elihu . . . became angry [his nose was enflamed]. He was angry [his nose was enflamed] at Job because he justified himself rather than God; he was angry [his nose was enflamed] also at Job's three friends because they had found no answer, though they had declared Job to be in the wrong (Job 32:2-3).

Of course the English Bible translations have "became angry" or "was angry" instead of a literal translation of the "enflamed nose" expression, but in the process, as so frequently happens, the metaphorical and anthropological features of the saying are lost.

We should think of the quality of the nose and its owner that commands respect and honor—and not of its size—when the nose of the beloved in the Song of Songs is compared with a tower raised up in Lebanon against the longed-for oasis city of Damascus (Song 7:4).

Of course, the First Testament speaks of the wrath (and therefore the nose) of God four times as often as it refers to human wrath. God's wrath is enkindled when God's long nose, that is, divine "patience," is exhausted. The nose then competes with the womb, whose life-giving mercy determines the basic character of the divine nature. The reason for God's wrath is always a historical event that thwarts God's plan, namely the protection of life. These connections are clearly exemplified at the time when Jerusalem is about to be destroyed by Nebuchadnezzar, after King Zedekiah has refused to pay him tribute. The prophet Jeremiah conveys the following words of God to Zedekiah:

> Thus says Yhwh, the God of Israel: I am going to turn back the weapons of war that are in your hands and with which you are fighting against the king of Babylon and against the Chaldeans who are besieging you outside the walls; and I will bring them together in to the center of this city. I myself will fight against you with outstretched hand and mighty arm, in anger, in fury, and in great wrath [with a nose snorting with rage]. . . . I will give King Zedekiah of Judah, and his servants, and the people in this city—those who survive the pestilence, sword, and famine—into the hands of King Nebuchadrezzar of Babylon . . . . He shall strike them down with the edge of the sword; he shall not pity them, or spare them, or have compassion [allow a womb to govern] (Jer 21:4-7).

When we consider that not once does the Bible speak of an outbreak of wrath on the part of a woman we can say that the enflamed nose, in contrast to the womb, embodies a masculine aspect of God.

In worship people attempted to calm God's irritable nose with the pleasant odor of animal sacrifices. Perhaps it is no

accident that it was precisely in the period of Assyrian domi-
nance, an era when God's nose was especially stressed, that it
became fashionable to burn expensive incense to intensify this
calming effect. To judge by Orthodox and Catholic worship,
this prescription is in use even today, while monasticism and
Protestantism relied solely on prayer as a means of soothing
God's nose and causing the divine face to shed light again.

The Hair: Vitality and Eroticism

The crown and ornament of the head is the hair. Have you,
dear readers, ever seen a picture of Jesus with a bald head?
That one is still waiting to be invented. It is part of the fixed
tradition of picturing Paul, but it is unimaginable for Jesus—
not because someone thirty-three years old could not be bald,
but because long hair is part of the program whose meaning
we will clarify in the following sequence of ideas.

The First Testament knows no less than thirteen technical
words for hair and haircare. It is not just a matter of proverbial
sayings about splitting hairs, hair standing on end, or people
tearing their hair. Hair was simply a separate topic, even a political matter. At any rate the Torah not only has a section on
healthy and sick hair for those who would become priests and
would therefore function as medicine men (Lev 13:40-44); the
priest's hairstyle was precisely regulated (Ezek 44:20), and the

Figure 36:
Picture from the Book of the Gates (Egypt, 13th–11th c. B.C.E.). Re as
shepherd of the nations (Egyptian, Asiatic, Nubian, Libyan), each typified
and identified by clothing, skin color, and hairstyle.

styles favored by the neighboring Arabs were strictly forbidden to Israelites (Lev 19:27-28; cf. Jer 9:25). The people of the Near East had their own typical ways of wearing their hair. Thus in Egyptian portraiture Egyptians, Asiatics, Nubians, and Libyans can be distinguished not only by their skin color and clothing, but also by their hairstyles (see Figure 36). Goddesses can also be recognized by their hairdos. Thus a center part and long, rolled locks are typical of Hathor (cf. Figure 32), the Egyptian goddess of love and eroticism. In general, women's ways of wearing their hair show more variety than do men's, although the latter also have different styles of beards (cf. Figures 40 and 49). In Judah a pointed beard was usually worn (cf. Figures 30 and 92), but under the Romans it nearly disappeared, at least in the upper class, since the Romans propagated the ideal of beardlessness. Thus among the secondary sexual characteristics the hair is the most important external sexual sign, and it is the occasion for the apostle Paul to write what is perhaps the most misogynistic theological argument in the New Testament:

> Any man who prays or prophesies with something on his head disgraces his head, but any woman who prays or prophesies with her head unveiled disgraces her head—it is one and the same thing as having her head shaved. For if a woman will not veil herself, then she should cut off her hair; but if it is disgraceful for a woman to have her hair cut off or to be shaved, she should wear a veil. For a man ought not to have his head veiled, since he is the image and reflection of God; but woman is the reflection of man. Indeed, man was not made from woman, but woman from man. Neither was man created for the sake of woman, but woman for the sake of man (1 Cor 11:4-9).

Paul brings other arguments to support this thoroughly man-centered argument justifying a requirement that women be veiled during worship. If we are to deal with this presumptuous passage from 1 Corinthians at all, we can only contradict it in the clearest terms—on the basis of the best biblical tradition.

Not only for women, but also for men cutting the hair was a great disgrace (2 Sam 10:4). Only in mourning did people resort to this drastic symbol of stripping away one's strength. In those cases men also veiled the hair of their beards, and mourning women tore out their hair (Figure 37). Hair has an entirely positive meaning, from the growing of pubic hair of young people (Ezek 16:7) to the gray hair of old people, which demanded respect:

> Gray hair is a crown of glory;
>   it is gained in a righteous life (Prov 16:31).

In the Song of Songs the loose hair of the beloved (Figure 38) is praised in the highest terms, with an image that expresses dynamism, fullness, and wild power:

> Turn away your eyes from me,
>   for they overwhelm me!
> Your hair is like a flock of goats,
>   moving down the slopes of Gilead (Song 6:5).

The billy goat, which is called "the hairy" in Hebrew, is a symbol of great vitality. To emphasize the destructive aspect of that kind of power one would refer to the goat demon (Figure 39). In this way the symbolism of the demonic also became associated with human hair.

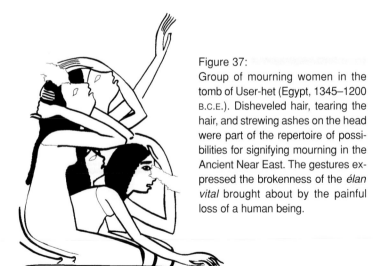

Figure 37:
Group of mourning women in the tomb of User-het (Egypt, 1345–1200 B.C.E.). Disheveled hair, tearing the hair, and strewing ashes on the head were part of the repertoire of possibilities for signifying mourning in the Ancient Near East. The gestures expressed the brokenness of the *élan vital* brought about by the painful loss of a human being.

Figure 38:
Dancer on an Egyptian clay shard (ca. 1400 B.C.E.). The rich hairdo of the dancer underscores her acrobatic movements and the vitality they express.

Last but not least, we should mention Samson, the hairy hero from the book of Judges (chs. 13–16), who—as the fable-like traditions report—had great strength because of letting his hair grow, but very little sense. Samson stands within a long Near Eastern tradition of long-haired heroes (Figure 40). In the Bible he embodies the type of the Nazirite, a man vowed to God (cf. Figure 42), who may never drink wine or touch corpses, and whose hair may never be touched by a razor (Num 6:2, 4, 5, 6).

We can say that from ancient times until today long, strong hair is a vivid, even a divine or demonic symbol of the life-force and eroticism, of the untamable, and of protest. This is true of the hair of Medusa, which in mythology was exaggerated

Figure 39:
Goat demon on an ivory tablet from Megiddo (Israel, 13th/12th c. B.C.E.). The billy goat is called "hairy" in Hebrew. Here the demonic is associated with hairiness. According to Leviticus 16, on the Day of Atonement the sins of the Israelites were to be laid on a billy goat and sent into the wilderness to the demon Azazel.

Figure 40:
Cylinder seal from the Akkadian period (Iraq, 2340–2150 B.C.E.). Long-haired heroes are a long tradition in the Near East. Sumerian seals from the early third millennium B.C.E. show a bearded, long-haired man, often a "six-lock hero," who subdues wild animals, here a lion, to protect the flocks. This is a common motif. The conspicuous hair represents his strength.

Figure 41:
"Medusa," 1990, photograph by Pierre and Gilles. Medusa ("ruler"), one of the three Gorgons, according to the myth changed everyone who looked at her to stone: this is the magical power of the erotic. Perseus succeeds, with divine help, in cutting off the Medusa's head. He gives the head to the goddess Athene, who thereafter bears it on her shield, where it assumes the original apotropaic role of the Medusa.

Figure 42:
"Eli Jah; Moses in the Burning Bush." Acrylic on linen (Kingston, Jamaica, 1992). The Jamaican artist paints Moses with Rastafarian "dreadlocks." The Rastafarians see themselves as successors to the Nazirites who, as a sign of their dedication to God, could not cut their hair, out of which their mysterious power (like that of Samson) grows.

and demonized as snakes (Figure 41), but also of the long hair of the Crucified in Christian art. It is true of the loose hair of the Magdalene imagery and medieval witches as well as of the dreadlocks of the Rastafarians in Jamaica (Figure 42), who appeal to the Bible for their practice. It is true of the long-haired minstrels and troubadours in the Middle Ages, but also of the Beatles, who brought fear to the bourgeois in the Sixties with their songs and their hairstyles. It holds true from the Song of Songs in the Bible to the musical "Hair."

"They Have Eyes, But Do Not See"

The average American spends eighteen years of her or his life in front of the television set. (The average for French people is about eight years.)[1] For them, listening to the radio, reading books, or even telling stories from memory are behaviors they only know about from seeing them on TV. Video stores are replacing libraries. At the same time, the number of illiterates in the developed nations of the world is increasing. The viewed world is replacing the world of experience. Simultaneously, consciousness of environmental problems is lessening (see Figure 43). Encounters and conversations, including the erotic aspects inherent in them, are being sacrificed to the time-consuming little screen. And at the same time the potential for frustration and for violence, susceptibility to neuroses, and isolation are on the increase.

Television and video at home, advertising billboards on the streets—our daily lives are marked by constant visual over-stimulation. News spots, interrupted more and more frequently by countless attractive images for purposes of entertainment and advertising, follow one another continually, at shorter and shorter intervals.[2] Even the worst information comes in entertaining form: the Persian Gulf war, carried live on television, acquired the appearance of a gigantic fireworks display. But that mere viewing by no means has the same quality as engaged, attentive seeing is evident, for example, from the almost-forgotten discussion of the question whether the televising of a Catholic eucharistic celebration was permissible and whether participation in such a TV Mass would be valid.

Figure 43:
Michael Böhme, "Der Segen des Fortschritts" [The Blessing of Progress],
acrylic on canvas. The German artist's contemporary-critical image urgently indicates that the television set has assumed the character of a fetish. It no
longer calls for broad vision, but causes its viewers to look away from reality to
a world that is only projected or has already vanished.

Overfed with this kind of image-salad, nowadays we more and more quickly forget how to look, how to observe closely, how to regard with love, and how to perceive the meaning of images. In the times of ancient Israel and at the beginnings of Christianity this was by no means the case. Perhaps the Bible holds some surprising knowledge for us, precisely as regards the eye and its seeing, because for us—in the case of the eyes as with most of the other organs—the discoveries and viewpoints of the Greeks have become standard. The very word "optician" on an eyeglass emporium in and of itself conveys that quite clearly. The learned Greeks were inspectors of nature who examined the component parts of what they observed with cool detachment. Alcmaeon of Crotona was one of these natural philosophers who lived around 500 B.C.E. He was the first to dissect living animals and thus made a discovery much honored in Western science:[3]

> There are narrow pathways from the brain, in which the highest and most crucial power of the soul is rooted, to the eye sockets; these contain a natural spirit *(pneuma)*. These pathways arise from one and the same origin and root, and are joined at the inmost base of the forehead for a time, but after forking and separating they reach the eye sockets, where the eyebrows form a crossing path; there they turn, where a fold of membrane absorbs the natural moisture, and fill globes that are protected by the eyelids . . . .

Eyes and Gaze

When the First Testament speaks of a person's eyes or, very frequently, of the eyes of God, what is in the foreground is never the form or physical function of the eye, but always the quality and dynamism of the gaze:

> Ah, you are beautiful, my love;
>   ah, you are beautiful;
>   your eyes are doves (Song 1:15; 4:1).

"Your eyes are doves," the lovers say to each other in the Song of Songs (cf. also 5:12). This means: your glances are messages of love; what your eyes tell me proclaims your love, just as the doves proclaimed the erotic emanations of the ancient Near Eastern love goddesses, to whom they were sacred (Figure 44). We can understand other love-declarations in the Song of Songs in the same sense:

> You have ravished my heart (inmost self, imagination, fantasy) with a glance of your eyes (Song 4:9).

> Turn away your eyes from me, for they overwhelm me! (Song 6:5).

In a transferred sense one can also speak of the eye of wine (Prov 23:31) or of a metal (Ezek 1:7; Dan 10:6). Thus shining and sparkling are associated especially with the eyes. The quality of the gaze was immensely important to the Hebrew people. Leah's disadvantage in comparison to her more beautiful sister Rachel was her dull eyes:

> Now Laban had two daughters; the name of the elder was Leah, and the name of the younger was Rachel. Leah's eyes

Figure 44:
Cylinder seal from ancient Syria (ca. 1750 B.C.E.). A dove flies away from the earth goddess, who is removing her veil, to the storm god who is advancing over the mountains, as a sign of the goddess's love. The dove was sacred to the Syrian goddess of love, Ishtar (Aphrodite in Greece; Venus in Rome). We find the same constellation in the gospel accounts of Jesus' baptism, where God sends forth a dove as a sign of love for the Son: "This is my Son, the Beloved . . ." (Matt 3:17 *parr.*).

were weak,[4] but Rachel was graceful and beautiful. Jacob loved Rachel . . . (Gen 29:16-18).

David's comeliness also consists primarily, according to 1 Samuel, in the beauty of his eyes (1 Sam 16:12).

God Sees

One of the most common types of amulet in ancient Egypt was the Eye of Horus (Figure 45). Anyone who prayed in the temple at Guzana was surrounded by statues of the gods with wide-open, staring eyes (Figure 46). The god Bes could even be portrayed as a figure covered with eyes (Figure 47). For the Israelites, too, it was a matter of course that God has eyes and sees. "He who formed the eye, does he not see?" (Ps 94:9). The text speaks much more often of YHWH's eyes than of YHWH's ears. The works of creation conclude, in the Priestly account, with the statement that "God saw everything God had made, and indeed, it was very good" (Gen 1:31).

Important places in the biblical tradition received explanatory names recalling that here God had seen and intervened in a special way. Thus the mountain on which Abraham bound his son Isaac, which was identified with the Temple mount in Jerusalem, was called Moriah, "God sees" (Gen 22:14), because at the last minute the "seeing" God prevented the human sacrifice and sent a ram in place of Isaac. The eyes of YHWH can be turned to the children of humanity or the people of Israel for good or ill; YHWH sees their ways, beholds the misery of the

Figure 45:
Eye of Horus. According to the myth the eye of Horus was wounded by his brother Seth. His mother, Isis, who possessed magical lore, healed it. The symbol stands for regeneration and can protect and designate the widest variety of things. Even a sacrificial offering could be considered the Eye of Horus, because it served the regeneration of the deity.

oppressed (Exod 3:7). The seeing implies a testing that can also become punishment, or it can lead to loving and concerned companionship. In this sense Job says of God:

> "Surely God is mighty and does not despise any;
>> he is mighty in strength of understanding.
> He does not keep the wicked alive,
>> but gives the afflicted their right.
> He does not withdraw his eyes from the righteous . . .
>> (Job 36:5-7).

In the interests of oppressive pedagogy and individualistic-pietistic morality the testing God who sees the injustice of the wicked was unfortunately twisted, all too often, into a heavenly controller who sees everything everywhere—even in the bedroom and under the covers. It is, of course, no accident that this very image of God, derived from a highly questionable

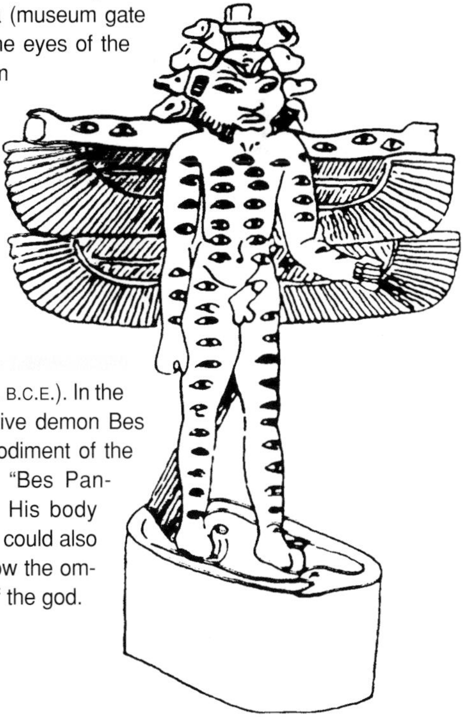

Figure 46:
Reconstruction of the entrance to the temple at Tel Halaf, ancient Guzana in Syria (museum gate at Aleppo, 9th/8th c. B.C.E.). The eyes of the gods and the beasts that form their pedestals are strongly emphasized as the most important element by means of stone inlays in the dark-gray basalt. The eyes lighted the pilgrims coming to the temple of Guzana from a long distance away.

Figure 47:
Bronze figure from Egypt (1st c. B.C.E.). In the late period the popular protective demon Bes could be regarded as an embodiment of the whole pantheon of gods. As "Bes Pantheos" he had seven heads. His body was covered with eyes, which could also be indicated by nails. They show the omniscience and omnipresence of the god.

catechesis, is disseminated throughout the world today on the backs of millions of U.S. one-dollar bills (Figure 48).

Faith Comes (Also) from Seeing

We can see a still more profound reason for increasing visual overstimulation on the one hand and the perverse God-image of the controlling eye on the other in a deficient culture of the eye, privileged in theology by a false or one-sided interpretation of the prohibition of images (Exod 20:4-5; Deut 5:8-9). The commandment "You shall not make for yourself an idol" did not refer, to begin with, to the plastic arts in general, but solely to the worship of cultic objects.[5] It was never aimed at people's mental images of God, either. Israelites loved to imagine Yʜᴡʜ in anthropomorphic, that is, humanlike images, and they could pray with joyful hope:

> As for me, I shall behold your face in righteousness;
>> when I awake I shall be satisfied, beholding your likeness
>> (Ps 17:15).

Figure 48:
United States one-dollar bill, verso. The "Great Seal of the United States" pictured there shows, on the left, above a pyramid with thirteen courses of stones (corresponding to the thirteen stars in the shield on the right) a shining eye of God as controller and guarantor of the "new order of the ages" *(novus ordo seclorum)*. The motto "In God We Trust," inscribed in the center of the banknote, reveals to critical (seeing) observers the fetishistic character of the money that, in the capitalist world order whose missionary the United States thinks itself to be, has long since taken the place of God.

The sense of the prohibition of images is therefore not met today when it is used as a way of protecting God's inaccessibility through radical abstinence from any kind of imagery applied to God. For the biblical God being inaccessible, unavailable for human use, was usually less worthwhile than communication, revelation. The sense of the prohibition of images was, rather, a matter of critique of idols, of symbols and representations of powers and forces that pretended to be gods and that maneuvered people to dependency and mortal danger rather than to a fulfilled life.

In contrast, in Israel as in the whole of the Ancient Near East seeing God played an extremely important role. The temple was the place where this immediate encounter was concretely possible. In the Mesopotamian temples the statues of people at prayer, with their overlarge, wide-open eyes, gaze with a kind of continual adoration at the cultic image of the god or goddess, and thus rejoice in the fullness of life and blessing that the deity gives (Figure 49). Israelite faith also found its summit, its joy, and its persuasive power in seeing. After YHWH has visited him personally Job can say: "I had heard of you by the hearing of the ear, but now my eye sees you" (Job 42:5). Faithful, prayerful people lift their eyes continually to this divinity in a longing, greedy gaze. The Israelite name Elienai (1 Chr 8:20) corresponds to this image: "to YHWH (are) my eyes (directed)." The Israelite who prays the psalms also hopes to receive help, and looks expectantly to the tops of the mountains, the place where the gods are enthroned on high:

> I lift up my eyes to the hills—
>   from where will my help come?
> My help comes from YHWH,
>   who made heaven and earth (Ps 121:1).

Finally, the ancient Simeon calls himself happy because shortly before his death he has been allowed to see the consolation of Israel, of whom he had heard so much and toward whom all his hope was directed, as he came to the Temple to be circumcised (Figures 50a–d):

> "Master, now you are dismissing your servant in peace,
>   according to your word;

for my eyes have seen your salvation,
   which you have prepared in the presence of all peoples,
a light for revelation to the Gentiles
   and for glory to your people Israel" (Luke 2:29-32).

The book of Proverbs recalls that God is the creator of the organs of sense:

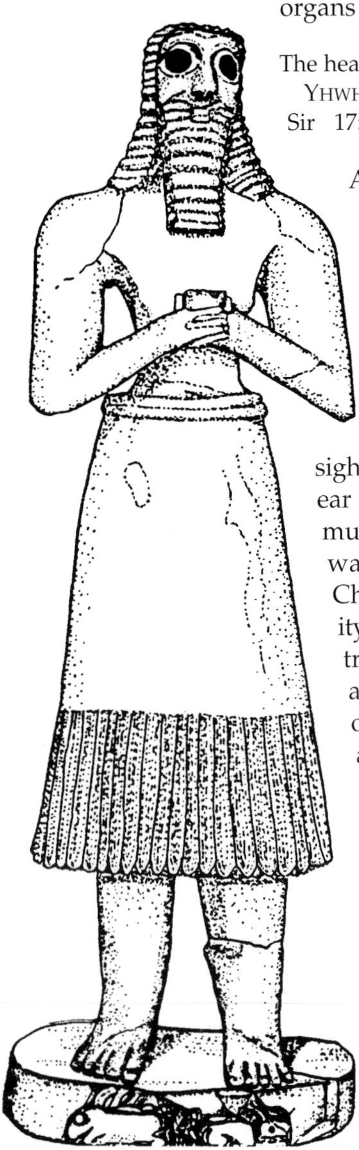

The hearing ear and the seeing eye—
   Y<small>HWH</small> has made them both (Prov 20:12; cf. Sir 17:6).

As early as Exod 4:11 Y<small>HWH</small> appears in this role. Ear and eye, hearing and seeing are differently, but equally important for human life. Blindness and deafness are a heavy fate, which is why both the blind and the deaf are accorded special protection under the Law (Lev 19:14; Deut 27:18). Unfortunately the insight into the divinely willed equality of ear and eye founded in creation, as formulated by Israel's Wisdom teachers, was lost to the great teachers of the Church and their theology. Christianity then, in the Lutheran and Reformed traditions with their hostility to images, became a thoroughly word-oriented religion in which hearing, and the faith that comes from hear-

Figure 49:
Adorer figure from the Abu temple at Tell Asmar, ancient Eshnunna, in Iraq (ca. 2800 B.C.E.). The figures with overlarge eyes frequently found in Mesopotamian temples, often inscribed, express the ardent desire of their donors to be able to look on God continually.

ing (Rom 10:17) were given almost absolute precedence over seeing. "The hearing of man [sic] represents correspondence to the revelation of the Word, and in biblical religion it is thus the essential form in which this divine revelation is appropriated," wrote Gerhard Kittel in 1933,[6] and the Old Testament scholar Hans-Walter Wolff, also Lutheran, devoted only a couple of lines in his otherwise exhaustive biblical anthropology to the eye—an unbelievable consequence of theological routine blindness, for the fact is that from a purely statistical point of view the First Testament accords a far greater importance to seeing and the eye than to hearing and the ear. The most important root for "seeing" (*r'ah*) appears 1300 times, the root for "hearing" only about 1160 times.[7] Seeing is thus the method of sensing most frequently mentioned. The word for "eye" (*'ayin*) occurs 866 times, while the text speaks of the ear only 187 times.

Seeing and Hearing as Recognizing and Understanding

Hence it is not surprising, either, that through the centuries Israel developed a real theology of the eyes and ears. An archaic word for Israel's prophets (*nabi*) really meant seer (*hose*). They see not only what is visible in the foreground; they see farther or deeper. Often they see events coming before they happen. In any case they see connections; their seeing is combined with knowing. Like a guiding thread there runs through the whole prophetic tradition and into the gospels the lament of the prophet over the people that has eyes to see and yet does not see:

> "Mortal, you are living in the midst of a rebellious house, who have eyes to see but do not see, who have ears to hear but do not hear; for they are a rebellious house" (Ezek 12:2-3).

A Jeremiah and an Ezekiel tried to attack this blindness with eye-catching symbolic acts, pantomimes, street theater. Thus Jeremiah, as a sign of the command to bow beneath the yoke of the Babylonian king, ran around the streets with a real yoke on his back (Jeremiah 27), and Ezekiel (4:1-8) produced a kind of city siege in a sandbox to set the threat from the Babylonians before the eyes of the people in as tangible and urgent a manner as possible.

Figures 50a–d:
In a remarkable sequence of sculptures above the north portal of the cathedral of Chartres (13th c.) Isaiah, Jeremiah, and Simeon stand in a row (a). Below Isaiah, who dreamed of Christ, there is a sleeping man (b); below Jeremiah, who heard of him, there is a listener (c); and below Simeon, who bore him in his arms, there is someone who sees (d). In this sequence seeing is evaluated as the most intensive and immediate means of perception.

The rabbi Jesus of Nazareth, six hundred years later, used a different method for opening the eyes of this stubborn people: he told parables. The one about the good Samaritan (Luke 10:25-37) is a narrative development of the Jewish belief that right seeing effects knowledge and action. The priest and Levite "see" the wounded man, but they pass by, while the Samaritan "sees" and then is seized by compassion, so that he does something. When Jesus was asked why he told parables he answered his disciples with a reference to the old eye-and-ear theology of the prophets (cf. Isa 6:9-10):

> "To you has been given the secret of the kingdom of God, but for those outside, everything comes in parables; in order that
> 'they may indeed look, but not perceive,
> and may indeed listen, but not understand;
> so that they may not turn again and be forgiven'"
> (Mark 4:11-12).

The telling of parables divides the sheep from the goats, for the one who takes the right standpoint and lives in solidarity with the poor whom God loves has the key to the right reading. But those who let sand be thrown in their eyes by the existing, unjust order of society, and see all reality only with the eyes of the powerful, do not understand anything, or if they do understand they fall victim to cynicism. The prerequisite for seeing is conversion, that is, a break with the existing praxis of death and a turn to the reign of God, which at first is still tiny and hidden. The community of those who believe in this alternative society: they are the ones who see.

Because those who believe and those who see are the same it is clear that the many healings of blind people in the Second Testament have a double meaning. This is especially clear in the healing of the man born blind in the Fourth Gospel, where there is a play on the two aspects of blindness. After this Sabbath healing there is a dispute between Jesus and the Pharisees, who suspect a trick, regard blindness as God's just punishment for the sins of the blind man's parents, and condemn Jesus' practice of healing on the Sabbath. Jesus on the one hand reveals their traditionalist know-it-all attitude as blindness, and on the other hand denies them even their blindness and therefore their ability to be healed, because they will not recognize their impenitence:

> Jesus said, "I came into this world for judgment so that those who do not see may see, and those who do see may become blind." Some of the Pharisees near him heard this and said to him, "Surely we are not blind, are we?" Jesus said to them, "If you were blind, you would not have sin. But now that you say, 'We see,' your sin remains" (John 9:39-41).

This identity of seeing and believing is pointedly argued again by John in the Easter story of Thomas, who was not present when Jesus appeared and who does not believe the other disciples who tell him "we have seen the Lord." He insists on seeing the marks of crucifixion (Figure 51). Thomas had learned his lesson. After all, it was this same Jesus who had opened his eyes to the fact that blessing must be concrete if it is to exist at all, that the body is God's temple, and that it is a good idea to look twice at what is being sold to us as salvation. The master's sympathy for his pupil, who takes his God-given physicality seriously, is still perceptible when he challenges him eight days later:

> "Put your finger here and see my hands. Reach out your hand and put it in my side. Do not doubt but believe" (John 20:27).

For the sake of later Christians a statement was attached to this marvelous homage that—frequently cited out of context— demands precisely the opposite attitude: "Blessed are those who have not seen and yet have come to believe" (John 20:29b). Against the background of biblical theology of the eyes and ears it is immediately obvious that this blessing is not meant to denigrate those who are concerned with things physical, but to praise those who exercise that praxis even though they have not seen the Lord himself. The whole proclamation, after all, rests on the witness of those who saw Jesus, or the Risen One, with their own eyes. Eyewitness, not word of mouth or fables (cf. Job 42:5) is the beginning of the Christian mission, as 2 Peter emphasizes:

> For we did not follow cleverly devised myths when we made known to you the power and coming of our Lord Jesus Christ, but we had been eyewitnesses of his majesty (2 Pet 1:16).

The Evil Eye

Seeing—as we have attempted to show—in the view of the First Testament is never merely a sense apprehension, an event without personal involvement or consequences. Seeing something always has consequences. One sees something and acts accordingly. Right seeing means knowing. If, on the other hand, it is only the eyes that cling to something, or if the heart (that is, the mind) simply follows the lust of the eyes,[8] the person is in danger:

> . . . if my step has turned aside from the way,
>   and my heart has followed my eyes,
>   and if any spot has clung to my hands;
> then let me sow, and another eat . . . (Job 31:7-8).

Thus the biblical theology of the eyes includes a critique of the eyes as well. In the work of the sage Jesus Sirach we find the following warning:

> Are you seated at the table of the great?
>   Do not be greedy at it,
>   and do not say, "How much food there is here!"
> Remember that a greedy eye is a bad thing.
>   What has been created more greedy than the eye?
>   Therefore it sheds tears for any reason (Sir 31:12).

The strengths of the eyes, namely the ability to grasp many things at once, whole constellations and combinations of things, and to externalize internal emotions, become weaknesses if they are used for their own sake. Then the eye becomes the symbol of unbridled, hard-to-control desires. The Second Testament suggests some especially radical means as therapy for this vice:

> "If your right eye causes you to sin, tear it out and throw it away; it is better for you to lose one of your members than for your whole body to be thrown into hell" (Matt 5:29).

Figure 51:
Pericope book from St. Erentrud, Salzburg, ca. 1140. Thomas touches the wounds of the Risen One. The attitude of the apostle, interpreted as unbelief, is seen on closer examination to be that of a pupil who has learned from his teacher to take the body seriously.

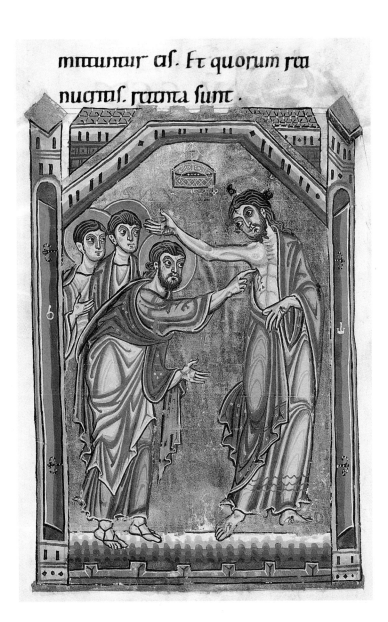

119

From the most ancient times and even now in the Near
East the evil eye or the evil glance, that is, enslavement to the
lust of a shameless eye, is something to be feared.[9] In the book
of Proverbs there is express warning against the evil eye, the
greedy and envious eye:

> The miser [the man with an evil glance] is in a hurry to get rich
> and does not know that loss is sure to come (Prov 28:22).

Various misfortunes throughout salvation history are as-
cribed to the evil eye by the Bible or Jewish tradition: Sarah's
jealous hatred of her maidservant Hagar, the animosity of
Jacob's sons against Joseph, Saul's suspicion of David, even
the destruction of the first tablets of the Law on Sinai. In
Egypt people tried to avert evil glances, that is, to shame
them and thus confine them, with
proverbs and amulets on which
as many eyes as possible were
shown (Figure 52). In spite of
continued Jewish polemic
against the magical practices

Figure 52:
Multiple Iret eyes with an Ujat eye
(cf. Figure 45) on the verso. Amulets
of this type served as protection
against the evil eye.

of the nations, amulets and sayings against the evil eye were
favored—and are still favored even today—in popular Judaism.
In Yiddish the words "evil eye" themselves are avoided; one
speaks placatingly instead of the *git-oyg* ("good eye").[10] Nothing
can more forcefully demonstrate the unique, intensive language
of the eyes and their opportunities for obscenity than the phenomenon of the evil eye. For this very reason priests in the con-
fessional and psychoanalysts behind the couches avoid direct
eye contact with their clients.

Human seeing is always seeing as in a mirror (1 Cor 13:12),
and according to 2 Cor 4:17-18 what people see is always lim-

ited to its time—mortal—while the endless or eternal remains invisible to our eyes. That was probably what Plato meant as well when he interpreted our seeing as the perception of shadow images, and Antoine de Saint-Exupéry's "Little Prince" when he says that the essential remains invisible to the eyes. As important as the senses are for enabling our inmost self, the heart, to enter into contact with the heart of another, they are dangerous to the same degree when they remain on the surface, when they declare the sign perceived to be the real thing, when they receive and devour signals without interpreting them or processing them. But this very temptation of the eyes to devouring—the evil eye—is exploited by our media to boost consumption and profits. In television programs nowadays sixty images per minute are not at all unusual. There are even sets with "picture in picture," a tiny screen set within the larger one. The paper with the highest circulation in Switzerland is called *Blick* ("look" or "glance"), which thus declares its program to be the brief, devouring, but never digesting and understanding kind of seeing. This superficial sensibility is so bad because it is loveless and without suffering. Even our language reveals this wisdom to us, as the sharp-eyed Eugen Rosenstock-Huessy very accurately wrote:

> When does our life ascend beyond its present consciousness? When our hearing and seeing are lost. When we suffer and when we love neither our eyes nor our ears help us. . . . Far be it from me to do injustice to the eye. But healthy is only the facing eye that lifts itself to another face. For only such an eye stares no longer at objects. Only the facing vis-à-vis pair of eyes attains the power of the other sense, letting the living thing live instead of stilling it and communicating to its viewers that lukewarmness of the stilling into which every holding still, every observing, setting up, and looking at forces us.[11]

"Let Anyone with Ears to Hear Listen!"

Machines, automobiles, airplanes, trains, jackhammers, television sets, radios, stereos . . . we live in a loud world. The rising swell of noise in our cities in the last hundred and fifty years has been a gigantic crescendo. There is usually no escape: we are delivered over to noise, even when we tune out, close our ears from within or just stop listening. Many people suffer from hearing disorders because they are continually at the mercy of loud noise. We need soundproof walls with thicker and thicker insulation; we study, work, or sleep with earplugs. The silence in which our own breathing or heartbeat suddenly sounds loud, the absolute quiet in which the small voices within can be heard—who knows such a thing? In the noise and confusion of voices of our time the ancient Near Eastern calls to prick up one's ears and listen seem almost a little naïve and silly. But perhaps it is precisely this listening to people who practiced hearing so well that offers a chance for us.

"Hearing Is Useful to Those Who Can Hear"

"To hear is of advantage for a son who hearkens. If hearing enters into a hearkener, the hearkener becomes a hearer. (When) hearing is good, speaking is good. Every hearkener (is) an advantage, and hearing is of advantage to the hearkener. To hear is better than anything that is, (and thus) comes the goodly love (of a man). How good it is when a son accepts what his father says! Thereby *maturity* comes to him. He whom god loves is a hearkener, (but) he whom god hates cannot hear. It is the heart which brings up its lord as one who hears or as one who does not hear. The life, prosperity, and health of a man is his heart."

So speaks the sage Ptah-hotep in the afterword to his teaching, which he gave to his court pupils 4300 years ago in Egypt.[1] According to him, in hearing there is life. Hearing has advantages; it is the precondition for being able to speak. The one who can listen is popular, and the ability to listen even says something about a person's religious nature. It shows whether the god loves this person, and vice versa. However, what is crucial for proper listening is a good cooperation with the heart, the intelligence (see Chapter 1 above). The ear and the heart are the external and internal aspects of the process of understanding.

According to Ptah-hotep, then, the quality of an Egyptian official lay in his ability to listen. The classic depiction is that of a man seated and concentrating (Figure 53). An official of the rather xenophobic Eighteenth Dynasty rightly celebrated his own special ability to receive, understand, and translate for Egyptian ears things that were foreign to them.[2]

> I am truly outstanding among all persons, one with a listening heart when seeking counsel among strangers, like one whose heart was present.

Yhwh, who according to Israel's faith was the creator of the whole world, rejoices that King Solomon, when invited to wish for any gift from God, asks only for a listening heart [NRSV "understanding mind"], so that he may know how to distinguish between good and evil and be able to rule such a numerous people (1 Kings 3:9). For this, God gives him long life.

> The proverbs of Solomon son of David, king of Israel:
> For learning about wisdom and instruction,
>   for understanding words of insight,
> for gaining instruction in wise dealing,
>   righteousness, justice, and equity;
> to teach shrewdness to the simple,
>   knowledge and prudence to the young—
> Let the wise also hear and gain in learning,
>   and the discerning acquire skill,
> to understand a proverb and a figure,
>   the words of the wise and their riddles (Prov 1:1-6).

Thus the sages of Israel taught their pupils, on the basis of a thousand years of Near Eastern tradition. The very possibility of such a handing on of tradition presupposed open ears. They are the fundamental requirement for the handing on of a teaching, and therefore the ancient Israelite Wisdom teachings are permeated with so-called admonitions:

> Listen to your father who begot you,
>> and do not despise your mother when she is old (Prov 23:22).

> Incline your ear and hear my words,
>> and apply your mind to my teaching (Prov 22:17).

In Israel they were accounted wise whose ears were open and who therefore had acquired knowledge and experience in their lives. Mention is made, for example, of the artisans and spinners who participated in building the tabernacle (Exod 35:25; 36:8; cf. also Jer 10:9), the women who mourned (Jer 9:17-22), and gave wise counsel (2 Sam 14:1-24; 20:14-22). Their knowledge was recorded in easily understood sayings that could be readily remembered in an oral culture dependent on hearing. The texts had to be right for hearing; otherwise they would quickly be forgotten. The tight form, the doubled character of almost all sayings (the so-called *parallelismus membrorum*), alphabetic poems, and many other rhetorical tricks served as "ear openers." Wisdom was handed on in the various artisanal guilds, among farmers, but especially among court officials and in the context of judicial decisions at the city gate. By no means least, many proverbs had an educational function.

Figure 53:
Limestone statue painted in several colors from Sakkarah, Egypt (ca. 2500 B.C.E.). In Egyptian tombs of the Old Kingdom the gentlemen enjoyed having themselves portrayed as scribes, because after the transition to a written language was fully accomplished ca. 3000 B.C.E. the scribe embodied the ideal of a model civil official. This little statue shows the judge and district commander Kai as a representative of the scribal class, seated with legs crossed and his writing materials in his lap. His left hand grasps the roll, his right the reed pen. Noteworthy is the scribe's alert gaze, aimed at the far distance, his tense concentration on what he hears and must write down.

The status of listening in Israelite society is shown by the draconian law regarding the stubborn son:

> If someone has a stubborn and rebellious son who will not obey [listen to the voice of] his father and mother, who does not heed them when they discipline him, then his father and his mother shall take hold of him and bring him out to the elders of his town at the gate of that place. They shall say to the elders of his town, "This son of ours is stubborn and rebellious. He will not obey us [listen to our voice]. He is a glutton and a drunkard." Then all the men of the town shall stone him to death. So you shall purge the evil from your midst, and all Israel will hear, and be afraid (Deut 21:18-21).

This law subjects inter-familial conflicts to public justice. If the grown son continually violates the norms of behavior in such a way that his parents, now grown old, feel themselves threatened, the community assumes social control, attempting in this way to prevent violent acts between members of a family. Such extreme cases must have been rare. Normally a young child learns at its mother's knee to listen to the elders of the tribe.

"Hear, O Israel!"

In the context of the deuteronomistic reform under King Josiah, which was also responsible for the law just mentioned, the whole cultic community of Israel, at that time threatened and in danger from the colonial power of Assyria, was conceived as a listening and learning community. The "Shema Israel," then, the passage from Deuteronomy prayed daily by Jews as their fundamental confession to this day, also begins with the admonition to hear:

> Hear, O Israel: YHWH is our God, YHWH alone. You shall love YHWH your God with all your heart, and with all your soul, and with all your might. Keep these words that I am commanding you today in your heart. Recite them to your children and talk about them when you are at home and when you are away, when you lie down and when you rise. Bind them as a sign on your hand, fix them as an emblem on your forehead, and write them on the doorposts of your house and on your gates (Deut 6:4-9).

The teaching and learning, the listening to the voice of God to which the text calls the Israelites, is clearly defined and institutionalized in the text itself. Thus even today phylacteries on the foreheads of people at prayer and mezuzahs, tiny boxes containing prayer scrolls placed on the doors and portals of Jewish houses and cities, all of them containing the "Shema Israel," (Figure 54) remind Jews to listen to the voice of God. Still more: they recall the loving relationship between God and the people that is the basis for this listening. And what is the foundation of that listening love? The answer to the question is clear and unmistakable:

Figure 54:
Mezuzah text, written in Hebrew with special ink on parchment. The mezuzah text, written in tiny letters by specialists, contains fundamental commandments from the Torah, which are partly fulfilled by placing the mezuzah box on the door of the house or the gate of the city (Deut 6:4-9; 11:13-20). This circle has an evocative character: the ear is directed to repetition.

> "We were Pharaoh's slaves in Egypt, but YHWH brought us out
> of Egypt with a mighty hand . . . to bring us in, to give us the
> land that he promised on oath to our ancestors. Then YHWH
> commanded us to observe all these statutes . . . (Deut 6:21-24).

The prophetic and Wisdom traditions agree that YHWH rejoices much more in followers who listen to God and keep the
commandments than in elaborate sacrificial rites in worship.
"Surely, to obey [listen] is better than sacrifice, and to heed
than the fat of rams," Samuel teaches King Saul (1 Sam 15:22).
According to Psalm 40, which is placed on the lips of David,
Israel's second king had thoroughly internalized this lesson
and says to God:

> Sacrifice and offering you do not desire,
>   but you have given me an open ear (Ps 40:6).

Ultimately it is God who opens and closes ears. The prophets are especially graced in this way. More than others, they are
open to the power of God working among us; they are able to
recognize God's signs, hear and interpret God's words. A pupil
of Isaiah who calls himself the servant of God says of himself:

> The Lord YHWH has given me the tongue of those who are taught,
>   that I may know how to sustain the weary with a word.
> Morning by morning he wakens—wakens my ear .
>   to listen as those who are taught.
> The Lord YHWH has opened my ear,
>   and I was not rebellious,
>   I did not turn backward (Isa 50:4-5).

Thus in the mouths of such listeners the word becomes God's
word, shown to be such by the fact that it brings fruit; that is,
it effects what it says. Hence Moses says:

> Give ear, O heavens, and I will speak;
>   let the earth hear the words of my mouth.
> May my teaching drop like the rain,
>   my speech condense like the dew;
> like gentle rain on grass,
>   like showers on new growth (Deut 32:1-2).

God Hears

By true hearing and being heard there arises, between human beings or between the human being and God, a close relationship, perhaps even attachment, belonging. A special Israelite ritual prescribed that the ear of a freed slave who freely chose to remain with the master or mistress should be fixed to the doorpost with an awl as a sign that this person now belongs wholly and entirely to the house (Exod 21:6; Deut 15:17). Also, in the Ancient Near East belonging to a particular deity was often signified by earrings (Gen 35:4; Exod 32:2-3).

The loving relationship between God and the human being of course presupposes that God also has ears with which to hear the voice of the beloved (Figure 55).

> The eyes of YHWH are on the righteous,
> and his ears are open to their cry (Ps 34:15; cf. 116:1-2).

The person praying the psalm urgently pleads:

> Out of the depths I cry to you, O YHWH,
> Lord, hear my voice!
> Let your ears be attentive
> to the voice of my supplica-
> tions! (Ps 130:1-2; cf. 4:2).

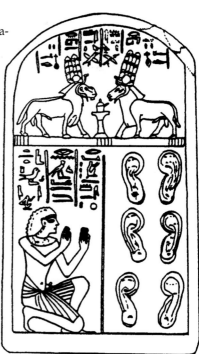

Figure 55:
Limestone stele from Thebes (ca. 1200 B.C.E.). In many Egyptian temples there are steles on which ears are supposed to make present the listening grace of a particular deity. By this multiplication of ears people hoped to emphasize their pleas. Here the kneeling worshiper, named Bai, hopes that his prayer will be heard by the god Amon, depicted as a ram.

Again and again the First Testament recalls that YHWH hears the cries of the oppressed (Exod 2:23-24; 22:22-23) and the laments of widows especially well:

> for the Lord is the judge,
>   and with him there is no partiality.
> He will not show partiality against the little ones;
>   and he will listen to the prayer of one who is wronged.
> He will not ignore the supplication of the orphan,
>   or the widow when she pours out her complaint.
> Do not the tears of the widow run down her cheek
>   and will no one hear as she cries out against the one who
>   causes them to fall?
> The weeping of those who are shattered will be accepted,
>   and their cry for help will reach to the clouds.
> The prayer of the humble pierces the clouds,
>   and it will not rest until it reaches [God] its goal . . .
>   (Sir 35:15b-21a*).

In Canaan it was especially the goddess who was supposed to have listening ears. The simple people trustingly brought her the prayers that arose out of their daily toil and trouble, as many amulets show (Figure 56). In the Bible YHWH takes over her role. YHWH is an Ishma-el and Samu-el, a God who hears, as attested by the names Hagar and Hanna, who in their misery had been heard by God, gave to their children (Gen 16:11; 1 Sam 1:20). Of course, it is not advisable to annoy the ears of the Most High without good reason, as the people of God, in their impatience, did again and again in the wilderness:

> Now when the people complained in the hearing of YHWH about their misfortunes, YHWH heard it and his anger was kindled. Then the fire of YHWH burned against them, and consumed some outlying parts of the camp (Num 11:1).

Figure 56:
Scarab from Palestine (1750–1550 B.C.E.). The typical Canaanite tree goddess is popularly characterized on amulets by especially large ears, a sign that she is a goddess who listens.

And yet attentive listening and gracious hearing are the very trademark of the living God that distinguishes this God from the false gods and their idols; these have ears but cannot hear (Pss 115:6; 135:17). The ridicule of human projections in the form of gods who really embody no effective power at all runs through the whole Bible. The contrast between God and the gods is given its most dramatic expression in the story of the contest between Elijah and the priests of Baal on Mount Carmel. When the priests are unable to cause their god Baal to send down fire Elijah heaps sarcastic mockery on them:

> "Cry aloud! Surely he is a god; either he is meditating, or he has wandered away, or he is on a journey, or perhaps he is asleep and must be awakened" (1 Kings 18:27).

Opening the Ears

The Jesus movement and the early Christian groups preserved the theology of the ears found in the First Testament and handed it on. Like Israel's prophets, they continually found that ears in good working order were no guarantee that people would hear. Countless times we find in the Second Testament the appeal: "Let anyone with ears listen." Nevertheless, closed ears and stubbornness hinder the spread of the message about the reign of God. Jesus therefore expressly calls those blessed who have ears *and* hear (Matt 13:16). He counts as his true family not his mother and brothers and sisters, but only those who hear the word of God and do it (Luke 8:21).

Hearing and doing: this is perhaps the most important axis of the New Testament's theology of the ears. Right hearing is proved in doing. But how can a person who is hard of hearing or deaf come to hear? A healing story in Mark's gospel gives a penetrating account of what Jesus did for a person who could neither hear nor speak:

> They brought to him a deaf man who had an impediment in his speech; and they begged him to lay his hand on him. He took him aside in private, away from the crowd, and put his fingers into his ears, and he spat and touched his tongue. Then looking up to heaven, he sighed and said to him, "Ephphatha," that is,

"Be opened." And immediately his ears were opened, his tongue was released, and he spoke plainly (Mark 7:32-35).

The deaf person, cut off from communication and so from community, and therefore a closed person, is touched by Jesus. Because he lets himself be touched he can open as he never could before. This openness in turn makes it possible for him to speak, to become a mature person (one who has a voice in things). The Church remembered for centuries how necessary it was for a Christian first, with divine help, to be opened in order to arrive at mature faith. The ancient Church's baptismal liturgy contained a ritual for opening the ears, the *apertio aurium*. The priest, during Lent, touched the ears of the baptizands with saliva and invited them, with the word *ephphatha*, to be open; this was the first precondition for baptism and confirmation, for full acceptance into the Christian community during the Easter night.

Jesus sought not only with miracles, but especially by telling parables, to open people's ears for the message about the reign of God. His disciples, and later the communities, compared this arduous work with that of a sower (Mark 4; Matthew 13; Luke 8):

The sower sows the word. These are the ones on the path where the word is sown: when they hear, Satan immediately comes and takes away the word that is sown in them. And these are the ones sown on rocky ground: when they hear the word, they immediately receive it with joy. But they have no root, and endure only for a while; then, when trouble or persecution arises on account of the word, immediately they fall away. And others are those sown among the thorns: these are the ones who hear the word, but the care of the world, and the lure of wealth, and the desire for other things come in and choke the word, and it yields nothing. And these are the ones sown on the good soil: they hear the word and accept it and bear fruit, thirty and sixty and a hundredfold (Mark 4:14-20).

The letter of James explains in a few verses how one may recognize the right hearing of the word:

. . . be doers of the word, and not merely hearers who deceive themselves. For if any are hearers of the word and not doers, they are like those who look at themselves in a mirror; for they look at themselves and, on going away, immediately forget what they were like. But those who look into the perfect law, the law of liberty, and persevere, being not hearers who forget but doers who act—they will be blessed in their doing (Jas 1:22-25).

Following these verses the author suggests care for widows and orphans as one opportunity for doing the word of God.

Thus in the biblical tradition the art of listening, much like that of seeing, leads to genuine understanding, and understanding to action. Liberation theology has taken this connection very seriously in seeking especially to listen to the people without having know-it-all answers prepared in advance, just as Proverbs demands:

> If one gives answer before hearing,
>   it is folly and shame (Prov 18:13).

It is a horrible short circuit, with evil consequences, to bypass understanding and insight and demand that hearing lead directly to faith or action. That kind of obedience without a process of understanding, whether demanded by secular or religious authorities, does not correspond to the biblical sense. Bertolt Brecht formulated it this way, in his usual concise manner, in his poem fragment "Höre beim Reden!" (Listen to What you Say):

> "Don't say too often 'You're right, teacher!
>   Let your pupils know it!'
> Don't put too much strain on the truth:
>   it can't take it.
> Listen to what you say."[3]

"My Mouth Shall Declare Your Praise"

The life of a child begins with a cry, and by crying it makes its wishes known during its earliest months. Crying reveals existential needs: hunger, thirst, fear. The infant experiences the world first through tasting, testing things with its mouth. Everything it can grasp is put into its mouth and tasted. Little by little babbling is added, then the ability to form words, and finally sentences. Thus the mouth is a central and complex organ for human life from the beginning. For the Bible it consists of lips, tongue, teeth, and gums.

Eating, Laughing, Kissing, Speaking

Because of the multifunctionality of the human mouth a broad spectrum of symbols attaches to it and its parts, ranging from contempt to the highest honor.

All human toil is for the mouth, yet the appetite is not satisfied (Qoh 6:7). The wise Solomon comes to this fatal conclusion in his reflections on God and the world in the book of Qoheleth. Israel's sages regard the devouring, insatiable mouth with no less distaste. The verses about greedy and effeminate Nineveh are disdainful:

> All your fortresses are like fig trees
> > with first-ripe figs—
> if shaken they fall
> > into the mouth of the eater (Nah 3:12).

The mouth can be full not only of food, but also of laughter. Bildad promises his friend Job such pleasure if he will only turn to God in humility:

134

"He will yet fill your mouth with laughter,
    and your lips with shouts of joy.
Those who hate you will be clothed with shame,
    and the tent of the wicked will be no more" (Job 8:21-22; cf.
    Ps 126:2).

What this passage illustrates is the typical biblical understanding of laughter. Laughter is almost always associated with triumph, namely joy at the fall of one's enemies: gloating is the finest joy, at any rate when it is justified gloating on the part of the poor (Ps 52:7). In this sense God also laughs from the heavenly throne at the raging of the nations and their kings (Pss 2:4; 37:13; 59:8), and Jesus promises those who mourn that they will laugh (Luke 6:21), namely when the powerful no longer have anything to laugh about (Luke 6:25; Jas 4:9).

The Hebrew Bible speaks much more lovingly of the kissing mouth. The first of the love songs collected in the Song of Songs begins (1:2) with the beloved's invitation to her partner to kiss her. "Let him kiss me with the kisses of his mouth!" Love's kisses can be accompanied by tears (Gen 29:11; 1 Sam 20:41; Luke 7:38; Acts 20:37), for the kiss affords a transparency in the face-to-face encounter that is physically unsurpassed. Kissing is a spontaneous expression of love, but also a sign of intimate family relationship (Figure 57). A kiss serves as a greeting between family members (Gen 29:13; Exod 18:7), and even more as a farewell (Gen 32:1; Ruth 1:9, 14), especially the last parting before death (Gen 33:4; 48:10). There is also a formal kiss by which public officials express their mutual loyalty, the fraternal kiss among statesmen (2 Sam 14:33), or the ritual kiss at anointing (1 Sam 10:1), which gives a living seal of legality to the official action and transfer of power. In Egypt the loyalty between the Pharaonic house and the temple could be expressed in this sense through a kiss exchanged between a god and the king (Figure 58). As far as YHWH is concerned, only a kiss of the divine foot, if anything, comes into consideration (Ps 2:11 LXX); this refers to a worshipful falling on one's face. For the Jewish prophets kissing a cultic image is a horror: "People are kissing calves!" (Hos 13:2). Almost as a replacement for this kind of kissing, so perverse in the eyes of the prophets, we find in the Psalms the astonishing metaphor:

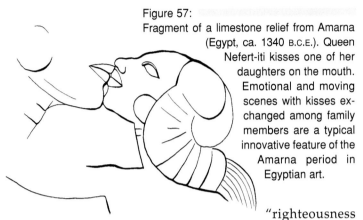

Figure 57:
Fragment of a limestone relief from Amarna (Egypt, ca. 1340 B.C.E.). Queen Nefert-iti kisses one of her daughters on the mouth. Emotional and moving scenes with kisses exchanged among family members are a typical innovative feature of the Amarna period in Egyptian art.

"righteousness and peace will kiss each other" (Ps 85:10). In view of the sensitivity to body symbolism it is not surprising that we are confronted in the Bible with a developed critique of kissing: a lying kiss is the symbol of diplomatic deceit (2 Sam 15:5), servile obsequiousness (Sir 29:5), even of the highest form of betrayal in the proverbial "Judas kiss" (Matt 26:49 *parr.*).

In the fairy tale of Snow White the queen wishes for a child "as white as snow, as red as blood, and as black as ebony." The blood-red color is for her lips. In the same sense the lover in the Song of Songs praises the richly contrasting color of his beloved's lips, as well as her white and unbroken rows of teeth. But what especially enchants him about this mouth, when he speaks and thus

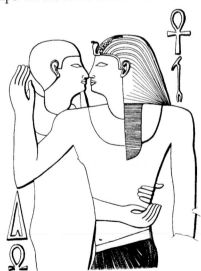

Figure 58:
Limestone relief from Karnak, from the reign of Sesostris I (1971–1930 B.C.E.). An embrace and kiss of greeting between the king and the god Ptah express their inner union and mutual loyalty.

reveals his mysterious and anticipatory inner desires, is her palate, which he compares to a pomegranate, a fruit that, like the inner part of the mouth, conceals a soft, red center beneath a hard, bright rind:

> Your teeth are like a flock of shorn ewes
>> that have come up from the washing,
> all of which bear twins,
>> and not one among them is bereaved.
> Your lips are like a crimson thread,
>> and your mouth is lovely.
> Your cheeks are like halves of a pomegranate
>> behind your veil (Song 4:2-3).

It is not cosmetics that make the mouth attractive, but first of all its way of speaking and the content of what it says:

> One who gives an honest answer
>> gives a kiss on the lips (Prov 24:26).

Hence in the First Testament the mouth, lips, and tongue are primarily organs of speech. Thanks to them a person can speak, call, order, teach, instruct, admonish, accuse, swear, bless, curse, sing, praise, rejoice, confess, pray, cry out, bemoan, murmur, and whisper. Moreover, grinding the teeth expresses the greatest rage or the despair of those who have missed entering into the reign of God (Matt 8:12).

The varied capabilities of the mouth for expression distinguish human beings from other animals. The rare passages in the Bible in which animals speak are to be regarded as literary travesties in which a special quality of the animal—the treachery of the serpent (Gen 3:1-15) or the reverence of the donkey (Numbers 22)—is depicted by having these animals speak in human words. The gift of speech is a human privilege that enables them to name the animals:

> So out of the ground YHWH God formed every animal of the field and every bird of the air, and brought them to the man to see what he would call them; and whatever the man called every living creature, that was its name. The man gave names to all cattle, and to the birds of the air, and to every animal of the field . . . (Gen 2:19).

Diplomatic and Wise Speech

Naming is merely the earliest form of speech. However, the more and more complex national entities in human civilization rest on a highly polished system of speech and language. Entire professions were soon developed to study this technique. Thus the tongue, mouth, and lips were a prominent topic even for Israel's Wisdom teachers. Countless sayings in the book of Proverbs are devoted to the beauty and balance of speech, the art of proper and timely speech and silence, and especially just and unjust speech:

> The tongue of the righteous is choice silver,
>   the mind of the wicked is of little worth (Prov 10:20).

> There is gold, and abundance of costly stones;
>   but the lips informed by knowledge are a precious jewel
>   (Prov 20:15).

> A word fitly spoken
>   is like apples of gold in a setting of silver (Prov 25:11).

For the Israelite sages only an intelligent word from the heart could be regarded as truly beautiful and persuasive:

> The mind of the wise makes their speech judicious,
>   and adds persuasiveness to their lips (Prov 16:23).

Again and again they admonish to honest speech, warn against glibness, lying, and the use of too many words or hasty speech:

> Whoever rebukes a person will afterward find more favor
>   than one who flatters with the tongue (Prov 28:23).

> Truthful lips endure forever,
>   but a lying tongue lasts only a moment (Prov 12:19).

> One who spares words is knowledgeable;
>   one who is cool in spirit has understanding (Prov 17:27).

> Do you see someone who is hasty in speech?
>   There is more hope for a fool than for anyone like that
>   (Prov 29:20).

Our modern society with its unstoppable and frequently superficial talk, the long speeches of economists and politicians

that often say nothing at all, the talk shows and other orga-
nized forms of sheer talkativeness—they would have had a
hard time facing the sages of the Ancient Near East, who had
developed their own economy of words. The elderly uncle of
Ahiqar, vizier at the court of the king of Assyria, warned him:

> My son, chatter not overmuch so that thou speak out every
> word that comes to thy mind . . . guard your mouth so that it
> will not become your accuser. More than all watchfulness watch
> thy mouth . . . . For a word is a bird: once released no man can
> recapture it . . . (Ahiqar 7.96-99).[1]

And Jesus Sirach expresses this wish:

> Who will set a guard over my mouth,
>   and an effective seal upon my lips,
> so that I may not fall because of them,
>   and my tongue may not destroy me? (Sir 22:27).

The Healing and Polluting Mouth

Idle talk brings the talker and others into danger, but to a
right and just speech is promised healing and community-
building power:

> Rash words are like sword thrusts,
>   but the tongue of the wise brings healing (Prov 12:18).

> The mouth of the righteous is a fountain of life,
>   but the mouth of the wicked conceals violence (Prov 10:11).

> A gentle tongue is a tree of life,
>   but perverseness in it breaks the spirit (Prov 15:4).

Jesus of Nazareth was also aware that words can make people
sick or well. In the face of the moral corruption of his time,
which cried out to heaven, he regarded the traditional purity
laws regarding food and washing as futile. Instead he asserted
that what comes out of people can be far more polluting to
them and to others than anything that enters into them through
their food. Jesus radically reinterpreted purity, understood as
concrete and physical. Now it was no longer the relationship
between hands (contact with objects) and mouth (consumption

of food) that was the center of attention, but the relationship between heart (intelligence, conscience) and mouth (speech). The multifunctional ambivalence of the mouth predestines it to be the crucial nexus between two attitudes:

> Then Jesus called the crowd to him and said to them, "Listen and understand: it is not what goes into the mouth that defiles a person, but it is what comes out of the mouth that defiles." . . . "Do you not see that whatever goes into the mouth enters the stomach, and goes out into the sewer? But what comes out of the mouth proceeds from the heart, and this is what defiles. For out of the heart come evil intentions, murder, adultery, fornication, theft, false witness, slander. These are what defile a person, but to eat with unwashed hands does not defile" (Matt 15:10-20 *par.*).

It is not surprising then that, given this evaluation of the mouth (that is, morally faultless speech and a good conscience) in Matthew's gospel, the last judgment weighs a person's every word. The Matthean Jesus warns the Pharisees, who were so adept with words:

> "You brood of vipers! How can you speak good things, when you are evil? For out of the abundance of the heart the mouth speaks. The good person brings good things out of a good treasure, and the evil person brings evil things out of an evil treasure. I tell you, on the day of judgment you will have to give an account for every careless word you utter; for by your words you will be justified, and by your words you will be condemned" (Matt 12:34-37).

The Speechless Mouth

Neither the Wisdom teachers' warnings about caution in speech nor Jesus' radical critique of the immoral mouth should be understood to mean that speaking is only silver and silence is always gold. In the book of Isaiah the time of salvation and the coming of God is associated not only with the blind seeing and the deaf hearing, but also with the leaping of the lame and the joyful singing of the tongues of those who had been speechless (Isa 35:5-6). Among Jesus' healing miracles those on behalf of those deprived of speech, or of both hearing and speech, play an important role:

> They brought to him a deaf man who had an impediment in his
> speech; and they begged him to lay his hand on him. He took
> him aside in private, away from the crowd, and put his fingers
> into his ears, and he spat and touched his tongue. Then looking
> up to heaven, he sighed and said to him, "Ephphatha," that is,
> "Be opened." And immediately his ears were opened, his tongue
> was released, and he spoke plainly (Mark 7:32-35).

In other healing stories inability to speak is attributed to the
influence of a demon and is considered a kind of possession
(Luke 11:14-15). Behind this is a deeply rooted knowledge on the
part of the storytellers that has been preserved in a number of expressions in our language as well. Horrible experiences can, as
we know, deprive a person of the ability to speak, usually for
only a moment, but in serious cases for life. Inability to speak
isolates people as scarcely any other handicap does. In the biblical view it is also associated with immaturity: "The theme of silence suggests a structure of mutism in face of the overwhelming
force of the limit-situations," according to the Brazilian peda-
gogue Paulo Freire.[2] Restrictive, limiting situations created by
greedy colonialist people rob the oppressed of their existence,
including their speech, their mouth. The result is silence, dumb-
ness, which keeps the oppression intact. People who cannot
speak on their own behalf, who are speech-less, who have no influence, who cannot break through their marginal situation:
these, according to the gospels, Jesus took for his own—but not
in a paternalist manner, so that he spoke for them. Instead he
gave them a voice by appealing to the creative potential of such
people: "Get up!" and by calling their own cause by name: not
the cause of silence in the Roman empire, but the cause of communication freed from oppression in the reign of God. Thus he
made them speakers, mature people who no longer had to be
flotsam and jetsam devoid of will, driven about on the waves of
Roman rule, and he freed them from their isolation.

The Violent Mouth

The mouth (that is, language) is thus also a primary power
factor. "Death and life are in the power of the tongue," according to the book of Proverbs (18:21). The Nazis misused language

as an instrument of propaganda for their ideology by, among other things, replacing words that were not originally German with archaic expressions or artificial, newly-coined German forms. The hegemony of the United States and its neo-liberal economic system reveals itself in countless Anglicisms in European languages, entering primarily by way of advertising and business. In the wake of the computer industry terms from programmers' language are spreading throughout the world; their purpose is the creation of a universal data net making possible new forms of communication, but also of data hoarding and thus of domination.

One of the primeval stories in Genesis, the first book of the Bible, is devoted to the topic of "language as an instrument of power." It tells of people's attempt—more properly *men's* attempt—to achieve world domination through a unification of language.[3] This is the biblical-prophetic commentary on an effort of the Assyrian King Sargon II to extend the conquered area of his world empire through a unifying language reform among the uprooted peoples from those places, and to build a mighty capital city with a huge acropolis at Der-Sharru-kin, close to Nineveh. Since the Israelites were among the nations affected, they saw the early death of Sargon as a sign that their God YHWH had put a stop to Sargon's ambitious and violent project:

> And YHWH said, "Look, they are one people, and they have all one language (literally "one lip"); and this is only the beginning of what they will do; nothing that they propose to do will now be impossible for them. Come, let us go down, and confuse their language there, so that they will not understand one another's speech." So YHWH scattered them abroad from there over the face of all the earth, and they left off building the city (Gen 11:6-8).

Thus God independently crushes the imperialist claim to unity in favor of a multiplicity of languages that even today supports a certain degree of resistance to occupation, annexation, and the oppression of peoples. What is bad about the multiplicity of languages, on the other hand, is that it makes it difficult for people to understand one another. It is the Spirit of God, after all, who on the first Pentecost led Christians out of that dilemma again, for the outpouring of the Holy Spirit made it possible for them to speak all languages, so that members of all language groups understood them (Acts 2:1-13). Thus global communication is possible, but not at the expense of variety and of minorities.

God's Mouth and Human Words

Not everyone who has a mouth can speak. As we know, acquiring the ability to speak and to use a language is a long, tedious process, and even that cannot guarantee that *what* a person says will make sense. And then there are people with insight and intelligence who are, nevertheless, not able to communicate with others through their mouths. There are quite a few biblical stories dealing with this problem. Probably the best known is the call of Moses at the burning bush. God tells Moses to lead the people of Israel out of Egypt. In addition, he is granted divine authority, namely the power to perform miracles. But that is still not enough for Moses, and the following dramatic dialogue with God ensues:

> But Moses said to YHWH, "O my Lord, I have never been eloquent, neither in the past nor even now that you have spoken to your servant; but I am slow of speech and slow of tongue." Then YHWH said to him, "Who gives speech to mortals? Who makes them mute or deaf, seeing or blind? Is it not I, YHWH? Now go, and I will be with your mouth and teach you what you are to speak." But he said, "O my Lord, please send someone else." Then the anger of YHWH was kindled against Moses and he said, "What of your brother Aaron, the Levite? I know that he can speak fluently; even now he is coming out to meet you, and when he sees you his heart will be glad. You shall speak to him and put the words in his mouth; and I will be with your mouth and with his mouth, and will teach you what you shall do. He indeed shall speak for you to the people; he shall serve as a mouth for you, and you shall serve as God for him" (Exod 4:10-16).

Moses regards not only his ability to speak, but also his way of talking, his dialect, as completely unsuitable for the enormous task God has devised for him, namely to be God for Aaron, the priest. The Temple personnel were chosen and paid for their rhetorical ability. This assignment in service of a higher power could be expressed in cultic worship by the wearing of masks.

It is disputed whether the mysterious *teraphim* in the Bible were cultic masks of this type. The *teraphim,* which were used in interpreting oracles, were at any rate sharply criticized by the post-exilic prophets (Ezek 21:26; Zech 10:2). What priests say is not from themselves, but from God, and God speaks through the prophets, who are called spontaneously: ecstatics, mystics, outsiders, crazy people. When the Moabite King Balak has the seer Balaam called and pays him a prophet's wage to curse Israel, Balaam sees visions that cause him instead to bless Israel (Numbers 22–24). The truth of his prophecy appears in the very fact that he does not say what his employer wants to hear, but what God wants—and thereby risks being fired. Anyone who takes pay for what she or he says is not a prophet, but a propagandist or, in biblical terms, a false prophet.

The Bible draws still finer distinctions, as the call story of the prophet Ezekiel shows:

> [God] said to me, "O mortal, eat what is offered to you; eat this scroll, and go, speak to the house of Israel." So I opened my mouth, and he gave me the scroll to eat. He said to me, "Mortal, eat this scroll that I give you and fill your stomach with it." Then I ate it; and in my mouth it was as sweet as honey. He said to me: "Mortal, go to the house of Israel and speak my very words to them. For you are not sent to a people of obscure speech and difficult language, but to the house of Israel—not to many peoples of obscure speech and difficult language, whose words you cannot understand" (Ezek 3:1-6).

In this passage the words "mouth, lips, tongue, words, speech" recur again and again. What is their relationship? The mouth is the organ of speech *per se,* the opening through which language emerges. This text describes the reverse process in the most strikingly material terms: the intellectual work of life is represented as words going in through the mouth into the inmost part of the body—in short, as eating. Making words one's own means ingesting them, making them part of oneself. For Ezekiel the scroll tastes like honey: this incorporation is in fact an act of oral pleasure. The prophet is to proclaim the words of God only to his own people, who speak Hebrew, not to the Babylonians among whom Ezekiel and the deported people are living. Their lips—that is, their expression or way of speaking—are dark, incomprehensible, obscure, and their tongue—that is, the idiom of their speech—is difficult, because it belongs to a foreign land. However, correct understanding is the precondition for the reception of God's word, even though there is no guarantee that it will be accepted.

The mouth and its parts (lips, tongue) thus stand in a differentiated and comprehensive sense for the special ability of human beings to speak.

> But the word is more than just an instrument which makes dialogue possible; accordingly, we must seek its constitutive elements. Within the word we find two dimensions, reflection and action, in such radical interaction that if one is sacrificed—even in part—the other immediately suffers. There is no true word that is not at the same time a praxis. Thus, to speak a true word is to transform the world.[4]

With this description of the transcendent character of the word Paulo Freire touches exactly what in biblical language is called "the word of God." Whoever speaks such words is a prophet; his or her mouth is a mouthpiece for the word of God. Thus speaking prophetically is not the privilege of a special class, but a particular liberating praxis. Such speaking is an act of creation. Therefore according to Genesis 1 all creation comes to be through God's speaking. Every "and God said" creates reality and living space. "The word of God" is hence nothing abstract or diffuse, neither propaganda (without action) nor activism (without reflection), but a transforming power, as expressed with special clarity in a passage from the hymns of the pupils of Isaiah after the Babylonian exile:

> For my thoughts are not your thoughts,
>   nor are your ways my ways, says YHWH.
> For as the heavens are higher than the earth,
>   so are my ways higher than your ways
>   and my thoughts than your thoughts.
> For as the rain and the snow come down from heaven,
>   and do not return there until they have watered the earth,
> making it bring forth and sprout,
>   giving seed to the sower and bread to the eater,

> so shall my word be that goes out from my mouth;
>> it shall not return to me empty,
> but it shall accomplish that which I purpose,
>> and succeed in the thing for which I sent it (Isa 55:8-11).

The prophets of this message believed unshakeably that "God's word" is active and effective. Here the word has an almost material character; it is not only hollow sound, but creates something new; it transforms the world. However, its effects are not sudden; they happen steadily and over time, like rain that soaks the earth, making it fruitful and causing seed to grow and nourish humankind. Thus these verses give us an important criterion for distinguishing God's word from other words, true prophecy from false. If a word is fruitful and nourishes it is really the word of God; otherwise it is not. The Second Testament, in this line, established the following rule for discerning prophets: "You will know them by their fruits" (Matt 7:16; cf. also Acts 5:38-39). Until the time of fruit and harvest we often remain in uncertainty.

The Mouth That Speaks Praise

Because of the dialectical relationship between human words and the word of God, the sense of the opening of all lips and every mouth lies ultimately in the praise of God. For the ancient Egyptians it was a nightmare to think of having to remain silent in the realm of the dead. Hence they assigned great significance to the so-called ritual for opening the mouth, which the gods (through their priests) had to perform on the mummy (Figure 59). The Israelites, rooted in the soil, could not believe that in the realm of the dead any mouth could still praise YHWH, as the sarcastic questions of the despairing in the Psalms show:

> Do the shades rise up to praise you?
> Is your steadfast love declared in the grave,
>> or your faithfulness in Abaddon?
> . . .
> But I, YHWH, cry out to you;
>> in the morning my prayer comes before you (Ps 88:10-11, 13).

Therefore they pressure their God to save them while they yet live, in order afterward to receive their prayers of thanksgiving

Figure 59:
Depiction of the mouth-opening ritual on the Hu-nefer papyrus (ca. 1300 B.C.E.). Before the entrance to the tomb of the deceased and a memorial tablet stands the mummy, held by a priest with an Anubis mask and mourned by women. The mouth-opening will be performed with adze-like tools. The complex ritual, involving a total of seventy-five individual actions, was also performed on scarabs, statues of gods, and entire temples.

Figure 60:
Ivory lyre-player from Kamid el-Loz (Lebanon, ca. 1400 B.C.E.). Most of the elements of the figure, which is about 7.3 centimeters tall, are weakly modeled in favor of the lyre and the emphatically expressive mouth.

in the Temple, especially the psalms performed by singers playing instruments (Figure 60):

> Deliver me from bloodshed, O God,
>   O God of my salvation,
>   and my tongue will sing aloud of your deliverance.
> YHWH, open my lips,
>   and my mouth will declare your praise (Ps 51:14-15).

But despite the significance of language it is ultimately not the mouth of adults that most powerfully speaks of God's glory. Marveling, we read in Psalm 8:

> Out of the mouths of babes and infants
> you have founded a bulwark because of your foes,
>   to silence the enemy and the avenger (Ps 8:2).

What comes from the mouths of babes and infants? Crying, not to be ignored, clear, demanding. They force us to decision and action. Their appeal is so urgent that in the Ancient Near East—for example when cities were besieged (Figure 61)—they were held out toward the enemy to appease the military forces.[5] Children are a protection that challenges the enemy and the avenger to cease. Biology interprets this human attitude as a determinant effected by tiny infants. The psalmist sees in it the power of God at work, before which the mighty of the world bow down[6] to the extent they have ears to hear, a heart to understand, and a belly to feel with.

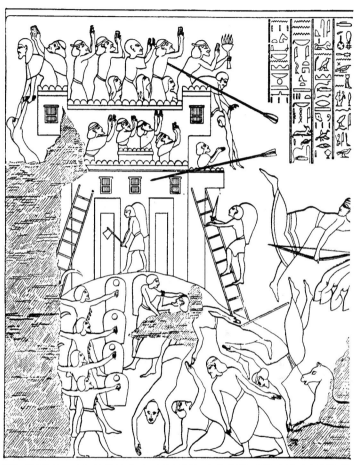

Figure 61:

Temple relief from Karnak in Egypt (ca. 1200 B.C.E.). Ramses III conquers a Canaanite city. To bring a halt to the attack the anxious inhabitants bring placatory offerings of incense and beg for mercy. At the moment of utmost peril a child is held out over the city wall, the sight of which, and its cries, are meant to arouse the sympathy of the attackers.

"With a Mighty Hand and an Outstretched Arm"

The Presocratic philosopher Anaximander is supposed to have said that the hand is the person. Without hands we cannot act humanly. With our hands we move, speak, and work. They are completely formed by the fourteenth week in the womb. The loss of a thumb is evaluated by modern insurance companies as a one-quarter disability, and anyone who loses an arm above the elbow is considered three-quarters disabled. With their hands people make countless signals and create works of art. Surgery is hand-work *par excellence.* Palmists read hands as if they were books. The hand is a universe in itself:[1] every hand, even every thumb, is unique, personal.

"Hand" (Hebrew *yad*), found 1600 times in the Hebrew Bible, is one of the most common words in the text. In Semitic languages *yad* originally referred to the hand and arm together. Over time the two parts came to be distinguished; in Akkadian the word was applied to the arm, in Hebrew to the hand.

Gestures: The Language of the Hands

The hands express relationships, moods, and messages. We can only mention a few examples from the rich treasure of biblical gestures. As with us, so also in ancient Israel a public handshake served as a sign of agreement, of contractual partnership (Figure 62), or of standing surety. This act of brotherhood was commonly performed before a large audience, like something done on television today. Thus Jehu allied with Jehonadab for battle against the dynasty of Ahab and the cult of Baal:

When [Jehu] left there, he met Jehonadab son of Rechab coming to meet him; he greeted him, and said to him, "Is your heart as true to mine as mine is to yours?" Jehonadab answered, "It is." Jehu said, "If it is, give me your hand." So he gave him his hand. Jehu took him up with him into the chariot. He said, "Come with me, and see my zeal for YHWH." So he had him ride in his chariot (2 Kings 10:15-16).

Gestures do not always have a clear meaning. Clapping the hands can be a sign of joy and applause: for example, the anointing and crowning of a king is affirmed by the acclamation of the people present (2 Kings 11:12). A pupil of Isaiah built this gesture into a metaphor to encourage the people returning from exile in Babylon:

> For you shall go out in joy,
>   and be led back in peace;
> the mountains and the hills before you shall burst into song,
>   and all the trees of the field shall clap their hands (Isa 55:12;
>   cf. Ps 98:4).

Figure 62:
Limestone relief from the throne room of Shalmaneser III in Nimrud (Iraq, 858–824 B.C.E.). The Assyrian king, on the right, seals an alliance with another king by shaking hands with the right hand.

Figure 63a:
Egyptian hand amulet (664–525 B.C.E.). This hand, made of blue glazed porcelain, comes from the 26th Dynasty; the silver frame and apparatus for hanging is much later, from the Islamic period (cf. Claudia Müller-Winckler, *Die ägyptischen Objekt-Amulette. Mit Publikation der Sammlung des Biblischen Instituts der Universität Freiburg, Schweiz, ehemals Sammlung Fouad S. Matouk* [Fribourg: Universitätsverlag; Göttingen: Vandenhoeck & Ruprecht, 1987] 48). Even today the protective so-called Fatima hand is very popular among Muslims. The Shiites interpret the five fingers as five great personalities, including Fatima; the Sunni interpret them as the five pillars of Islam.

Figure 63b:
Underside of an Egyptian scarab. One sees a large crocodile and a hand—a brief, but urgent image of prayer for protection against enemies.

Figure 64:
Nomadic weli above a sheikh's tomb in central Sinai with apotropaic handprints, photographed in 1986. The family that made pilgrimage to this little shrine to beg the blessing of children from God and the ancestors adorned the tiny sanctuary with the prints of their hands, which they had dipped in the blood of the sacrificial animals. To be protected from the destroying angel who killed the firstborn of the Egyptians, the Israelites before the Exodus smeared the doors of their houses with signs drawn in the blood of the Passover sacrifice (Exod 12:7, 12).

Depending on the context, however, clapping can express rejection rather than affirmation, or even expulsion. For example, in this apotropaic sense it was customary to clap in the presence of someone stricken by misfortune in order not to be drawn into the sphere of his or her accursedness (Job 27:23), or at sight of a ruined city (Lam 2:15). Ezekiel is ordered to clap his hands over Israel and to stamp his feet because Israel has become a demonic horror to YHWH (Ezek 6:11) that must be driven out publicly, like wild beasts in the field. Or he is to clap his hands and raise the war cry like a warrior armed with the sword, and YHWH will do the same (Ezek 21:14, 17). On the other hand, YHWH threatens to destroy the Ammonites because they have clapped their hands and stamped their feet over the destruction of Israel by the Assyrians (Ezek 25:6). Shaking one's fist or waving one's hand also signified repelling, in the sense of a threatening gesture (Isa 10:32; 11:15; 19:16; Zech 2:9;

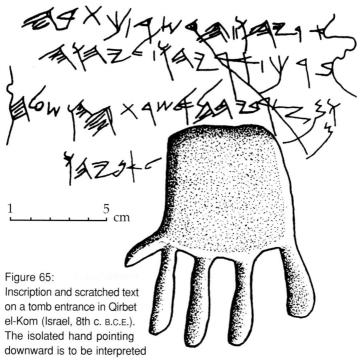

Figure 65:
Inscription and scratched text
on a tomb entrance in Qirbet
el-Kom (Israel, 8th c. B.C.E.).
The isolated hand pointing
downward is to be interpreted
as apotropaic; it was to prevent even illiterate grave robbers from violating
the tomb. The inscription reads: "Uriah the singer has written it. Uriah is
blessed by YHWH, and out of his distress he praises the God he serves, who
helps him." (For the translation see Siegfried Mittmann, "Die Grabinschrift
des Sängers Uriahu," *ZDPV* 97 [1981] 139–52; for the hand Silvia Schroer,
"zur Deutung der Hand unter der Grabinschrift von Chirbet el Qôm," *Ugarit
Forschungen* 15 [1983] 191–99.) There is another interpretation of the
hand, as the protecting and rescuing hand of YHWH (though without any
analogy before the Roman period), in Siegfried Mittmann, "Das Symbol der
Hand in der altorientalischen Ikonographie," in René Kieffer and Jan
Bergman, eds., *La Main de Dieu. Die Hand Gottes* (Tübingen: Mohr, 1997)
19–48.

Job 31:21) or for the purpose of warding off something dangerous (Zeph 2:15). Apotropaic hands for the warding off of
hostile forces were extremely popular in the Ancient Near East
at all periods, either as amulets for the neck or wrist (Figures

63a, b), bloody handprints on the walls of houses (Figure 64), or figures scratched at the entrance to a tomb (Figure 65).

Gestures could also be made political. Washing one's hands is in the first place not a gesture, but a need or a hygienic requirement after work, using the toilet, or eating, to remove dirt. However, this action can also symbolize moral integrity. Thus Pilate demonstrates by washing his hands in public that he is not guilty of the execution of Jesus of Nazareth (Matt 27:24; cf. Deut 21:6; Pss 26:6; 73:13). The Jewish custom of washing hands before prayer, which continues in Islam as well as in Christian priests' washing their hands during the celebration of the Eucharist, was first explained in the *Letter of Aristeas* (ca. 120 B.C.E.), in an account of the translation of the Hebrew Bible into Greek by seventy-two scholars in Alexandria:

> When they had washed their hands in the sea, as is the custom of all Jews, and had offered prayer to God, they addressed themselves to the interpretation and clarification of each passage. I questioned them on this point too, why it was that they washed their hands before praying. And they explained that it was in witness that they had done no wrong, since the hands are the organs of all activity; in such beautiful and holy spirit do they make all things symbols of righteousness and truth (*Letter of Aristeas* 305–306).

Jesus and his disciples deliberately omitted hand-washing before eating. When Jesus was questioned about this offense against pious custom he criticized such gestures as externalities that conceal one's real attitudes. The latter are shown, instead, by people's concrete speech and actions (Matt 15:1-20; Mark 7:1-23).

In Palestine it was usual to lift one's hands in prayer (Ps 44:20; see Figure 66), expressing praise (Ps 63:4) or urgent petition (Isa 1:15; 2 Macc 14:34). Extended hands could also evoke the witness of heaven when an oath was sworn (Deut 17:7; 32:40; Ps 106:26; Ezek 36:7). To do something with an uplifted hand was to do it deliberately. While sins committed unintentionally could be atoned with a purifying sacrifice, a deed done on purpose and later regretted required a sin offering (Leviticus 4–5). On the other hand, it may seem odd that when taking a solemn oath the one swearing had to place his hand under the testicles of the one to whom he was making oath (Figure 67):

> Now Abraham was old, well advanced in years; and YHWH had blessed Abraham in all things. Abraham said to his servant, the oldest of his house, who had charge of all that he had, "Put your hand under my thigh and I will make you swear by YHWH, the God of heaven and earth, that you will not get a wife for my son from the daughters of the Canaanites, among whom I live, but will go to my country and to my kindred and get a wife for my son Isaac." . . . "But if the woman is not willing to follow you, then you will be free from this oath of mine; only you must not take my son back there." So the servant put his hand under the thigh of Abraham his master and swore to him concerning this matter (Gen 24:1-9; cf. 47:29-31).

Behind this archaic custom[2] may lie the notion that the oath-taker swears by his manly strength, which will dry up if he breaks the oath. (For further connections between the hand and the penis see below, pp. 164–68.)

Hands are laid on in blessing (Figure 68; Gen 48:13-14; Mark 10:16), to convey the Spirit (Deut 34:9; Acts 8:18-19), and to heal (Mark 5:23; 16:18). This is to be distinguished from the gesture by which the person bringing a sacrifice lays a hand on the sacrificial animal in presenting it to the priest (Lev 1:4), or the one by which sins are laid on the scapegoat (Lev 16:21). Royal heads were anointed with the hands (1 Sam 10:1). A tenderly loving hand can also be a blessing and produce a feeling of well-being. So the beloved says in the Song of Songs:

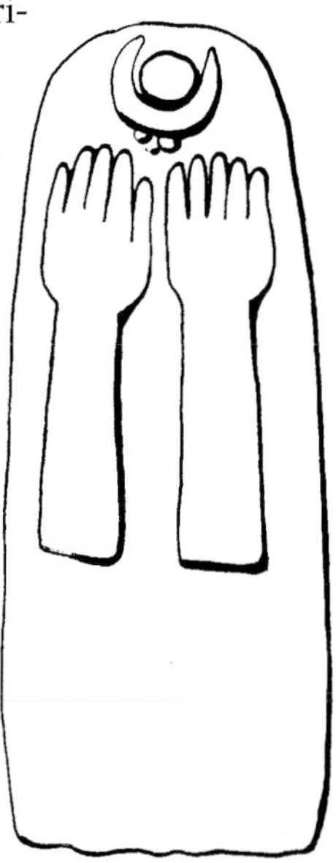

Figure 66:
Praying hands below a sickle moon and disk on a basalt stele from the Late-Bronze-Period stele sanctuary in the city of Hazor (13th c. B.C.E.). Alongside this decorated stele were found others lacking any decoration but the figure of a seated man. It is not clear whether he is the king, a deity, or a dead person.

Figure 67:
Underside of a scarab, supposedly from Jordan (1750–1550 B.C.E.). It probably depicts a scene in which a contract is being made, when each man lays his hand under the testicles of his partner (Othmar Keel, *Studien zu den Stempelsiegeln aus Palästina/Israel.* Vol. 4 [Fribourg: Universitätsverlag; Göttingen: Vandenhoeck & Ruprecht, 1994] 221). Between the partners to the contract is a branch or tree. Trees are also mentioned in the Bible as popular places for making contracts (cf. Josh 24:26). They make the divine witness present.

Figure 68:
Middle-Syrian cylinder seal from Latakia (Cyprus, 13th c. B.C.E.). A male deity blesses the "holy play" of a couple in bed by laying on of hands. The power and joy of life inherent in the erotic are under the special protection of the deity.

> O that his left hand were under my head,
>   and that his right hand embraced me! (Song 2:6).

A hand laid on the mouth meant silence, as it does for us. After God's first speech Job acknowledges God's greater authority and decides from now on to keep his mouth shut (cf. Mic 7:16; Job 21:5):

> "See, I am of small account; what shall I answer you?
>   I lay my hand on my mouth" (Job 40:4).

Of course hands with extended fingers also denoted pointing. A pointer in the shape of a hand (cf. Figure 79) is used even today in synagogal worship, since touching the Sacred Scriptures makes one unclean *(b. Šabb.* 14a). Behind this is concern for not mixing the sacred and profane spheres, and a certain fear of the power of the holy, as evidenced especially by Moroccan Torah pointers, which can take the form of a hand of Fatima (see Figure 63a).

Left and Right Hands

The zones of responsibility of the left and right hands were clearly regulated, as they are today in many societies in which one eats and writes with the right hand and cleans oneself with the left. In fact we could almost speak of two separate, hostile realms. The left should not know what the right is doing (Matt 6:3); what the right hand discreetly gives in mercy should not be boastfully put on display by the left. Therefore to be left-handed was something suspect and promised no good (Judg 3:15-29).

Especially in prescriptions for ritual, where every action has a symbolic character, the distinction between the right and left hand was elementary. Thus it was ordered that the Israelite priests, when purifying a leper, should hold the vessel with the oil in the right hand, pour some of the oil into the cupped left hand, and then use the finger of the right hand to sprinkle the oil before YHWH and to anoint the recovered leper (Lev 14:15-18). The function of the cupped left hand could be assumed by an artificial hand, for example an oil spoon of expensive material (Figure 69).

When Joseph brought his children to his father to be blessed he placed Manasseh, his firstborn, at Jacob's right hand and Ephraim at his left. But his father crossed his hands and thus, to Joseph's displeasure, gave the second-born the primary blessing of the right hand (Gen 48:13-20).

Seizing the right hand or being led by the right hand is an expression of friendly and trusting relationship (Figure 70; cf. Ps 63:8). Thus someone praying Psalm 73 can say to Yʜwʜ:

> Nevertheless I am continually with you;
> you hold my right hand (Ps 73:23).

As the right hand was preferred, so the right side was the side of honor. The order of seating near the throne of a king or god expressed orders of power and relationships. Jesus considered such distinctions and privileges among human beings out of place. He sarcastically criticized the quest for honor on the part of the scribes who sit on Moses' seat (Matt 23:1) and love to take the best places at meals (Luke 20:46). James and John, the sons of Zebedee, ask Jesus for the places of honor in the world to come; Jesus tells them that they do not know what they are asking for, since those places are reserved for the martyrs and no one but God knows to whom they belong. Anyone who is asked

Figure 69:
Oil spoon from Beth-zur (Palestine, ca 1000 B.C.E.). The handle shows a belted man with arm and wrist jewelry standing in front of a lotus flower and raising his right hand, extending the finger used for anointing. This gesture also has apotropaic significance. Anointing was an expression of joy and thus presupposed the complete banishing of the demonic, or accomplished it. One might also consider the lion bowl from Kinnereth (750–70 B.C.E), of "Egyptian blue," the underside of which depicts a cupped hand whose function is assumed by the vessel, to which tiny sacks of salve could be attached.

Figure 70:
Cylinder seal, Akkadian period, from Mesopotamia (ca. 2200 B.C.E.). A person bringing sacrifice is accompanied to the throne and altar of the goddess Ishtar. A middle-level goddess leads the visitor by the right hand. The seal also shows other significant hand-gestures, such as greeting by lifting the hand, holding a scepter as a symbol of power, and bearing gifts.

to take a seat of honor should instead be humble and take a lower place with the slaves (Mark 10:35-45 *parr.*). For this very reason, that Jesus did not concern himself about having a place of honor, but became a slave, he has inherited the place of honor before God, the throne of David at God's right hand (Matt 22:41-46 *parr.;* cf. Ps 110:1; see Figure 71). Thus it is said of him in the Apostles' Creed that "he is seated at the right hand of God."

In the Near East the right hand of God, the hand that blesses and governs all destiny, over time became the symbol of the highest god, a concept that the Jews also applied to YHWH. On Punic steles the hand is frequently the topmost symbol, with nothing above it but the stars, the visible signs of God in the heavens (Figure 72). From Asia Minor and Phoenicia we have bronze hands dedicated with an inscription to "the highest god," to whose protecting power the donors entrusted themselves (Figure 73).

God's left hand, in contrast to the right (see below) was never mentioned, even though, for example, the psalmist thanks God for having made him or her with "your hands" (plural:

Ps 119:73). However, it is clear from a fresco in the synagogue at Dura-Europos that God was imagined as having two hands, and that the left hand was associated with punishment and misfortune, the right with grace and blessing (Figure 74), as also in a midrash on the book of Exodus:

> May peace be upon both Thy hands! Both on the one with which Thou dost save us from the sea, and on the other with which Thou dost overthrow the Egyptians (*Beshallach* 22.2).

Creative and Destructive, Powerful and Violent Hands

Human action is concentrated in the hands. Action means "doing." Our doing gives information about our thoughts and desires; it is their expression. In the hand, reflection takes shape. It becomes productive. We work; something new comes into being. (Work, biblically speaking, is the work of our hands.) In our work we continue God's creative task. Therefore doing/working is service to God. Work without reflection (heart) is only reproduction. Then the hands are no

Figure 71:
Egyptian statues with the Pharaoh Haremhab (1345–1318 B.C.E.) to the right of Horus, the divine protector of the royal house. The Egyptians have given us pictorial evidence for what the texts of the Bible and the Christian creeds tell us: that the king or the son sits at God's right hand.

Figure 72:
Punic Tophet stele from Carthage (period of Tanit III). The symbol of the highest god, a hand, appears frequently on the Tophet steles in the highest segment, even above the stars. The hand corresponds to the hand of the petitioner or donor in the lowest register, as also found frequently in the later cult of Jupiter Dolichenus.

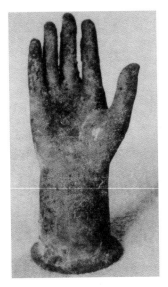

Figure 73:
Votive hand from Asia Minor (2nd/3rd c. C.E.). An inscription dedicates this petitioner's gift "to the highest god." The right hand of the god promises blessing and the preservation of the world. The motif of the hand of god became popular in Europe especially through the cult of Jupiter Dolichenus (successor deity to the Hittite storm god Teshub), which originated in Asia Minor and was spread primarily by Syrian immigrants; in this cult the god was acclaimed far and wide as "preserver of the world."

longer ours, but merely parts of a machine. We speak of alienated work. In a human hand it is determined whether a piece of wood or stone will be used for plowing, grinding grain, or killing someone (cf. Num 35:16-17). The work of our hands, involving toil (cf. Gen 3:17; 5:29), nourishes the person if God sees it (Gen 31:42) and allows it to succeed (Gen 39:3). Whether God blesses the work of the hands depends on whether the one working fears God. It is not efficiency that matters, but a socially appropriate, solidary attitude. Deuteronomy says in the context of the laws for the "Levite tax":

Figure 74:
God's left and right hands in a wall fresco from the synagogue at Dura-Europos in Syria (ca. 250 B.C.E.). While the right hand leads the people Israel through the Reed Sea, the left hand causes the destruction of the Egyptian army.

> Every third year you shall bring out the full tithe of your produce for that year, and store it within your towns; the Levites, because they have no allotment or inheritance with you, as well as the resident aliens, the orphans, and the widows in your towns, may come and eat their fill so that YHWH your God may bless you in all the work that you undertake (Deut 14:28-29).

In contrast, people who have no regard for the good of the community but rely entirely on the work of their hands, their own strength and cleverness, who even glorify the products of their hands and worship them, are considered wanton and sinful. This danger occurs especially with regard to the weapons of war, which rob their possessors of reverence for the God of life. For this reason Isaiah, for example, criticizes the people of Israel as idolatrous:

> Their land is filled with silver and gold,
>   and there is no end to their treasures;
> their land is filled with horses,
>   and there is no end to their chariots.
> Their land is filled with idols;
>   they bow down to the work of their hands,
>   to what their own fingers have made (Isa 2:7-8).

Spears, swords, and lances, but also plows, sickles, and the tools of the vinegrower are properly extensions of the hand and thereby "superhuman" expansions of its power or violence, something the hand symbolizes especially well. Kings rule their people with their hands, whose power-symbolism is underscored by the scepter (Judg 5:14; Jer 48:17; Esth 4:11; 5:2). But possessions (Lev 25:28) and wealth (Lev 5:7; 25:47; 27:8) as well as political rule can be symbolized by the hand. Woe to the person who must suffer under such a "hand," whose hands are bound by the violence of the godless! These are they whom the Psalms tirelessly beg God to free from the power of their enemies:

> For dogs are all around me;
>   a company of evildoers encircles me.
> They bind my hands and my feet.
>   . . .
> Deliver my throat from the sword,
>   my life from the power ["hand"] of the dog! (Ps 22:16, 20*).

Hence the hand is very often a synonym for power, violence, and tyranny. But it is always YHWH whose power determines the destiny of these forces. It is YHWH who gives Canaan into Israel's hand, Israel into the hand of the Philistines, or Egypt into the hand of Assyria; YHWH's hand controls the history of the powerful and the powerless.

Hand and Penis

Remarkably enough, there is no word in Hebrew for penis; the same is true of German and English (not counting all the childish, vulgar, and slang expressions). "Penis" is a loanword from Latin; the best we can do in English is "male organ." The Bible substitutes words such as "feet," "loins," "thing," "belly," or "tail," most frequently using "flesh" (see p. 212), or for the phallus "hand." This is the case in the Song of Songs, where a "sexual pantomime"[3] at the door of the beloved's chamber is described this way:

> My beloved thrust his hand into the opening [in the door],
> and my inmost being yearned for him (Song 5:4).

It is true that in Egypt the (ejaculating) phallus had a written symbol of its own, but even there the erect penis was equated with the "hand." Thus the fertility god Min, always depicted with erect phallus, also always raises his right hand (Figure 75). The Theban creator god Aton, according to an

Figure 75:
Relief from the propylaeon of the temple of Chon erected by Ptolemy II in Karnak (Egypt, 246–221 B.C.E.). The Pharaoh carries out a fertility rite with threshing oxen before Min. The raised arm and erect organ of the god clearly demonstrate the correspondence of the power-symbols hand and penis.

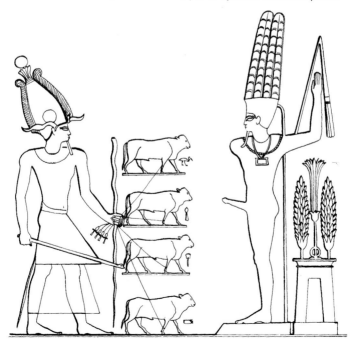

Egyptian myth, lacking a partner, produced his first creatures, Shu (air) and Tefnut (moisture) through masturbation. In the late Egyptian period his procreative organ was worshiped both as a goddess and also as hand and phallus (Figure 76). The connection of hand and phallus with power is also expressed in the fact that both organs were cut off the men captured in war and gathered in great heaps as trophies of victory.

The circumlocution "hand" emphasizes the mighty and powerful aspect of the male organ; German has a corresponding archaic word, "Gemächt" (related to "Macht," "power"). The potency resulting in posterity and thus associated with life was also invoked in Egypt through amulets, some of which have a humorous or comical character (Figures 77a, b). A relaxed and humorous approach to power represents a measure of liberation from it. In contrast, a machistic and phallocratic cult of male potency, dominant everywhere in the world today, leads to violence, not in loving relationships but in perpetrator/victim

Figure 76:
Relief from the temple of Amon at Hibis in the Charga oasis, Persian period (Egypt, ca. 500 B.C.E.), with two busts of the goddess Hathor guarded by cats. The Hathor-head on the right, under the decorated *naos,* rests on a hand, the left on a hand grasping a phallus. Hathor thus appears here as Hetepet. While the emblem at the left recalls the creation myth of Aton, the right emphasizes the powerful aspect of the goddess (cf. Claude Sourdive, *La main dans l'Egypte pharaonique. Recherches de morphologie structurale sur les objets égyptiens comportant une main* [Bern, Frankfurt, and New York: Peter Lang, 1984] 281–82).

Figure 77a
Fully modeled Egyptian faience amulet (1st c. B.C.E.). This amulet may have served as a potency stimulator. It is uncertain whether the clashing of cymbals was supposed to drive away demons (cf. Tob 8:1-3) or to serve as an aphrodisiac.

Figure 77b:
Fully modeled Egyptian limestone amulet (1st c. B.C.E.). The grotesque motif makes present-day viewers laugh; it may have done so even when it was new. Probably such amulets, popular in this later period, were the reason why Ezekiel ridiculed the Egyptians as "neighbors with big organs" (Ezek 16:26; cf. Othmar Keel and Christoph Uehlinger, *Altorientalische Miniaturkunst. Die ältesten visuellen Massenkommunikationsmittel* [2nd ed. Fribourg: Universitätsverlag, 1996] 105).

structures. This form of idolatrous worship of sexual power is probably what the school of Isaiah had in view when, in a passage difficult to understand (Isa 57:8, 10) it wrote a polemic against the worship of the "hand."

When the "hand" failed or was violently mutilated, a "hand" in the sense of a monument could replace the endurance of one's name in posterity. Having no children, David's son Absalom had a monument erected in the Kidron valley during his own lifetime, in the place where Judah's kings were buried (2 Sam 18:18). Thus "hand and name" *(yad vashem)* in Hebrew stand for the whole person. The memorial in Jerusalem to the victims of the Holocaust takes its name, Yad Vashem, from a passage from the school of Isaiah:

> . . . do not let the eunuch [the infertile or the castrated] say,
>   "I am just a dry tree."
> For thus says YHWH:
>   "To the eunuchs who keep my sabbaths,
>   who choose the things that please me
>   and hold fast my covenant,
>   I will give, in my house and within my walls,
>   a monument ["hand"] and a name
>   better than sons and daughters;
>   I will give them an everlasting name
>   that shall not be cut off" (Isa 56:3b-5).

The Finger of God

When God, through Moses and Aaron, struck the Egyptians with gnats, the Egyptian magicians were unable to master this plague.

> And the magicians said to Pharaoh, "This is the finger of God!" (Exod 8:19).

They were saying that the evil was caused by a god, thus a matter of fate that could not be combatted by human devices. In order to protect themselves against demonic blows the Egyptians, when in dangerous situations, stretched out the first and middle fingers to turn the demons aside, and they danced exorcistic dances while holding their fingers in that position. Stone or iron fingers showing the same gesture were placed in sarcophagi with mummies (Figure 78). In Mesopotamia this gesture was used to approach and pray to a deity. In the synagogue the Torah scroll is touched only with a pointer in the shape of a hand, the so-called Torah pointer (Figure 79).

The rabbis employed the fact that the Egyptians regarded the plagues as the work of the finger of God as the occasion for a practical interpretation of the miracle at the Reed Sea, to the greater glory of God. It is found also in the Passover Haggadah, read at the family Seder:

Rabbi Jose the Galilean said: "How do I know that the Egyptians were visited with ten plagues in Egypt, but with fifty plagues at the sea? Of those in Egypt Scripture says: The masters of hieroglyphics said to Pharaoh: 'It is a finger of God.' But of those at the sea Scripture says: When Israel saw the great hand that the Eternal laid upon Egypt, the people feared the Eternal, but they also believed in the Eternal and his servant Moses. But how many plagues did they receive with the finger? Ten! Hence ten plagues in Egypt, but fifty at the sea."

The evangelist Luke, in his version of the exorcism of a man with impaired speech, plays on the same passage in the book of Exodus.[4] Jesus is accused of driving out demons with the aid of Beelzebul, the ruler of the demons. In other words, he was accused of being in bed with the devil and not acting with divine authority. Jesus responds that Satan's kingdom could not stand if it fought against itself; furthermore:

Figure 78:
Egyptian two-finger amulet of steatite (664–525 B.C.E.). The significance of the extended first and middle fingers of the left hand is disputed. When placed with mummies they may have secured the closed edges of the wounds that had to be made in the process of mummification. That these are the fingers of the left hand points to an apotropaic gesture: evil is driven away by evil (the left).

"Now if I cast out the demons by Beelzebul, by whom do your exorcists cast them out? Therefore they will be your judges. But if it is by the finger of God that I cast out the demons, then the kingdom of God has come to you" (Luke 11:19-20).

Jesus' words rely on their knowing the Exodus passage, for only then can one understand why Jesus speaks of the finger of God in this context. He uses a typical rabbinic move, from the lesser to the greater: Moses, with the finger of God, conquered a political power and thus brought liberation; Jesus, with the finger of God, drives out demons, and where that happens the reign of God is breaking in. As Moses' plagues, wrought through the finger of God, indicated the coming of God's liberating hand in the Exodus, so Jesus' healing through the finger of God proclaims that very soon the rule of God will begin.

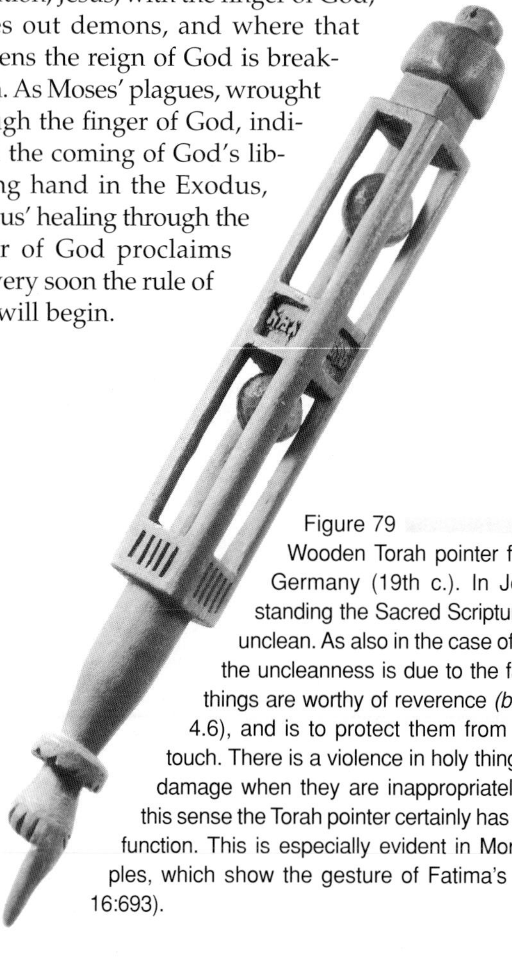

Figure 79

Wooden Torah pointer from southern Germany (19th c.). In Jewish understanding the Sacred Scriptures make one unclean. As also in the case of dead people, the uncleanness is due to the fact that these things are worthy of reverence *(b. Yadayim* 3.5, 4.6), and is to protect them from unauthorized touch. There is a violence in holy things that can do damage when they are inappropriately handled. In this sense the Torah pointer certainly has an apotropaic function. This is especially evident in Moroccan examples, which show the gesture of Fatima's hand (cf. *EJ* 16:693).

The Church Fathers' exegesis, much like that of the rabbis, was disturbed by the anthropomorphic innocence of the biblical texts. That God's finger would write the Law on tablets (Exod 31:18; cf. Deut 10:2), or that God would produce the whole of creation with a divine finger (Ps 8:3) seemed ridiculous to them. They almost always interpreted the finger as a symbol of the Holy Spirit, as did, for example, Rabanus Maurus in his famous Pentecost sequence, *"Veni, creator spiritus"*:

Tu septiformis munere	Thou, sevenfold in gifts,
dexterae Dei tu digitus	Thou finger on God's right hand.

With a Mighty Hand and an Outstretched Arm

It is striking that the Bible, while it speaks of the powerful shaking hands, never talks of the powerful hand or the mighty arm of the king. And yet it is just this image of a powerful, uplifted, and violently attacking arm that in the Ancient Near East was associated with a strong and effective king. On many temple walls in Egypt the Pharaoh is depicted, monumental in size, with his left hand seizing a bundle of enemies by the hair and with his uplifted right hand holding a club (Figure 80). The Egyptians even carved this scene on cliffs in the most distant regions of their kingdom in order to discourage possible enemies from desiring to attack the Nile valley. At certain times the same motif was carved on amulets even in Palestine; these guaranteed the one who wore or carried them of the striking power of divine strength. Only in this way—but never as a symbol of human strength—the same motif entered the Bible. The book of the prophet Ezekiel has some satirical fun with the omnipresent arm of Pharaoh's power. YHWH, Israel's God, is the only one who gives power. It is YHWH who puts Israel's enemies in its hands, that is, hands them over to Israel's power. Anyone powerful on earth (as, in Ezekiel's time, the king of Babylon was) owes that power to God alone, without whom we can do nothing:

> Mortal, I have broken the arm of Pharaoh king of Egypt; it has not been bound up for healing or wrapped with a bandage, so that it may become strong to wield the sword. Therefore thus says the Lord YHWH: I am against Pharaoh king of Egypt, and

Figure 80:
Temple of Horus in Edfu (Egypt, 3rd–1st c. B.C.E.). The pylon, 64 meters wide and 36 meters high, is decorated with the motif of the king's destruction of his enemies. Ptolemy XII Neos Dionysos (80–51 B.C.E.) seizes a group of enemies by their heads and strikes them dead in the presence of the temple deities. The ancient and common motif was especially widely used in the period of the Ramses kings (14th–13th c. B.C.E.) in a highly simplified form; it is found on large numbers of scarabs in the Palestinian region.

> will break his arms, both the strong arm and the one that was broken; and I will make the sword fall from his hand. . . . I will strengthen the arms of the king of Babylon, and put my sword in his hand; but I will break the arms of Pharaoh, and he will groan before him with the groans of one mortally wounded. I will strengthen the arms of the king of Babylon, but the arms of Pharaoh shall fall. And they shall know that I am YHWH, when I put my sword into the hand of the king of Babylon. He shall stretch it out against the land of Egypt . . . (Ezek 30:21-25).

While the strength and power of human arms can give rise to ridicule, the mighty hand and outstretched arm of God (Deut 4:34; 5:15; 7:19; 11:2; 26:8) cannot be too highly praised. The most praiseworthy of all God's deeds, of course, is bringing the Hebrews out of the Egyptian house of slavery. In a dramatic climax the book of Exodus tells how Moses leads the people out of Egypt but quickly finds himself trapped between the sea and Pharaoh's army. And yet it is in just this moment that the miraculous might of God proves itself superior to all powers; it is symbolized by the outstretched hand of God's servant Moses (cf. Figure 74):

> Then Moses stretched out his hand over the sea. YHWH drove the sea back by a strong east wind all night, and turned the sea into dry land; and the waters were divided. The Israelites went into the sea on dry ground, the waters forming a wall for them on their right and on their left. The Egyptians pursued, and went into the sea after them, all of Pharaoh's horses, chariots, and chariot drivers. . . . Then YHWH said to Moses, "Stretch out your hand over the sea, so that the water may come back upon the Egyptians, upon their chariots and chariot drivers." So Moses stretched out his hand over the sea, and at dawn the sea returned to its normal depth. . . . Thus YHWH saved Israel that day from the Egyptians . . . (Exod 14:21-30).

To this day God's liberating deed is proclaimed in the Christian Easter Vigil, and of course it is also remembered in the Jewish celebration of Passover. After the people had again experienced the mighty hand of God in being led back from the Babylonian exile, the arm or hand of God became God's most popular attribute (Isa 59:16; 62:8; 63:5, 12). Until the high Middle Ages a hand extending from heaven was for both Jews and Christians the only permissible representation of God in art, and the motif itself was restricted to a few chosen scenes: the binding of Isaac (cf. Gen 22:11; Figure 81), God's giving the inscribed tablets of the Law to Moses (Exod 31:18), and the raising of the dead bones in Ezekiel's vision (Ezekiel 37; cf. Figure 108).

The World-Creating and World-Sustaining Hands of God

In addition to all these recollections of the mighty interventions of God in human history with *a* hand, however, there is also the idea of a divinity who formed the whole world by hand, like a potter, and who keeps all created things alive by an act of continuing new creation (cf. Deut 33:27). The book of Job expresses it this way:

Figure 81:
Floor mosaic from Beth Alpha (Israel, 6th c. C.E.). As an etiology for the sacrificial cult in Jerusalem (Moriah), the binding of Isaac was one of the most popular synagogal motifs in the Roman and Byzantine periods. YHWH's intervention through an angel to prevent the sacrificing of Isaac is marked by a divine hand. Below it are the words *al tishlah* ("do not stretch out [your hand]") (Gen 22:12).

> But ask the animals, and they will teach you;
>   the birds of the air, and they will tell you;
> ask the plants of the earth, and they will teach you;
>   and the fish of the sea will declare to you.
> Who among all these does not know
>   that the hand of the LORD has done this?
> In his hand is the life of every living thing
>   and the breath of every human being (Job 12:7-10).

All living things depend on the giving hand of God. It is present in the yield of the harvest and the offspring of the sheep and goats. As Israel could speak of trees that clap their hands (see p. 153), so in Egypt people liked to emphasize the fertile character of the tree goddesses through giving hands emerging from the trunk (Figure 82). Jesus Sirach describes divine wisdom as a tree rooted in the people, more precisely a wealth of trees that yield fruit in abundance (Sir 24:1-22). The motif is applied in the Fourth Gospel to Jesus, who gives the water and bread of life (John 4:10-14; 6:35; 7:37).

It is also said of Y<small>HWH</small>: "you open your hand, satisfying the desire of every living thing" (Ps 145:16). In Psalm 104, strongly influenced by Egyptian hymns to the sun, we read:

> when you give to them, they gather it up;
>> when you open your hand, they are filled with good things (Ps 104:28).

Figure 82:
Stele for the dead, from Abusir in Egypt (ca. 1300 B.C.E.). A sycamore by a pool gives water and a richly laden platter of sacrifices to the dead and their ba-birds (soul birds). Above the deceased is a reference to a corresponding proverb in the Book of the Dead: "Spell for drinking water in the realm of the dead."

Under King Akh-en-Aton, who attempted a religio-political revolution by commanding that all worship in the land be given to Aton, the divine sun, large numbers of pictures were made depicting the royal family, the people, and even the animals beneath the graciously protecting and giving rays from the hand of the sun god (Figure 83). Yet this daily being-blessed by the divinity presumes that the world will be permanently preserved, that the order of creation will not be broken, that the cosmos will not sink back into chaos. This sustaining power of the universal god could be portrayed differently in Egypt: through the hands of the elevating power, Ka, and the primal ocean on the one hand, or through the outspread arms of the sky-goddess Nut on the other (Figure 84). In Israel YHWH and divine Wisdom took the place of these individual aspects of the cosmos:

> YHWH by wisdom founded the earth;
>   by understanding he established the heavens . . . (Prov 3:19).

The tender image of the protecting and sustaining hand of God could also bring comfort in a world in which a hand, shown on billboards holding a credit card, is adored (Figure 85). For again and again people are surprised by the life-creating power of God when they are threatened with destruction by the consequences of human power and violence. Jesus must also have been sustained by that power when he accepted martyrdom on the cross. The evangelist Luke therefore has him say at the last: "Father, into your hands I commend my spirit" (Luke 23:46).

God's Hidden Hand

In postbiblical times as well the hand remains the most important symbol of God in Judaism.[5] According to the visionary Hekhaloth literature of the Jewish mystics in late antiquity, in which God's sacred halls are described, the holy presence (Shekinah) of the divine power rests on the palm of God in the eighth heaven—that is, higher still than the traditional seven heavens. Fantastic measures of size, such as "fifteen thousand myriad parasangs in height" for a single finger also serve to emphasize the incomprehensible omnipotence of God, as do

Figure 83:
Limestone relief from a temple at Tel-el-Amarna, the residence of the reforming king Akh-en-Aton (1377–1358 B.C.E.). The *do ut des* ("give that you may receive") between human and god is expressed by a symbolism of hands that is typical of the Amarna period. The sun-god Aton accepts the gifts of the royal family, which they present in their hands and on altars. In return the god gives life to the humans' noses, symbolized by ankh-symbols in the hands of the sun.

Figure 84:
Relief on the lid of an Egyptian sarcophagus from Sakkarah (4th c.). The earth, depicted as a round disk, is held by a pair of hands resting on feet ànd with an eye at the center, where the arms meet. It is the life-force Ka that lifts all living things out of darkness into light. Above Ka a figure consisting only of head and arms symbolizes the primal ocean (Nun), who surrounds the earth and the realm of the dead (oval and circle). Above the earth the heaven goddess (Nut) extends her arms both in a frontal view, directly above the earth-disk, and as a deity portrayed from the side, bent to encircle everything. She also appears twice within the earth-disk, sending forth the sun's boat in the morning and receiving it again at evening.

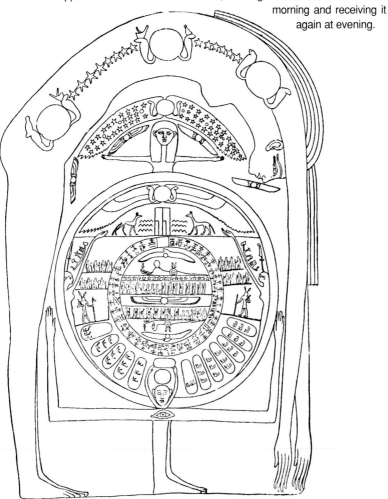

Figure 85:
Billboard advertising a credit card that permits its owners to hold the whole world in their hands. The play on the words of the spiritual, "He's Got the Whole World in His Hands," sets human beings in the place of God.

surrealistic images: the world is hung on God's arm "like an amulet on the arm of a hero." But in spite of this immeasurable power, God is helpless because since the destruction of the Temple God mourns with the Jewish people. As a sign of this mourning God has stretched out God's right hand backward. Mourning means making oneself like the dead, giving oneself up to helplessness. The same God who in wrath permitted the destruction of the Temple now suffers with God's people. The Jewish mystics deliberately set against the apathetic God of Aristotle and the Stoics a pathetic God capable of mourning. For this, too, they found an almost bizarre image:

> Then the right hand of the Omnipresent One wept, and five
> rivers of tears flowed from its five fingers, and, falling into the
> Great Sea, made the whole world to tremble, as it is written:
>> The earth will split into fragments,
>> the earth will be riven and rent.
>> The earth will shiver and shake,
>> the earth will stagger like a drunkard,
>> sway like a shanty
> —five times, corresponding to the five fingers of his great right
> hand (3 Enoch 48A:4; cf. Isa 59:16).

This text makes it clear that mourning is not seen as a sign of divine weakness, but of strength. There is no contradiction between the omnipotent creator of the world and the loving Father moved by sympathy. The mourning God waits for advocates, for people who will mourn with God from upright hearts. Yet at the end of time, if there are no advocates, God will lift up God's hand for the sake of the divine name, deliver Israel, and—when the Messiah comes—reveal the divine power to the whole world.

Christianity has refashioned the God who suffers with the people in the image of Christ, the man of sorrows (Figure 86). With fettered hands on his knees and thorn-crowned head he sits, in the tradition of Job-imagery, on a dung heap, tortured and taunted by the powerful of this world. So God, by completely laying aside the divine glory, descended to the level of God's suffering people, in order to be known and acclaimed by believers as their Savior.

Figure 86:
Suffering Christ with hands bound. Devotional sculpture from Osnabrück in Westphalia (ca. 1400). The bound hands reveal the powerlessness of the Redeemer. In his very solidarity with the powerless, Jesus becomes their liberator.

"You Have Placed Everything Under His Feet"

Our feet bind us to the earth. They enable us to stand, but also to walk. Of course a good deal of time must elapse before the fledgling human stands on its own feet—in a broad sense often twenty years or more. Many have no solid ground under their feet, others have cold feet or keep their feet under their parents' table, and all too many have to endure someone else's foot on their necks. But anyone who stands on his or her own two feet, stands fast, or accomplishes something that has "legs" probably has little need to put her or his enemies underfoot. Like the hand, the foot also embodies the human world in its own way and in the foot the human body is fully present, according to an ancient conviction that is enjoying new popularity in the practice of therapy of the reflex zones of the foot. Still, it is rather remarkable that the foot, almost constantly subjected to pressure and friction, at the same time demonstrates a high degree of sensitivity and even erotic excitability that has brought opprobrium on it within the anti-erotic Christian tradition. The paradox of sensitivity and exposure is also connected with the fact that, at least in the Bible, no other part of the human body is thought of so constantly in connection with its clothing: sandals or shoes.

Standing and Walking

The First Testament speaks about two hundred fifty times of feet or legs. The Hebrew language does not distinguish between the two: *regel* can mean one or the other, depending on

Figure 87:
Bronze figure of a storm god from Megiddo in Israel (13th c. B.C.E.). Bronze figurines of gods usually had pegs on the soles of their feet so that they could be set in wooden stands, few of which have survived. The prophet Isaiah therefore teased the owners of these images: they "[seek] out a skilled artisan to set up an image that will not topple" (Isa 40:20; cf. 41:7, and Silvia Schroer, *In Israel gab es Bilder. Nachrichten von darstellender Kunst im Alten Testament* [Fribourg: Universitätsverlag; Göttingen: Vandenhoeck & Ruprecht, 1987] 210–14).

circumstances. In some discreet circumlocutions the word occasionally also refers to the region between the legs, the male or female genitals.

In the first instance the feet are considered functionally: they are used for walking or standing. Lameness or the fragility of old age limit this ability, and it is a fundamental difference between the living and the dead. The skeletons that are awakened to life in the great vision in Ezekiel 37 immediately stand on their feet (cf. 2 Kings 13:21). Sneering ridicule is directed at the statues of gods that have feet but cannot walk (Ps 115:7; Jer 10:5; see Figure 87). The fate of lameness or injury to the legs could happen to anyone, young or old, poor or royal, for example Saul's son Meribbaal (2 Samuel 9) or King Asa (1 Kings 15:23). One of the obligations of a god-fearing person was to be feet for the lame (Job 29:15). The Church Fathers said that after the death of Jesus the apostles were Christ's feet. The Egyptians provided their mummies with carnelian leg amulets to give a magical guarantee that the legs would function after death (Figure 88).

Nevertheless, walking, running, or hiking are not, even today, among the favored activities of a Near Easterner. Anyone who can manage it remains sitting at home or in the shade and delegates the necessary daily errands. People who

Figure 88:
Carnelian leg amulet (Egypt, end of the 3rd c. B.C.E.), placed in the sarcophagus with the mummy. The Book of the Dead 92, "Saying to open the grave for the ba and for the shadow to go forth by day and to have command of the feet," could fulfill this purpose. There we read: "I have walked far and have stretched my knees, I have gone a long way and my flesh is calmed . . . . The way is open for the one who has command of his feet, so that he may behold the great god within the sun's bark."

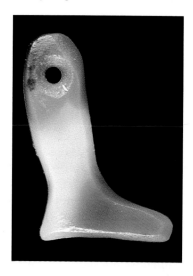

ran too fast in ancient Israel aroused suspicion of being spies; in fact, the word *meraggel,* "runner," also means "messenger" (Josh 2:1; 6:22-23; 1 Sam 26:4; 2 Sam 15:10) or "spy" (Gen 42:9, 14, 31, 34). Only the feet of the joyful messenger who announces the end of the time of exile have a positive image:

> How beautiful upon the mountains
>> are the feet of the messenger who announces peace,
> who brings good news,
>> who announces salvation,
>> who says to Zion, "Your God reigns" (Isa 52:7).

When anyone speaks of the beauty of the feet or legs it is, as with the other parts of the body, not the form but the expression and function that are foremost:

> How graceful are your feet in sandals,
>> O queenly maiden!
> Your rounded thighs are like jewels,
>> the work of a master hand (Song 7:1).

Rural women in Israel, even those of high rank, went barefoot as a rule.[1] Sandals were therefore regarded as equivalent to jewelry (Ezek 16:10; Jdt 10:4; 16:9). The epithet "queenly maiden" indicates the woman's proud, self-confident way of walking. It is thus her elegant, sure stride, not the shape of her feet, that fascinates the man. The woman praises especially the man's strong, solid calves, which she compares to alabaster columns on bases of gold (Song 5:15; but see also Sir 26:18).

The Enemy Beneath One's Feet

The foot, much like the hand, had a symbolic power of its own in Israel: it was associated with subjugation, domination, and the seizure of others' property. To "tread someone or something under foot" (Figure 89) was regarded even then as an act of the greatest humiliation. Within a patriarchal order it was especially important for men that no one, and certainly no woman, would tread upon their dignity (thus Sir 9:2).

In the arts of the Ancient Near East we find throughout the millennia the motif of the ruler who strides firmly over the enemies of the land (Figure 90) and subjugates them, or whole heaps of whose enemies already lie beneath his feet (Figures 91 and 92). Thus YHWH promises King David of Israel:

> "Sit at my right hand
> until I make your enemies your footstool" (Ps 110:1).

Such drastic ideas of subjection and domination are part of the *pathos* of Near Eastern kingship and appear not to have created any revulsion in Israel either, for kingship was always associated with the idea of "right ruling." However, there was severe criticism of the overestimation of the warrior's strong legs (representative of personal strength; see Figure 93), which his profession requires that he use to trample on his enemies (Ps 147:10; cf. Isa 9:4-5 and Jdt 9:11-14).

In the metaphorical language of the Psalms those who pray them identify, after surviving a crisis, with the victorious king under whose feet the enemies fall:

> You gave me a wide place for my steps under me,
> and my feet did not slip.
> I pursued my enemies and overtook them;
> and did not turn back until they were consumed.
> I struck them down, so that they were not able to rise;
> they fell under my feet (Ps 18:36-38).

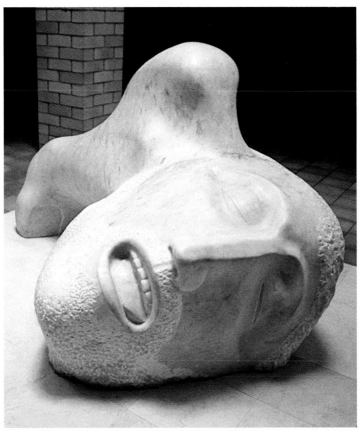

Figure 89:
White marble sculpture, "The Suffering Human" (1986), by Joseph Wyss, in the Romero-Haus, Luzerne, Switzerland. The foot, lowest part of the body and symbol of oppression, is in direct contrast to the head, the highest part and symbol of the human itself. Throughout the world the human face is being trodden upon by the feet of the powerful. People in authority who—like Archbishop Oscar Romero of El Salvador—do not accommodate themselves to the acceptable pose of the powerful, but instead resist their terror and pay for it with their lives are called martyrs in Christian tradition and are celebrated as followers of Christ.

Figure 90:
Life-size stone relief on a cliff face near Sarpol-i Zohab, where the Alwand breaks through the Zagros (Iran, 19th c. B.C.E.?). The heavily armed, sandal-clad King Anubanini of the Lulubians stands in a triumphant pose on a naked enemy. The goddess Ishtar is dragging more enemies to him, using a rope attached to rings in their noses; she hands the king a ring. In the lower register we see a column of prisoners of war.

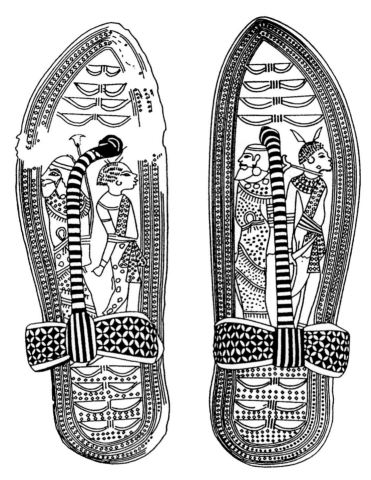

Figure 91:
Tut-ankh-Amon's sandals from his tomb (ca. 1330 B.C.E.). This intimate look into the ruler's sandals reveals to us that day in and day out he stood on the fettered enemies of his kingdom. The Old Testament scholar Othmar Keel calls this Pharaonic (and still prevalent) activity "maintaining the world order by trampling" (Othmar Keel, *Deine Blicke sind Tauben. Zur Metaphorik des Hohen Liedes* [Stuttgart: Katholisches Bibelwerk, 1984] 107).

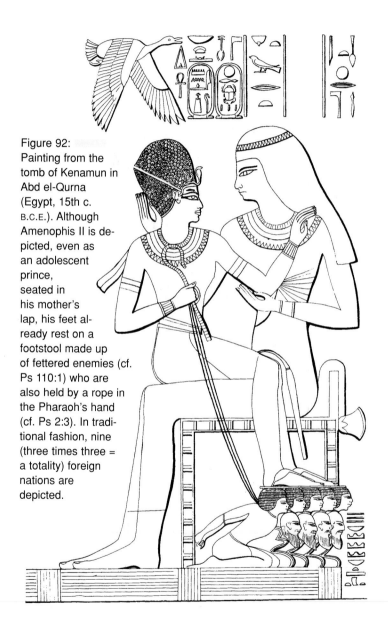

Figure 92:
Painting from the
tomb of Kenamun in
Abd el-Qurna
(Egypt, 15th c.
B.C.E.). Although
Amenophis II is de-
picted, even as
an adolescent
prince,
seated in
his mother's
lap, his feet al-
ready rest on a
footstool made up
of fettered enemies (cf.
Ps 110:1) who are
also held by a rope in
the Pharaoh's hand
(cf. Ps 2:3). In tradi-
tional fashion, nine
(three times three =
a totality) foreign
nations are
depicted.

Figure 93:
Wall painting from the Neo-Assyrian governor's palace at Tell Achmar in Syria (original destroyed; 8th c. B.C.E.). It represents a heavily armed Assyrian warrior with sharply emphasized leg muscles. Part of the tradition of YHWH faith that was critical of military might was God's aversion to warriors' legs (Ps 147:10b).

Of course there are also prayers by people who are still in the midst of crisis, whose whole desire is a righteous life but who must behold how the right is daily twisted by arbitrary rulers so that God is denied. Their powerless rage and despair wrings from them the dreadful hope:[2]

> The righteous will rejoice when they see retribution,
>   when they bathe their feet in the blood of the wicked.
> And people will say, "Surely there is a reward for the righteous;
>   surely there is a God who does justice on earth" (Ps 58:10-11).

The eschatological hope related to this wish, that someday God will crush Satan under their feet (Rom 16:20), inspired Christians also. The concrete political facts connected to the hope were then disclosed (to those who were initiated in its symbolic language) in the Revelation of John.

One of the signs of the inbreaking of the reign of God is that the halt and the lame are healed (Matt 15:30). Perhaps the New Testament miracle stories about lame people who were able to walk again need to be augmented with background from the Near Eastern experience of domination. When the things told in these stories were happening Palestine lay both under the (taxation) foot of Rome, which turned the people of the land into debt slaves, and the foot of a corrupt Temple aristocracy who made the great majority of the population politically lame. Jesus healed a lame man in Capernaum (Mark 2:1-12 *par.*) by declaring his debts (sins), which had apparently lamed him, null and void. Peter and John, on the steps of the Temple in Jerusalem, in the name of Jesus set on his feet a man who had been lame from birth (Acts 3:1-11): they did not participate in the practice of almsgiving that was expected even by the sick, but instead— poor and free as they were—in the spirit of Jesus defied the restrictions and customs of the Temple authorities; in doing so, of course, they also provoked the latter's opposition.

What Lies at People's Feet

One way of countering the despotism of violent rulers was to subjugate oneself willingly to them. The physical and perceptible expression of such subjugation was falling on one's face, so-called *proskynesis*, at the feet of the ruler (cf. Figure 30). Significantly, this is rarely told of anyone in relation to a king in Israel (1 Sam 25:24), but it is something one would do before YHWH (Pss 2:12; 99:5; 132:7) or as a sign of honor for YHWH's prophets when ordinary people asked help from them (2 Kings 4:27, 37).

For Israelites the fact that YHWH had given human beings such an advantaged place over all living things was always a reason for marveling:

> . . . what are human beings that you are mindful of them,
> mortals that you care for them?
> Yet you have made them a little lower than the divine beings,
> and crowned them with glory and honor.
> You have given them dominion over the works of your hands;
> you have put all things under their feet . . . (Ps 8:4b-6).

Domestic and wild animals, birds and fish are given over to the governance, but therefore also to the responsibility of human beings. In the plastic arts the gesture of conquering is often emphasized by having the conqueror place a foot on the neck of the enemy (cf. Josh 10:24) or the conquered creature; at the same time, however, the protective role of the hero over subjected life is also depicted (Figure 94).

People placed their feet not only symbolically on living things, but also on a piece of ground or a land that, by this action, was taken possession of, and of which, if possible, one would not surrender even a foot's breadth (Josh 14:9). In Genesis, God tells Abraham to walk through the land of Canaan:

> "Rise up, walk through the length and the breadth of the land,
> for I will give it to you" (Gen 13:17).

At the Feet of God

In the sense just indicated the sun god Shamash was celebrated in Near Eastern iconography as the owner of the whole earth when sunrise was depicted as the foot of the god demonstratively placed on the mountains (Figure 95). Consequently, YHWH in the form of the sun (1 Kings 8:12-13 LXX)[3] rests on the empty cherubim-throne prepared for YHWH in the Jerusalem Temple (1 Kings 6:23-30).

It appears that people imagined the entry of God into the sanctuary in human form in the Syrian temple of ʿAin Dara in the fertile Afrin valley, where huge footprints were carved into the threshold, pointed toward the sanctuary interior (Figure 96). The threshold was regarded as the borderline of a house, where the inner and outer spheres meet. Throughout antiquity the crossing of this border was therefore connected with special rituals. The worshipers of Dagon at Ashdod, for example, avoided touching the threshold of the temple by jumping over it. In Israel people made fun of that custom and thus, in polemical fashion, explained the custom by saying that when the people of Ashdod carried Yhwh's Ark of the Covenant as a trophy into Dagon's temple the statues all fell down and their heads and hands lay on the threshold (1 Sam 5:4-5). In reality the custom may well have been associated with the idea that when the deity entered a sanctuary he or she stopped on the threshold, thereby hallowing it; as a result, one should avoid

Figure 94:
Neo-Assyrian cylinder seal from Iraq (9th–7th c. B.C.E.). "The foot placed up on the weaker animal expresses dominion (cf. Ps 8:6[7]). As in the case of the king, however, this dominion consists not only in holding the subject, but also in defense of the weaker animal against the attacking lion" (Othmar Keel, *The Symbolism of the Biblical World: Ancient Near Eastern Iconography and the Book of Psalms.* [New York: Seabury, 1978] [58]).

touching it. In any case, a similar custom seems to have been observed in certain circles in Jerusalem (Zeph 1:9). The theology of Ezekiel also expresses the idea that the threshold is a special place. According to Ezekiel the glory of God abode on the threshold of the Temple before; in face of the sinful behavior of the Israelites, it left the place of its rest (Ezek 9:3; 10:4, 18). And in his vision of the new Temple the prince stands in prayer on the threshold, the source of divine blessing (Ezek 47:1). In this sense the feet at ʿAin Dara could also be regarded as liturgical directions for the cultic personnel; their nakedness favors this interpretation, but the gigantic (divine) size of the feet is against it.

Figure 95:
Akkadian cylinder seal from Iraq (ca. 2200 B.C.E.). The sequence on the unrolled seal shows a sunrise in Mesopotamian iconography: the sun god

Shamash strides through the gate of heaven, a key in his left hand, a rod as scepter in his right, and places his foot on the earth as a sign of his rule over the whole world, on which he shines each day.

In Jerusalem the Ark of the Covenant could be regarded as God's footstool (1 Chr 28:2). However, the image of God's footstool was also applied, in a critique of the cult, to the Temple itself (Ps 132:7; cf. Isa 6:1), to the Temple mount, Zion (Lam 2:1), and even to the whole earth:

> "Heaven is my throne
>   and the earth is my footstool;
> what is the house that you would build for me,
>   and what is my resting place?" (Isa 66:1).

What in human eyes is the holy of holies, is in the eyes of those who fear God only the lowest, most distant reflection of the unimaginable majesty of God—an insight that was reserved not only to the pious of Israel, and that has only been more and more appreciated as a result of the scientific exploration of the universe.

Figure 96:
Threshold of the temple at ʿAin Dara in Syria (9th/8th c. B.C.E.). Feet (97 x 35 centimeters) were carved into the huge plate of the threshold, a pair of feet in the foremost plate and a left foot in the one to the rear. There is a plate of *terra sigillata* from the same place in the Hellenistic period with a foot in relief in the center.

Jesus of Nazareth taught his disciples in the context of this theology (Matt 5:34-35), but in the gospels he also sometime takes the place of God. Frequently the miracle stories tell how petitioners throw themselves at Jesus' feet (Matt 15:30, and frequently elsewhere). Behind this customary posture of petition there is probably a reference on the part of the authors of the gospels to Jesus' divinity, for the spontaneous reaction to an encounter with a deity is throwing oneself down. When the Risen One encounters his disciples and greets them they fall down and grasp his feet (Matt 28:9). The story of the prostitute who comes into the house of Simon (Luke 7) to anoint Jesus' feet also reveals a deeper meaning against this religious background.

> One of the Pharisees asked Jesus to eat with him, and he went into the Pharisee's house and took his place at the table. And a woman in the city, who was a sinner, having learned that he was eating in the Pharisee's house, brought an alabaster jar of ointment. She stood behind him at his feet, weeping, and began to bathe his feet with her tears and to dry them with her hair. Then she continued kissing his feet and anointing them with the ointment (Luke 7:36-38).

With her actions of washing and drying, anointing and kissing Jesus' feet the woman sets up a sign. She touches the human being and at the same time she touches the feet of God, who gives protection and mercy.

Removing One's Shoes

Taking off one's sandals, both really and symbolically joined to the feet in the closest possible way, accordingly means renouncing possession. Boaz can only marry the widowed Ruth, in the book of that name, when a closer relative removes his sandal and hands it to Boaz. In doing so he renounces the field, but is also relieved of the levirate duty to beget and rear progeny for his relative. If a brother-in-law, in the absence of another claimant to the widow, refuses to fulfill that duty, the widowed sister-in-law is permitted to take off his sandals in the presence of the elders. His house is called "barefoot" in Israel (cf. the corresponding legal ordinances in Deut 25:5-10).

Taking off one's shoes and going barefoot is always associated in the Bible with experiences of powerlessness, mourning

(Mic 1:8), poverty, or imprisonment. Weeping and barefoot, David leaves the city of Jerusalem after his son Absalom's rebellion (2 Sam 15:30). The poor whom the prophet Amos seeks to protect often have scarcely a pair of sandals to pawn (Amos 2:6; 8:6). According to the gospel of Luke, Jesus sends his disciples barefoot on mission as a sign of their total renunciation of possessions (Luke 10:4; 22:35). Those who are captured in the course of war must expect to go naked and barefoot into exile. Thus the prophet Isaiah, on God's orders, has to go about naked and barefoot for three years as a sign of the humiliation involved in the exile and imprisonment of many nations by the Assyrians:

> . . . at that time YHWH had spoken to Isaiah son of Amoz, saying, "Go, and loose the sackcloth from your loins and take your sandals off your feet," and he had done so, walking naked and barefoot. Then YHWH said, "Just as my servant Isaiah has walked naked and barefoot for three years as a sign and a portent against Egypt and Ethiopia, so shall the king of Assyria lead away the Egyptians as captives and the Ethiopians as exiles, both the young and the old, naked and barefoot, with buttocks uncovered, to the shame of Egypt" (Isa 20:2-4).

The Israelites willingly took off their sandals when they entered a holy place. The biblical model of this is Moses, who is told by the voice from the burning bush:

> "Come no closer! Remove the sandals from your feet, for the place on which you are standing is holy ground" (Exod 3:5).

This became a sign of humbling oneself, of respect for the deity, and also a ritual that helped to separate the spheres of the profane and the holy. As is well known, this custom has been retained in Islam to this day.

Shoes, in constant contact with dust and filth, were *the* expression of lowliness and impurity, which is why the office of sandal-bearer, or of the one who loosens the straps of someone's sandals, was regarded even in the Second Testament as the lowliest form of service—and yet John the Baptizer says that before the Messiah he himself is unworthy even of that office (Matt 3:11; John 1:27).

Washing Feet

Throughout the Mediterranean basin, where people went about in sandals or barefoot, washing one's feet was part of daily cleansing. Excavations have revealed special basins for footwashing (Figure 97). Washing feet was one of the friendly gestures extended to one's guests (Gen 18:3-5; 19:1-2; 24:32; 43:24; Luke 7:44; John 2:6). The classic form of this action has been immortalized in a beautifully developed scene in Homer's *Odyssey,* when the old nursemaid, while washing his feet, recognizes Odysseus, who has returned home in disguise, as her nursling when she sees a scar on his foot (*Odyssey* 19.343–507). Footwashing was considered the lowest service of a slave. Thus it was one of the daily activities that reflected social classes and structures of domination. Anyone who had to wash others' feet was counted among the losers, as the oracle of Delphi indicated in announcing to the Milesians that the Greeks had been defeated by the Persians:

> In that day, Miletus, thou planner of works that are evil,
> Thou for a banquet shalt serve and a guerdon rich of the spoiler;
> Many the long-locked gallants whose feet shall be washed by thy women;
> Woe for my Didyman shrine! No more shall its ministers tend it.
> (Herodotus, *Hist.* VI.19)

This is not altered by the fact that the action was understood as a loving gesture when a wife or children performed it for the *paterfamilias,* or as a sign of respect when disciples washed the feet of their teacher. While footwashing was one of the indispensable

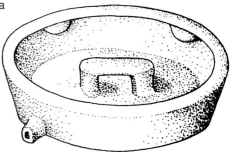

Figure 97:
Footwashing bowl from Samaria (9th/8th c. B.C.E.) with shelf for the foot and a drain that can be stoppered. Similar basins are in use even today and in Muslim countries are called "the mother of prayer," because they are used especially before praying.

obligations of the wife, it was unimaginable that a free man would bow to this slavish work. All the more revolutionary must it have seemed when Jesus himself, in complete freedom, undertook the inglorious task of washing feet (John 13:1-14; Figure 98). It is not a coincidence that it was a man, namely his disciple Simon Peter, who had the most difficulty with this exchange of roles, which upset the whole system of rank: "Lord, are you going to wash my feet?" he cries in disgust, and he makes it clear that he will never allow it. But Jesus teaches his disciples that it is only through mutual footwashing, the constant overturning of the system of rank, that they can become a true community in the reign of God, and only in this way can they have community with him and with God.

In the Fourth Gospel footwashing takes the place of the Lord's Supper as described in the synoptic gospels. While the

Figure 98:
Section of a miniature in the illuminated manuscript Marcianus Graecus 538, probably from Asia Minor, containing the text of the book of Job with a commentary by Olympiodoros (10th c. C.E.). The LXX reads: "and great were Job's works on earth" (Job 1:3c). Olympiodoros interpreted the verse in terms of Job's good works, which led the illustrator to represent him in a singular way as a type of Christ, who washed others' feet.

latter became a sacrament of the Church and the consecration of the body of Christ was stylized as a priestly privilege, footwashing never became a Church sacramental institution: the contrast between this action and the quickly restored patriarchal order in Christianity would have been too obvious. Instead, as early as the Pastorals footwashing was made part of the catalogue of duties for widows (1 Tim 5:10), and on that basis it became in some churches a privileged act to be done for those men who walk in the footsteps of the apostles. One exception was the church in Milan, where in the fourth century Ambrose required that the feet of the newly baptized should be washed; this custom endured until the fourteenth century. In contrast, Augustine insisted on an allegorical interpretation of the action, confirming the opinion of Origen, who in turn could refer to a spiritual interpretation of footwashing already present in Judaism; we find it in Philo of Alexandria:

> The washing of feet, however, means that we should no longer walk on the earth, but sweep through the heights of the ether (*Spec. leg.* 1.207).

Footwashing, it was taught, frees us from the fetters of sin that bind the feet of our soul; it completes the effects of baptism, secures Peter a share in Christ, and equips the disciples to be messengers of the Gospel. Only on Maundy Thursday is footwashing celebrated physically in some churches in memory of Christ's loving service to his disciples. Patriarchs, bishops, and abbots then wash the feet of their fellow workers (Figure 99).

Thus in the framework of the ethicizing of the monotheistic religions by the prophets, the daily action of footwashing acquired a moral dimension. But while in Christianity footwashing as a ritual action has practically disappeared, in Islam it is one of the obligations of pious people (Figure 100), and has always remained connected to the demands for concrete purification of the body, as an oral tradition makes clear:

> Abu Huraira said: "The messenger of God said: 'The prayer of a person who is unclean is not accepted until he completes the little washing.'" A man from Hadramaut asked him: "O Abu Huraira, how does one become unclean?" He responded: "By flatulence, for example" (*Sahih al-Buhari* IV.2).

Figure 99:
Solemn footwashing on Maundy Thursday in the Armenian Orthodox Cathedral of St. James in Jerusalem. On this day only, the patriarch washes the feet of twelve other ecclesiastical dignitaries, recalling with this action Christ's washing the feet of the disciples (John 13).

The Footsteps of Christ

Besides the theological tendency to spiritualization, however, there was also the popular need for concrete visibility and assurance. The pious crowd of pilgrims who visited the Holy Land sought to obey the apostle's admonition to walk in the footsteps of the Lord (1 Pet 2:21) literally, and they looked for the Lord's footprints. Muslims point to the impression of Muhammad's foot on the sacred stone in the Dome of the Rock in Jerusalem, supposed to have been left by the prophet when he began his ascent into heaven. The model for this was on the Mount of Olives, where Christians even today point to the last impression of the foot of the risen Christ in the Chapel of the Ascension (Figures 101a, 101b). This footprint is of course more than merely an expression of naïve pilgrim piety. It indicates that on that very spot the disciples fell before Jesus (Luke 24:52), on the spot where according to 2 Sam 15:32 people had already worshiped God, where Jesus had wept over Jerusalem (Luke 19:43-44), and

Figure 100:
Wellhouse in the Oma-yaden mosque in Damascus. Every mosque has a wellhouse or a large public toilet facility. Before prayer, in the so-called "little washing," the head, arms, and feet are washed.

where even in Ezekiel's time the glory of God paused one last time to take leave of its city (Ezek 11:23). But above all the footprint is meant to show that Jesus is the eschatological Savior, the Messiah, who according to a vision of Zechariah will stand

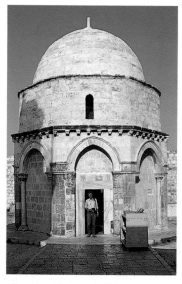

Figures 101a and 101b:
Christ's last footprint in the Ascension mosque on the Mount of Olives near Jerusalem: testimony to a materialist pilgrim piety of following in the footsteps of the Holy One.

on the Mount of Olives on the last day (Zech 14:4). There the elect will gather under his protection, while the nations will be judged.[4]

Of course these material efforts at finding traces drew criticism from Gnostic-spiritual groups:

> . . . I often wished, as I walked with him [Jesus], to see his footprint in the earth, whether it appeared—for I saw him raising himself from the earth—and I never saw it (*Acts of John* 93).

However, such a bodiless theology could not withstand even the interpretation of the Church Fathers, despite their tendencies to hatred of the body, because they repeatedly asserted that Jesus not only appeared to suffer, but was nailed to the cross by his hands and feet. The biblical God is a God with hands and feet, a God who acts powerfully in history, suffers with God's people, is concrete and can be touched—even if be only God's feet that we touch.

"All Flesh Is Like Grass"

Carne vale!—Flesh, farewell! The freewheeling festivities preceding Lent are known by this ambiguous phrase (*carne vale* = English "carnival"). It means, on the one hand, "Flesh, may it be well with you!" but on the other hand also "Flesh, away with you!"—namely for the period of forty days until Easter, the feast of the Resurrection. The flesh is a symbol of joy and life, but also of vulnerability and death. During carnival life is revealed to be a great masquerade behind which death is hiding. But it is especially in face of death that life is most joyful and exuberant. In the Baroque period death, portrayed as a bizarre skeleton on the walls of churches and city houses, shamelessly reminded believers of their mortality and so evoked a lust for living (Figure 102). Anyone today who talks too concretely about death is considered indecent. We don't want the Church's ministers to remind us of death, but to console us with talk of everlasting life. Death and dying are scarcely regarded as suitable themes for public discourse in our progressive world, and only a few specialists in mortuaries and cemeteries deal with dead bodies.

Bones as Sober Evidence of Death

The Hebrew Bible knows neither technical nor spiritual fantasies of eternal life. Instead, human mortality is acknowledged and described with disarming clarity and honesty:

> You turn us back to dust,
> and say, "Turn back, you mortals."
> For a thousand years in your sight
> are like yesterday when it is past,
> or like a watch in the night.

Figure 102:
"Berner Totentanz" [Bern Dance of Death] by Niklaus Manuel (1484–1530), painted between 1516 and 1517 in twenty-four lifesize pictures on the wall of the Dominican convent. We see death taking possession of the widow and the virgin. The slogan on the picture of the daughter is "Daughter, now the hour is come,/white will be your red mouth;/your body, your face, your hair and breast/all must become foul filth."

> You sweep them away; they are like a dream
> 　　like grass that is renewed in the morning;
> in the morning it flourishes and is renewed;
> 　　in the evening it fades and withers.
> For we are consumed by your anger;
> 　　by your wrath we are overwhelmed.
> 　. . .
> The days of our life are seventy years,
> 　　or perhaps eighty, if we are strong;
> even then their span is only toil and trouble
> 　　they are soon gone, and we fly away (Ps 90:3-7, 10).

In light of these bitter truths the psalm gives us a recipe by which we can nevertheless go on living without despair. It is neither a pointer to a medical solution of the problem nor consolation in terms of a world beyond this one; instead, it is wisdom for a limited lifespan:

> So teach us to count our days
>   that we may gain a wise heart (Ps 90:12).

For the time after this life people can only hope for rest for their bones. Thus the household manager of a king of Jerusalem had written over the door of his rock tomb outside the city:

> Here is no silver and gold, (for) only (his bones) and the bones of his slaves are with him. Cursed be the man who opens *this.*[1]

This educated Israelite apparently died trusting that grave robbers also knew how to read. In fact, they would have found in his tomb, besides a few little oil lamps to light the dead in the land of darkness, and a couple of water jugs to refresh him in the land of thirst, only a couple of pieces of personal jewelry or a little icon for blessing (Figure 103). According to ancient Israelite ideas people did not need much after death. As long as the flesh was still moldering on the bones the dead were conceded to have a certain existence. People talked of the corpse's "chirping" and were unwilling to get near it. When there was nothing left but bones they were, after a certain length of time, removed to a corner of the tomb to make room for the next corpse.

In the mortal remains of a human being the story of men and women is made concrete, and in their relationship to those remains lies also the relationship of the world beyond to their story. So the biblical histories strove for a picture of a conciliatory, pious, and magnanimous King David, who permitted the corpse of his archenemy Saul to be placed in the tomb belonging to his family (2 Sam 21:12-14). On the other hand, the break with the past in the religious reforms under King Josiah is nowhere more obvious or more violent than in the exhuming and burning of the bones of the believers who had been buried near the controversial temple at Bethel (2 Kings 23:16).

Skin and Bones

During life human bones are something like a barometer of health. Even today images of emaciated people whose bones

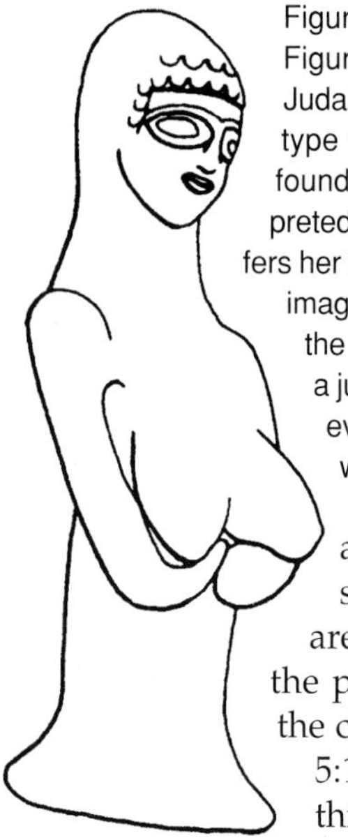

Figure 103:
Figurine from a column (Jerusalem, 8th c. B.C.E.). In Judah in the 8th and 7th centuries clay figurines of this type were enormously widespread. They have been found in dwellings and in graves and are to be interpreted as images of blessing. The woman or goddess offers her full breasts, which in biblical texts also represent an image of blessing as such. Placing such figurines with the dead in the grave, and also perhaps a tiny lamp or a jug, expressed the great need to give the deceased, even in this dark place of rest, some light, refreshing water, and a small share in the vital forces of life.

are clearly visible evoke blank horror and sympathy (Figure 104). The more the bones are embedded in sound flesh, the healthier the person appears, and the more they show, the closer that person is to death (Lam 3:4; 4:8; 5:10). The pain in Job's limbs makes him think of this:

> They are also chastened with pain upon their beds,
>   and with continual strife in their bones,
> so that their lives loathe bread,
>   and their appetites dainty food.
> Their flesh is so wasted away that it cannot be seen;
>   and their bones, once invisible, now stick out (Job 33:19-21; cf. 7:5; 30:30).

In the prologue to the book of Job, Satan bets for the skin, flesh, and bones of Job, so that in the end Job really cannot even take his own skin to market:

> Then Satan answered YHWH, "Skin for skin! All that people have they will give to save their lives. But stretch out your hand now and touch his bone and his flesh, and he will curse you to your face" (Job 2:4-5).

"Is my strength the strength of stones, or is my flesh bronze?" the driven Job demands of God (Job 6:12). That is: "am I perhaps an immortal god, that you mistreat me this way?!" The substance of the gods is of precious metals rather than "flesh,"

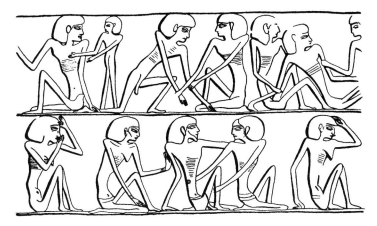

Figure 104:
Figures of nomads from the exit corridor of the Unas pyramid in Sakkarah (Egypt, 2480–2350 B.C.E.). This is the oldest surviving depiction of nomads in the art of the settled Egyptians. It is chiseled in the limestone inner wall of the exit from the Unas pyramid, and shows a group of emaciated, dehydrated, hungry nomads whom the king in his generosity (praised in this documentation) has rescued from death. At the upper left a child begs a woman for milk, but her breasts are completely dried up. Below, another eats the lice from her own head. The smaller groups of men seem to show both conflict and mutual support.

and so that word *basar* is the only one among the many Hebrew words for the body and its parts that is *never* applied to God, and is frequently contrasted to YHWH as the very symbol of all that is mortal:

> "Cursed are those who trust in mere mortals
>   and make mere flesh *(basar)* their strength,
> . . .
> Blessed are those who trust in YHWH,
>   whose trust is YHWH" (Jer 17:5, 7; cf. 2 Chr 32:8).

The skin, the hide is, like the flesh, something that people and animals have in common. Neither can get out of its own skin; a person with black skin will always be black just as a leopard cannot change its spots (Jer 13:23). In Israel a black skin could evoke widely differing associations. On the one hand, it could be an indication of sickness and death. The defeated and suffering princes of Israel are described in Lamentations as black-skinned:

> Her [Israel's] princes were purer than snow, whiter than milk;
> their bodies were more ruddy than coral, their hair like sapphire.
> Now their visage is blacker than soot;
> they are not recognized in the streets.
> Their skin has shriveled on their bones;
> it has become as dry as wood (Lam 4:7-8; cf. Job 30:30).

Only in Song of Songs 1:5-6 is there a more positive association with black skin. The black-skinned beloved here has the image of a black goddess (Figure 105) who evokes the "wholly other" (cf. the black Madonnas in our cultural context).

Job, in his despair, appeals urgently to God's care for the fragile human creature, which God had so lovingly made of skin, flesh, bones, and sinews (Job 10:11). The prophet Micah, in the most drastic language possible, accused the responsible people of his time of literally tearing the skin and flesh from the bones of the poor (Figure 106), making them lifeless skeletons:

> . . . you who hate the good and love the evil,
> who tear the skin off my people,
> and the flesh off their bones;
> who eat the flesh of my people,
> flay their skin off them,
> break their bones in pieces,
> and chop them up like meat in a kettle,
> like flesh in a caldron (Mic 3:2-3).

The psalms have quite a bit to say about the terror that gnaws one's bones, the dread of death that strikes a chill in the bones of those who pray (Pss 6:2; 22:14, 17; 31:10; 32:3; 38:3; 42:10; 102:3), and there are a remarkable number of sayings in the book of Proverbs that establish psychosomatic connections between one's way of life or experiences and the state of one's bones:

> A good wife is the crown of her husband,
> but she who brings shame is like rottenness in his bones
> (Prov 12:4).

The light of the eyes rejoices the heart,
  and good news refreshes the body [bones] (Prov 15:30).

A tranquil mind gives life to the flesh,
  but passion makes the bones rot (Prov 14:30).

Flesh and Bone Related

As the last saying in particular makes clear, flesh and bones can be said to have a physical common destiny. Only when flesh surrounds the bones are the conditions present that make it possible for spirit, motion, life to enter the body (cf. Ezekiel 37). But flesh and bones are not only the fundamental requirements for life, their shape and form constitute the unmistakable sign of the human, making it possible for us to recognize a human being when we see one. The second creation account describes the forming of Eve as being like an artist's shaping of a statuette, a living work of art (Figure 107):[2]

Figure 105:
Painting from the tomb of In-her-cha in western Thebes (12th c. B.C.E.). The transfigured queen mother Ahmes-Nefertari, the mistress of the necropolis of Thebes, is regularly depicted as black. Black evokes the "wholly other."

210

So YHWH caused a deep sleep to fall upon the man, and he slept; then he took one of his ribs and closed up its place with flesh. And the rib that YHWH God had taken from the man he made into a woman and brought her to the man. Then the man said,

"This at last is bone of my bones and flesh of my flesh; this one shall be called Woman (ʾishshah), for out of Man (ʾish) this one was taken."

Therefore a man leaves his father and his mother and clings to his wife, and they become one flesh (Gen 2:21-25).

Here, and in many other places (Gen 29:14; Judg 9:2-3; 2 Sam 5:1; 19:12-13) flesh and bones express the closest relationship, such as is felt by members of the same tribe. In a general way the expression "all flesh" can stand for the whole of humanity, even for every living thing, including the animals (Gen 6:17; 9:15). People have their fleshliness in common with the animals, but it radically distinguishes them from God, who has neither flesh nor bones. Nevertheless it is God who gives flesh to human beings, especially a heart of flesh, that is, a living capacity for intelligence to understand God's instruction:

Figure 106:
Drawing by Friedrich Dürrenmatt for the World Hunger Year 1967, "Cruel Father with Hungry Children." Like Micah, Dürrenmatt depicts the unscrupulous profiteers of his own time as people who eat other people. In a nice bourgeois ambience, with a crucifix on the wall and a fist on the table, the father, before the eyes of his horrified children, holds a cannibalistic meal, complete with wine. (Cf. Othmar Keel, *Die Bibel mischt sich ein. Predigten und "Worte zum Sonntag"* [Zürich, Einsiedeln, and Cologne: Benziger, 1984a] 127ff.).

Figure 107:
Statuette from ʿAin Ghazal near Amman (7th c. B.C.E.). This neolithic statuette is made of mortar modeled around a central reed or piece of rush. These two materials correspond to the biblical "flesh and bone," the basic substances that make up the human body.

> Thus says the Lord YHWH: "I will give them one heart, and put a
> new spirit within them; I will remove the heart of stone from their
> flesh and give them a heart of flesh, so that they may follow my
> statutes and keep my ordinances and obey them (Ezek 11:19-20).

Signs of Mortality

The flesh is thus altogether a symbol of God-willed humanity and an expression of life. But while normally the bones
of the dead endure and even after death bear witness that they
once belonged to a living soul, soon after death there is nothing of the flesh left to see. Therefore the flesh, even more than
the bones, is a symbol of mortality, seen in sharp contrast to
the immortality of the divine power:

For

> "All flesh is like grass
>   and all its glory like the flower of grass.
> The grass withers,
>   and the flower falls,
>   [when the breath of the LORD blows upon it]
> but the word of the Lord endures forever" (1 Pet 1:24; cf. Isa
>   40:6-7).

Because it is so close to the sphere of death, the flesh is easily susceptible to all that is sickly and impure. No illness is
mentioned more frequently in the First Testament or treated at
greater length than leprosy in the flesh (Leviticus 13–14).
Those who suffer from that illness are counted among the
dead, because they have to live cut off from the living. When
the Priestly purity texts speak of a discharge "of the flesh"
they are referring to the male organ (Lev 15:2-3, 7). The
prophet Ezekiel uses the same word to refer to the penis in his
image of the nations, interpreted as males, with whom Israel,
the bride of YHWH, is whoring:

> You played the whore with the Egyptians, your lustful neigh-
> bors [lit.: your neighbors with the swelling member] . . . (Ezek
> 16:26; cf. 23:20).

Here, as in the famous Flood story, we see a tendency to asso-
ciate the flesh with sinfulness.

In the figure and the life of Jesus of Nazareth the paradox of the flesh's positioning between healthful life and vulnerability reaches its apex. For his enemies he is a glutton and a drunkard: that is, a person who cares too much for his flesh. He himself, in the consistency of his prophetic life in the service of righteousness, takes no care for his flesh and risks crucifixion. However, the gospels portray him during his lifetime as a man who likes to sit at table in company, who lets himself be anointed, who evokes the reign of God in the image of a great feast, who, finally, leaves his spiritual testament in fleshly form, namely in the form of a meal in which bread and wine, as body and blood, are central, the food that gives life to the flesh.

Paul, in contrast, had little use for the fleshly aspect of his body: on the contrary, he finds it a hindrance, even a burden in the realization of his image of the human. For him Near Eastern skepticism toward the vulnerable flesh is coupled with Greek body-soul dualism to form a pointed disparagement of the flesh. It becomes the essence of sinful, death-consumed human nature, the opposite pole to spirit, which is the only category in which Christians can be one with Christ, as Paul explains in his letter to the Romans:

> For those who live according to the flesh set their minds on the things of the flesh, but those who live according to the Spirit set their minds on the things of the Spirit. To set the mind on the flesh is death, but to set the mind on the Spirit is life and peace. For this reason the mind that is set on the flesh is hostile to God; it does not submit to God's law—indeed it cannot, and those who are in the flesh cannot please God. But you are not in the flesh; you are in the Spirit, since the Spirit of God dwells in you. Anyone who does not have the Spirit of Christ does not belong to him. But if Christ is in you, though the body is dead because of sin, the Spirit is life because of righteousness (Rom 8:5-10).

Whereas Paul, following the Greek tradition, regards what is physical and bodily as problematic *as such* in contrast to the spirit, the *pneuma*, and devalues it, we can find in the First Testament neither such a deep-seated contempt for physicality nor such a clear counter-function of spirit. In the first place the human being is flesh—but as long as one lives, as long as one is a life-hungry throat, one's flesh is moved, driven about, buoyed and winged by vital forces. To these forces the First Testament gives the name *rūaḥ*. *Rūaḥ* is collectively the spirits of life that begin to rule when the starving finally have food to eat or the dehydrated have water to drink (1 Sam 30:12; Judg 15:19), or when the will to live, which can be thrown to the ground, destroyed, or extinguished, is revived by good news (Gen 45:27).

Rushing Wind as the Spirit of God

The Hebrew notion of *rūaḥ* has been introduced to many Christians, especially women, through feminist theology. In Woman-Church *rūaḥ* has become a feminine synonym for the Holy Spirit, the stormy-creative Spirit-power that moves the daughters and sons of God. In fact the Hebrew word, almost always given in feminine form, is related to the concept of "breadth." *Rūaḥ* creates room, puts in motion, leads out of narrowness into broad space, and gives life. The word almost always appears in connection with verbs of motion, and describes wind or storm, but also life force, creative force, and divine power. Never is *rūaḥ* immobile; it is always active, producing dynamism. Thus in Gen 1:2 God's *rūaḥ* flutters over the waters of chaos at the very beginning of the work of creation. It is this same *rūaḥ* of YHWH that causes humans to become living beings, as the creation Psalm 104 is aware:

> When you hide your face, they are dismayed;
>> when you take away their breath *(rūaḥ),* they die
>> and return to their dust.
> When you send forth your spirit *(rūaḥ),* they are created;
>> and you renew the face of the ground (Ps 104:29-30).

From time to time YHWH is explicitly addressed as the God of the "spirits of life" of all flesh (Num 16:22, and frequently elsewhere). The prophet Ezekiel sees in a vision a vast field full of bones of the dead, symbolizing the hopeless, dead people of Israel (Figure 108). He is told to prophesy to the bones:

> Then he said to me,
> "Prophesy to the breath *(rūaḥ),* prophesy, mortal,
> and say to the breath *(rūaḥ):* 'Thus says YHWH God:
> Come from the four winds, O breath *(rūaḥ),*

Figure 108:
Fresco from the synagogue at Dura-Europos in Syria (250 C.E.). This section from the lengthy illustration of the waking of the dead in Ezekiel 37 shows how God's *rūaḥ* comes into the dead in the form of winged angelic beings, so that they are able to stand on their feet again. Thus the valley of death becomes a valley of life.

> and breathe upon these slain, that they may live.'"
> I prophesied as he commanded me,
> and the breath *(rūaḥ)* came into them,
> and they lived, and stood on their feet,
> a vast multitude (Ezek 37:9-10).

This vision is not about a realistically understood raising of the dead. Rather, the image of the bones represents the hopeless, even dead condition of Israel in exile. Only God's *rūaḥ* will lead the people out of this deathlike condition and restore them to life, give them courage and hope and joy in living. The Holy Spirit has the same effect in the Acts of the Apostles (2:17-18) when it suddenly gives the discouraged disciples new enthusiasm, new abilities, and new perspectives (Figure 109). *Rūaḥ* overcomes all laziness and slackness, everything that is lethargic and dead.

Figure 109:
Modern depiction of Pentecost from Serima, Zimbabwe, executed on a clay tablet. The Spirit, as an abstract entity, is depicted in abstract form, as triangles over the heads of Mary and the apostles.

While it is true that in a great many cases the positive effects of divine *rūaḥ* are described, the Israelites were not always entirely certain whence the living spirits that dwell in human beings came. *Rūaḥ* itself remained as incomprehensible as the origin of the wind, which also can only be observed in its effects. Thus much later Jesus taught the curious Nicodemus, who was trying to understand the difference between birth according to the flesh and birth from the Spirit, Greek *pneuma:*

> The wind *(pneuma)* blows where it chooses, and you hear the sound of it, but you do not know where it comes from or where it goes (John 3:8).

The Evil Spirit

In the understanding of the First Testament it appears that not every *rūaḥ* is sent from YHWH. In all cases, however, these are forceful impulses that do not come from within the human person itself, but have a powerful influence on him or her from outside. Among the less-pleasant experiences of *rūaḥ* are attacks of rage and anger. Jealousy is described as such a spirit that primarily attacks men and shakes them, and the prophet Hosea describes all of Israel's wicked goings-on as the work of a spirit of whoredom and immorality.

Thus the word *rūaḥ* embraces psychic components. This is especially evident when 1 Samuel reports of Saul's illness:

> Now the *rūaḥ* of YHWH departed from Saul, and an evil *rūaḥ* from YHWH tormented him. And Saul's servants said to him, "See now, an evil *rūaḥ* from YHWH is tormenting you. Let our lord now command the servants who attend you to look for someone who is skillful in playing the lyre; and when the evil *rūaḥ* from YHWH is upon you, he will play it, and you will feel better" (1 Sam 16:14-16).

We would now say that Saul suffered from clinical depression; here music therapy is prescribed for it, and at first it is successful. Later, however, his depressions are increasingly accompanied by manic episodes. Then, when the *rūaḥ* seizes him, Saul rushes about with his spear in his hand and tries to kill his young adversary, David. As a charismatic who, like a prophet, can be seized by YHWH's *rūaḥ* (1 Sam 19:21-24), Saul is apparently vulnerable to other kinds of spirits as well. In this case the text attributes even the evil *rūaḥ* to YHWH, who had already withdrawn divine favor from Israel's first king. However, its effects are similar to those of demonic powers that influence human beings against their will.

The description of impressive changes in a person's mood and spiritual condition as the work of unknown, dangerous powers may seem naïve and archaic, but this kind of language may not be at all remote from the experiences of those affected. The Second Testament assigned far more importance to destructive powers that undermine human vitality and *joie de vivre* than the First Testament did. Under Roman occupation the greatest variety of demons multiplied in Palestine, many of them capable of causing illness and possession. Jesus of Nazareth's authority was therefore shown especially in healings and the driving out of evil spirits who delayed the coming of the reign of God.

Figure 110:
Graphic by Klaus Staeck (1979), "Nord-Süd-Konferenz" [North-South
Conference]. Invisible managers negotiate at the conference table over
the fate of starving people.

Thus in the whole Bible it is not the vulnerability and mortality of all flesh that blocks full humanity. Even in the eschatological time of salvation people die, although only at a great age (Isa 60:20-22). But a person can perish of insufficient dynamism, lack of motivation, resignation, failure of nerve, depressions, and above all of the spirit of our times, that of murderous capitalism (Figure 110). When we battle against these anti-spirits we stand within the tradition of all those who believe in the life-giving *rūaḥ* of God and in life *before* death.

Notes

INTRODUCTION

¹ Cf. Christian Duquoc, "Mensch/Ebenbild Gottes," *NHThG* 3 (1985) 83–94.

² Thomas Aquinas, *Summa theologiae* I.93, Prologue to I/II. Karl Barth still postulated an *analogia relationis* (analogy of relation) between God and the human being, and saw the *imago Dei* not as an attitude, but as a way of being (cf. *Church Dogmatics* III/1, 183–206).

³ "Spiritual birth is the result of a free choice, and thus we are in a sense our own parents; we create ourselves as we wish to be; through our wills we model ourselves on the model we choose" (*Life of Moses*, PG 44.328B; quoted from Duquoc).

⁴ Cf. Ruth Groh and Dieter Groh, *Weltbild und Naturaneignung. Zur Kulturgeschichte der Natur* (Frankfurt: Suhrkamp, 1991).

⁵ Cf. Especially Paul Humbert, *Etudes sur le récit du paradis et de la chute dans la Genèse*. Mémoires de l'Université de Neuchâtel 14 (Neuchâtel: Secrétariat de l'Université, 1940) 153–75 (Chapter V: "L'Imago Dei dans l'Ancient Testament); Johann Jakob Stamm, "Die Imago-Lehre von Karl Barth und die alttestamentliche Wissenschaft," in *Antwort. Karl Barth zum siebzigsten Geburtstag am 10 Mai 1956*. (Zollikon-Zürich: Evangelischer Verlag, 1956) 84–98 (bibliography!).

⁶ See most recently Erich Zenger, *Gottes Bogen in den Wolken. Untersuchungen zu Komposition und Theologie der priesterschriftlichen Urgeschichte*. SBS 112 (Stuttgart: Katholisches Bibelwerk, 1983); Silvia Schroer, *In Israel gab es Bilder. Nachrichten von darstellender Kunst im Alten Testament*. OBO 74 (Fribourg: Universitätsverlag; Göttingen: Vandenhoeck & Ruprecht, 1987); Walter Groß, "Die Gottebenbildlichkeit des Menschen nach Gen 1,26.27 in der Diskussion des letzten Jahrzehnts," *BN* 68 (1993) 35–48.

⁷ But then, neither are the lexicon articles! Nevertheless, we will mention several, each with bibliography: "Adam," *TRE* 1:414–37; *EJ* 234–45; "Mensch," *TRE* 22:458–577.

⁸ Cf. Wis 10:1, and similarly in apocryphal texts: *Apoc. Mos.* 21:6; *4 Ezra* 6:53-54; *1 Enoch* passim.

⁹ *b. Sanh.* 38b.

¹⁰ See Plato, *Symposium* 189–193; thus also in the rabbinic literature: *BerR* 8.1 and elsewhere.

¹¹ Thus, for example, the Apocryphon of John, the Apocalypse of Adam, or the Gospel of Philip.

¹² *The Koran.* Translated with notes by N. J. Dawood (Rev. ed. Harmondsworth: Penguin, 1999). This motif appears frequently (Sura 7:11-12; 15:29-33; 20:116; 38:71-88), even apart from the context of the creation account (Sura 17:61; 18:50).

¹³ "Anthropologie," *Wörterbuch der Feministischen Theologie* 16. See also Kristen E. Kvam, "Anthropology, Theological," in Letty M. Russell and J. Shannon Clarkson, eds., *Dictionary of Feminist Theologies* (Louisville: Westminster/John Knox, 1996) 10–12.

¹⁴ On this see Hartmut Böhme and Gernot Böhme, *Das Andere der Vernunft. Zur Entwicklung von Rationalitätsstrukturen am Beispiel Kants.* stw 542 (Frankfurt: Suhrkamp, 1985) 83–168 (Chapter 2: "Materie und verdrängter Leib).

¹⁵ Franz Rosenzweig, *The Star of Redemption.* Translated from the 2d ed. of 1930 by William W. Hallo (New York: Holt, Rinehart and Winston, 1971) 422–23.

¹⁶ Emmanuel Lévinas, *Totality and Infinity. An Essay on Exteriority.* Translated by Alphonso Lingis (Pittsburgh: Duquesne University Press, 1969) 291.

¹⁷ Enrique Dussel, *Philosophy of Liberation* (Maryknoll, N.Y.: Orbis, 1985) 189.

¹⁸ See, among others, Leonardo Boff, *When Theology Listens to the Poor* (San Francisco: Harper & Row, 1988).

¹⁹ Frantz Fanon, *The Wretched of the Earth* (New York: Grove Press, 1965).

²⁰ Boff, *Sacraments of Life: Life of the Sacraments* (Washington, D.C.: Pastoral Press, 1987).

²¹ José Comblin, *Retrieving the Human: a Christian Anthropology* (Maryknoll, N.Y.: Orbis, 1990); José Ignacio González Faus, "Anthropology: The Person and the Community," in Ignacio Ellacuría and Jon Sobrino, eds., *Mysterium liberationis: fundamental concepts of liberation theology* (Maryknoll, N.Y.: Orbis, 1993) 497–521.

²² Ivone Gebara, "El cuerpo, nuevo punto de partida de teología," *Solidaridad* (Bogotá) 14 (May 1990); Doris Strahm, *Vom Rand in die Mitte: Christologie aus der Sicht von Frauen in Asien, Afrika und Lateinamerika* (Luzern: Edition Exodus, 1997) 354–84; João Batista Libânio, "Zur Entwicklung der Befreiungstheologie," in Raúl Fornet-Betancourt, ed., *Befreiungstheologie: Kritischer Rückblick und Perspektiven für die Zukunft 1: Bilanz der letzten 25 Jahre (1968–1993)* 60 (bibliography!). See also the bibliography in J. Jakob Stamm, "Die Imago-Lehre von Karl Barth und die alttestamentliche Wissenschaft," in *Antwort. Karl Barth zum siebzigsten Geburtstag am 10 Mai 1956* (Zollikon-Zürich: Evangelischer Verlag, 1956) 84–98.

²³ See the bibliography in Stamm, "Die Imago-Lehre von Karl Barth."

[24] See the following articles in the *Wörterbuch der Feministischen The-ologie:* "Körper der Frau/Leiblichkeit," 219–24; "Gewalt," 153–56. (And see the relevant articles in Russell and Clarkson, eds., *Dictionary of Feminist Theologies:* Susan A. Ross, "Body," p. 32; Susan Brooks Thistlethwaite, "Violence, Institutionalized," pp. 307–309; Marie M. Fortune, "Violence, Sexual," pp. 309–311.) For women's christological projects on several continents see Doris Strahm, *Vom Rand in die Mitte,* especially pp. 389ff. for the subject of the female body.

[25] Hans Walter Wolff, *Anthropology of the Old Testament.* Translated by Margaret Kohl (Philadelphia: Fortress, 1974).

[26] Among the few works of this type that anticipated Wolff's anthropology were those of Georges Pidoux (*L'homme dans l'Ancien Testament* [Neuchâtel: Delachaux & Niestlé, 1953]) and Ludwig Köhler (*Hebrew Man. Lectures delivered at the invitation of the University of Tübingen, December 1–16, 1952. With an appendix on justice in the gate.* Translated by Peter R. Ackroyd [London: S.C.M., 1956]).

[27] Wolff, *Anthropology of the Old Testament* [118].

[28] On this see Silvia Schroer and Othmar Keel, "Von den schmerzlichen Beziehungen zwischen Christentum, Judentum und kanaanäischer Religion," *Neue Wege* 88 (1994) 71–78.

[29] See Silvia Schroer and Thomas Staubli, "Saul, David und Jonatan eine Dreiecksgeschichte? Ein Beitrag zum Thema 'Homosexualität im Ersten Testament,'" *BiKi* 51 (1996) 15–22.

[30] Frank Crüsemann, Christof Hardmeier, and Rainer Kessler, eds., *Was ist der Mensch? Beiträge zur Anthropologie des Alten Testaments. H. W. Wolff zum 80. Geburtstag* (Munich: Kaiser, 1992). We would like to point out, however, that Jürgen Kegler devoted a major section of his essay to the symbolism of the womb.

[31] James Barr, *The Semantics of Biblical Language* (London: Oxford University Press, 1961).

[32] See the extensive treatment of this topic in Helen Schüngel-Straumann, *Rûah bewegt die Welt. Gottes schöpferische Lebenskraft in der Krisenzeit des Exils.* SBS 151 (Stuttgart: Katholisches Bibelwerk, 1992), especially 9–21.

[33] See Heinrich Schäfer, *Principles of Egyptian Art.* Edited, with an epilogue by Emma Brunner-Traut. Translated and edited, with an introduction by John Baines (Oxford: Clarendon Press, 1974); Emma Brunner-Traut, *Frühformen des Erkennens. Am Beispiel Altägyptens* (Darmstadt: Wissenschaftliche Buchgesellschaft, 1990); Othmar Keel, *The Symbolism of the Biblical World: Ancient Near Eastern Iconography and the Book of Psalms* (New York: Seabury, 1978).

[34] John Macmurray, *The Clue to History* (London: S.C.M. Press, 1938).

[35] "Androzentrismus," *Wörterbuch der Feministischen Theologie* 14; see Mary E. Hunt, "Androcentrism," in Russell and Clarkson, eds., *Dictionary of Feminist Theologies* 7.

[36] "Anthropologie," *Wörterbuch der Feministischen Theologie* 16–22 (and see n. 13 above); "Eva," ibid. 90–97; Helen Schüngel-Straumann, *Die Frau am Anfang. Eva und die Folgen* (Freiburg: Herder, 1989).

[37] Franz Josef Stendebach, *Der Mensch, wie ihn Israel vor 3000 Jahren sah* (Stuttgart: Katholisches Bibelwerk, 1972).

[38] For this see Cornelia Klinger, "Was ist und zu welchem Ende betreibt man feministische Philosophie?" in Lynn Blattmann, et al., eds., *Feministische Perspektiven in der Wissenschaft*. Zürcher Hochschulforum, vol. 21 (Zürich: Zürcher Hochschulforum, 1993) 7–22.

[39] I am grateful to Ina Praetorius for this suggestion (in a letter, 1994).

[40] Cf. Gesa Lindemann, "Zeichentheoretische Überlegungen zum Verhältnis von Körper und Leib," in Annette Barkhaus, M. Mayer, N. Roughley, and D. Thürnau, eds., *Identität–Leiblichkeit–Normativität. Neue Horizonte anthropologischen Denkens* (Frankfurt, 1996) 146–75.

[41] Enrique Düssel, "The Bread of the Eucharistic Celebration as a Sign of Justice in the Community," in Mary Collins and David Power, eds., *Can We Always Celebrate the Eucharist? Concilium* 152 (2/1982) 56–65.

[42] Ibid., 62.

[43] Fernando Belo, *A Materialist Reading of the Gospel of Mark* (Maryknoll, N.Y.: Orbis, 1981) 244–52, 334.

CHAPTER 1

[1] Robert North, "Brain and Nerve in the Biblical Outlook," *Biblica* 74 (1993) 577–97.

[2] Cf. Wilfred G. E. Watson, "The Unnoticed Word Pair 'eye(s)'//'heart,'" *ZAW* 101 (1989) 389–408.

[3] Cf. Hellmut Brunner, *Das Hörende Herz. Kleine Schriften zur Religions- und Geistesgeschichte Ägyptens,* edited by Wolfgang Röllig. OBO 80 (Fribourg: Universitätsverlag; Göttingen: Vandenhoeck & Ruprecht, 1988) 11–12.

[4] Cf. Adrian Schenker, "Die Tafel des Herzens," *VHN* 48 (1979) 236–50.

[5] See Raymond O. Faulkner, translator, *The Ancient Egyptian Book of the Dead.* Edited by Carol Andrews (New York: Macmillan, 1972) 29–31.

[6] 𓊪 Ani, quoted from Evelyn Rossiter, ed., *The Book of the Dead: Papyri of Ani, Hunefer, Anhai* (New York: Miller Graphics, 1979) 57.

[7] Plato, *Timaeus* 70b. LCL 7 (London: Heinemann; New York: G. P. Putnam's Sons, 1929).

[8] "On Detachment" (Tractate 9).

[9] Dorothee Sölle, *Verrückt nach licht: Gedichte* (Berlin: W. Fietkau, 1984).

CHAPTER 2

[1] Thus Nikolaus Pan Bratsiotis, "שֶׁפֶנ–ΨΥΧΗ. Ein Beitrag zur Erforschung der Sprache und der Theologie der Septuaginta," *VT Suppl.* XV (1966) 58–89; for Greek ideas of the soul see also Erwin Rohde, *Psyche. The Cult of Souls and Belief in Immortality Among the Greeks* (London, Routledge and Kegan Paul, 1950).

[2] Homer, *The Iliad.* Translated by Robert Fagles (Harmondsworth: Penguin, 1990) 23.117-26 (pp. 562–63).

[3] Wilhelm Capelle, *Die Vorsokratiker. Die Fragmente und Quellenberichte* (Stuttgart: A. Kröner, 1968) 243, fr. 182.

[4] According to Cicero, *De Republica* 3.11.19.

[5] Eugen Rosenstock-Huessy, *Die Sprache des Menschengeschlechts. Eine leibhaftige Grammatik in vier Teilen.* 2 vols. (Heidelberg: L. Schneider, 1963) 1:739–810. See also idem, *Speech and Reality* (Norwich: Vt.: Argo Books, 1970) 59.

CHAPTER 3

[1] *TUAT* 2:21.

[2] Motosuke Ogushi, "Ist nur das Herz die Mitte des Menschen?" in Frank Crüsemann, Christof Hardmeier, and Rainer Kessler, eds., *Was ist der Mensch? Beiträge zur Anthropologie des Alten Testaments. H. W. Wolff zum 80. Geburtstag* (Munich: Kaiser, 1992) 42–47.

[3] Thus, for example, it is absent from Wolff's work, which is otherwise strongly oriented to concepts and etymologies: see pp. 14–15 above.

[4] Phyllis Trible, *God and the Rhetoric of Sexuality* (Philadelphia: Fortress, 1978).

[5] The translation follows that of Helen Schüngel-Straumann, "God as Mother in Hosea 11," in Athalya Brenner, ed., *A Feminist Companion to the Latter Prophets* (Sheffield: Sheffield Academic Press, 1995) 194–218, at 195–96.

[6] *TUAT* 3:453, and Othmar Keel, "Jahwe in der Rolle der Muttergottheit," *Orientierung* 53 (1989) 89–92.

[7] Anne Cameron, *Daughters of Copper Woman* (Vancouver, B.C.: Press Gang, 1981) 61–62.

CHAPTER 4

[1] Joseph Reindl, *Das Angesicht Gottes im Sprachgebrauch des Alten Testaments* (Leipzig: St. Benno Verlag, 1970).

[2] Christoph Uehlinger, "Israelite Aniconism in Context," *Biblica* 77 (1996) 540–49.

[3] A complete example from Sendshirli (in southern Turkey) is in the Near Eastern museum in Berlin.

[4] Christoph Uehlinger, "Das Image der Großmächte. Vorderasiatische Herrschaftsikonographie und Altes Testament. Assyrer, Perser, Israel," BiKi 40 (1985) 165–72.

CHAPTER 5

[1] *Le Monde diplomatique,* from the German edition for the second week of May 1997.

[2] Neil Postman, *Amusing Ourselves to Death: Public Discourse in the Age of Show Business* (New York: Viking, 1985).

[3] Chalcidius, *Comm. Tim.*, quoted from Wilhelm Capelle, ed., *Die Vorsokratiker. Die Fragmente und Quellenberichte* (Stuttgart: A. Kröner, 1968) 110–11.

[4] Translator's note: The meaning of the Hebrew adjective here is uncertain; most English Bible translators give Leah the benefit of the doubt and translate "lovely," while the German translator chooses to render the word as "weak" or "dull" *(matt)*.

[5] Silvia Schroer, *In Israel gab es Bilder. Nachrichten von darstellender Kunst im Alten Testament* (Fribourg: Universitätsverlag; Göttingen: Vandenhoeck & Ruprecht, 1987), especially 3–17; eadem, "Du sollst Dir kein Bildnis machen . . . oder: Welche Bilder verbietet das Bilderverbot?" in G. Miller and F. W. Niehl, eds., *Von Batseba – und andere Geschichten. Biblische Texte spannend ausgelegt* (Munich, 1996) 29–44.

[6] Gerhard Kittel, ἀκούω, κτλ., *TDNT* 1:216.

[7] Jesus Arambarri, *Der Wortstamm "hören" im Alten Testament. Semantik und Syntax eines hebräischen Verbs* (Stuttgart: Katholisches Bibelwerk, 1990).

[8] For the word pair "eyes/heart," see also Wilfred G. E. Watson, "The Unnoticed Word Pair 'eye(s)'//'heart,'" *ZAW* 10:1(1989) 398–408.

[9] On this see the stimulating chapter "A>yin Har>—Das Böse Auge," in Aaron R. Bodenheimer, *Verstehen heisst antworten* (Stuttgart, 1987) 207–29.

[10] *Encyclopedia Judaica* 6:997–1000.

[11] Eugen Rosenstock-Huessy, *Die Sprache des Menschengeschlechts. Eine leibhaftige Grammatik in vier Teilen.* 2 vols. (Heidelberg: L. Schneider, 1963) 1:160–61.

CHAPTER 6

[1] "The Instruction of the Vizier Ptah-hotep," *ANET* 414.

[2] Stele of Amenophis, son of Hapu, in the temple at Karnak (18th Dynasty), quoted from Hellmut Brunner, *Das Hörende Herz. Kleine Schriften zur Religions- und Geistesgeschichte Ägyptens,* edited by Wolfgang Röllig (Fribourg: Universitätsverlag; Göttingen: Vandenhoeck & Ruprecht, 1988) 4–5.

[3] Quoted from *Die Gedichte von Bertolt Brecht in einem Band* (Frankfurt: Suhrkamp, 1981) 1017.

CHAPTER 7

[1] "The Words of Ahiqar," translated by H. L. Ginsberg, *ANET* 427.

[2] Paulo Freire, *Pedagogy of the Oppressed* (New York: Herder and Herder, 1970) 87.

[3] Christoph Uehlinger, *Weltreich und "eine Rede." Eine neue Deutung der sogenannten Turmbauerzählung (Gen 11,1-9)* (Fribourg: Universitätsverlag; Göttingen: Vandenhoeck & Ruprecht, 1990).

[4] Freire, *Pedagogy of the Oppressed* 68.

[5] Othmar Keel, "Kanaanäische Sühneriten auf ägyptischen Tempelreliefs," *VT* 25 (1975) 413–69.

[6] On this see Frank Crüsemann, "Die Macht der kleinen Kinder. Ein Versuch, Psalm 8,2b.3 zu verstehen," in Frank Crüsemann, Christof Hardmeier, and Rainer Kessler, eds., *Was ist der Mensch? Beiträge zur Anthropologie des Alten Testaments. H. W. Wolff zum 80. Geburtstag* (Munich: Kaiser, 1992) 48–60.

CHAPTER 8

[1] Cf. Claude Verdan, *La Main – cet univers* (Denges, 1994), with an inventory of the newly-opened "Museum of the Hand" in Lausanne, Switzerland.

[2] Meir Malul, "More on *pahad yishaq* (Genesis XXIV 42,53) and the oath by the thigh," *VT* 35 (1985) 192–200; idem, "Touching the Sexual Organs as an Oath Ceremony in an Akkadian Letter," *VT* 37 (1987) 491–92.

[3] Othmar Keel, *The Song of Songs* (Minneapolis: Fortress, 1994) 192.

[4] For what follows see Martin Hengel, "Der Finger und die Herrschaft Gottes in Lk 11,20," in René Kieffer and Jan Bergman, eds., *La Main de Dieu. Die Hand Gottes* (Tübingen: Mohr, 1997) 87–106.

[5] For what follows see Beate Ego, "Trauer und Erlösung. Zum Motiv der Hand Gottes in 3 Hen §§68–70," in Kieffer and Bergman, eds., *La Main de Dieu. Die Hand Gottes* 171–88. The quotations are from so-called Third Enoch, which was certainly written before 900 C.E.

CHAPTER 9

[1] Othmar Keel, *The Song of Songs* (Minneapolis: Fortress, 1994) 231 and Fig. 105.

[2] Translation from Erich Zenger, *A God of Vengeance? Understanding the Psalms of Divine Wrath* (Louisville: Westminster/John Knox, 1996) 34. This book contains a great many ideas on understanding the psalms of cursing that are worthy of consideration.

[3] On this see the extensive treatment in Othmar Keel, "Sturmgott–Sonnengott–Einziger. Ein neuer Versuch, die Entstehung des judäischen Monotheismus historisch zu verstehen," *BiKi* 49 (1994a) 82–92.

[4] Max Küchler, "Die 'Füsse des Herrn' (Eus. DE 6,18). Spurensicherung des abwesenden Kyrios an Texten und Steinen als eine Aufgabe der historisch-kritischen Exegese," in idem and Christoph Uehlinger, eds., *Jerusalem. Texte, Bilder, Steine* (Fribourg: Universitätsverlag; Göttingen: Vandenhoeck & Ruprecht, 1987) 11–36, at 32–34; cf. Eusebius, *Demonstratio evangelica* 6.18.

CHAPTER 10

[1] Quoted from Othmar Keel, *The Symbolism of the Biblical World: Ancient Near Eastern Iconography and the Book of Psalms* (New York: Seabury, 1978) 67, on Figure 73.

[2] Christoph Uehlinger, "Eva als 'lebendiges Kunstwerk.' Traditionsgeschichtliches zu Gen 2,21-22(23.24) und 3,20," *BN* 43 (1988) 90–99.

Bibliography

Arambarri, Jesus. *Der Wortstamm "hören" im Alten Testament. Semantik und Syntax eines hebräischen Verbs.* SBB 20. Stuttgart: Katholisches Bibelwerk, 1990.

Assmann, Jan. *Ägypten. Theologie und Frömmigkeit einer frühen Hochkultur.* Stuttgart, Berlin, Cologne, and Mainz: Kohlhammer, 1984.

Barkay, Gabriel, and Amos Kloner. "Jerusalem Tombs from the Days of the First Temple," *Bar* 12/2 (1986) 22–39.

Barr, James. *The Semantics of Biblical Language.* London: Oxford University Press, 1961.

Barth, Karl. *Church Dogmatics.* Authorized translation by G. T. Thompson. 4 vols. in 12. London: T & T Clark, 1936–1963.

Belo, Fernando. *A Materialist Reading of the Gospel of Mark.* Translated from French by Matthew O'Connell. Maryknoll, N.Y.: Orbis, 1981.

Bergman, Jan. "Darstellungen und Vorstellungen von Götterhänden im Alten Ägypten," in C. L. Ransom, *A Late Egyptian Sarcophagus: The Metropolitan Museum of Art Bulletin* 9 (1914) 112–20.

Boardman, Sir John. *Athenian Red Figure Vases, the Classical Period: A Handbook.* New York: Thames and Hudson, 1989.

Bodenheimer, Aaron R. *Verstehen heisst antworten.* Stuttgart: Reclam, 1987.

Boehmer, Rainer Michael. *Die Entwicklung der Glyptik während der Akkad-Zeit.* Berlin: Walter de Gruyter, 1965.

Boff, Leonardo. *Sacraments of Life: Life of the Sacraments.* Translated by John Drury. Washington, D.C.: Pastoral Press, 1987.

_____. *When Theology Listens to the Poor.* Translated by Robert R. Barr. San Francisco: Harper & Row, 1988.

Böhme, Hartmut, and Gernot Böhme. *Das Andere der Vernunft: zur Entwicklung von Rationalitätsstrukturen am Beispiel Kants.* stw 542. Frankfurt: Suhrkamp, 1985.

Bomann, Thorleif. *Das hebräische Denken im Vergleich mit dem griechischen.* Göttingen: Vandenhoeck & Ruprecht, 1952; 6th ed. 1977.

Börker-Klähn, Jutta. *Altvorderasiatische Bildstelen und vergleichbare Felsreliefs.* 2 vols. Mainz: P. von Zabern, 1982.

Boucher, Stephanie. *Bronzes Romains Figurés du Musée des Beaux-Arts de Lyon.* Lyon: en dépôt aux Éditions de Boccard, Paris, 1973.

Bratsiotis, Nikolaus Pan. "בָּשָׂר–נֶפֶשׁ. Ein Beitrag zur Erforschung der Sprache und der Theologie der Septuaginta," *VT Suppl.* XV (1966) 58–89.

Brunner, Hellmut. *Das Hörende Herz. Kleine Schriften zur Religions- und Geistesgeschichte Ägyptens,* edited by Wolfgang Röllig. OBO 80. Fribourg: Universitätsverlag; Göttingen: Vandenhoeck & Ruprecht, 1988.

Brunner-Traut, Emma. *Frühformen des Erkennens. Am Beispiel Altägyptens.* Darmstadt: Wissenschaftliche Buchgesellschaft, 1990.

Bühlmann, Walter. *Vom rechten Reden und Schweigen. Studien zu Proverbien 10–31.* OBO 12. Fribourg: Universitätsverlag; Göttingen: Vandenhoeck & Ruprecht, 1976.

Bukhari, Muhammad ibn Isma'il. *Selections from the Sahih of al-Buhari.* Edited with notes by Charles C. Torrey. Semitic Study Series 6. 2nd ed. Leiden: Brill, 1948.

Cameron, Anne. *Daughters of Copper Woman.* Vancouver, B.C.: Press Gang, 1981.

Capelle, Wilhelm, ed. *Die Vorsokratiker. Die Fragmente und Quellenberichte.* Stuttgart: A. Kröner, 1968.

Catalogue of the Institute for Archaeology and Anthropology, Irbid, Jordan. Irbid, Jordan: Museum of Jordanian Heritage, 1988.

Comblin, José. *Retrieving the Human: a Christian Anthropology.* Translated from the Portuguese by Robert R. Barr. Maryknoll, N.Y.: Orbis, 1990.

Crüsemann, Frank. "Die Macht der kleinen Kinder. Ein Versuch, Psalm 8,2b.3 zu verstehen," in Crüsemann, Hardmeier, and Kessler, eds., *Was ist der Mensch?* 48–60.

Crüsemann, Frank, Christof Hardmeier, and Rainer Kessler, eds., *Was ist der Mensch? Beiträge zur Anthropologie des Alten Testaments. H. W. Wolff zum 80. Geburtstag.* Munich: Kaiser, 1992.

Das Ägyptische Museum Berlin. Mainz: P. von Zabern, 1991.

Das Ägyptische Museum Kairo (Offizieller Katalog). Mainz: P. von Zabern, 1986.

Davies, Norman de Garis. *The Temple of Hibis in El Khargeh Oasis.* New York: Metropolitan Museum of Art, 1953.

Dayagi-Mendels, Michal. *Perfumes and Cosmetics in the Ancient World.* Jerusalem: Israel Museum, 1989.

Duquoc, Christian. "Mensch/Ebenbild Gottes," *NHThG* 3:83–94.

Dürrenmatt, Friedrich. *Bilder und Zeichnungen.* Zürich: Diogenes, 1978.

Dussel, Enrique. "The Bread of the Eucharistic Celebration as a Sign of Justice in the Community," in Mary Collins and David Power, eds., *Can We Always Celebrate the Eucharist? Concilium* 152 (2/1982) 56–65.

_____. *Philosophy of Liberation.* Translated from the Spanish by Aquilina Martinez and Christine Morkovsky. Maryknoll, N.Y.: Orbis, 1985.

_____. *History and the Theology of Liberation: A Latin American Perspective.* Translated by John Drury. Maryknoll, N.Y.: Orbis, 1976.

Ego, Beate, "Trauer und Erlösung. Zum Motiv der Hand Gottes in 3 Hen §§68–70," in René Kieffer and Jan Bergman, eds., *La Main de Dieu. Die Hand Gottes.* WUNT 94. Tübingen: Mohr, 1997, 171–88 (bibliography!).

Encyclopaedia Judaica. Corrected ed. 18 vols. Jerusalem: Encyclopaedia Judaica: Keter Publishing House, 1996.

Erman, Adolf, and Hermann Ranke. *Ägypten und ägyptisches Leben im Altertum.* Tübingen: Mohr, 1923.

Fanon, Frantz. *The Wretched of the Earth.* Preface by Jean-Paul Sartre. Translated from the French by Constance Farrington. New York: Grove Press, 1965.

Freedberg, David. *The Power of Images. Studies in the History and Theory of Response.* Chicago: University of Chicago Press, 1989.

Freire, Paulo. *Pedagogy of the Oppressed.* Translated by Myra Bergman Ramos. New York: Herder and Herder, 1970.

Galling, Kurt, ed. *Biblisches Reallexikon.* HAT 1st ser. 1. 2nd ed. Tübingen: Mohr, 1977.

Gebara, Ivone. "El cuerpo, nuevo punto de partida de Teología," *Solidaridad* (Bogota) 14 (May 1990) 3–6.

González Faus, José Ignacio. "Anthropology: the Person and the Community," in Ignacio Ellacuría and Jon Sobrino, eds., *Mysterium liberationis: fundamental concepts of liberation theology.* Maryknoll, N.Y.: Orbis, 1993, 497–521.

Goodenough, Erwin R. *Jewish Symbols in the Greco-Roman Period.* 13 vols. Vol. XI/1. New York: Pantheon, 1964.

Grappe, Christian. "Main de Dieu et mains des apôtres. Réflexions à partir d'Actes 4,30 et 5,12," in René Kieffer and Jan Bergman, eds., *La Main de Dieu. Die Hand Gottes.* WUNT 94. Tübingen: Mohr, 1997, 117–34 (bibliography!).

Gressmann, Hugo, ed., *Altorientalische Texte und Bilder zum Alten Testamente.* Tübingen: J.C.B. Mohr (Paul Siebeck), 1909.

Groh, Ruth, and Dieter Groh. *Weltbild und Naturaneignung. Zur Kulturgeschichte der Natur.* stw 939. Frankfurt: Suhrkamp, 1991.

Groß, Walter. "Die Gottebenbildlichkeit des Menschen nach Gen 1,26.27 in der Diskussion des letzten Jahrzehnts," *BN* 68 (1993) 35–48.

Hengel, Martin. "Der Finger und die Herrschaft Gottes in Lk 11,20," in René Kieffer and Jan Bergman, eds., *La Main de Dieu. Die Hand Gottes.* WUNT 94. Tübingen: Mohr, 1997, 87–106 (bibliography!).

Homer, *The Iliad.* Translated by Robert Fagles. Introduction and Notes by Bernard Knox. Harmondsworth: Penguin, 1990.

Hornung, Erik. *The Ancient Egyptian Books of the Afterlife.* Translated from the German by David Lorton. Ithaca, N.Y.: Cornell University Press, 1999.

_____. *The Valley of the Kings: Horizon of Eternity.* Translated by David Warburton. New York, N.Y.: Timken Publishers, 1990.

Huber, Paul. *Hiob–Dulder oder Rebell? Byzantinische Miniaturen zum Buch Hiob in Patmos, Rom, Venedig, Sinai, Jerusalem und Athos.* Düsseldorf: Patmos, 1986.

Humbert, Paul. *Etudes sur le récit du paradis et de la chute dans la Genèse.* 1940. Mémoires de l'Université de Neuchâtel 14. Neuchâtel: Secrétariat de l'Université, 1940.

Keel, Othmar. *Die Welt der altorientalischen Bildsymbolike und das Alte Testament. Am Beispiel der Psalmen.* Zürich, Einsiedeln, and Cologne: Benziger; Neukirchen: Neukirchener Verlag, 1972 (5th ed. 1996). English: *The Symbolism of the Biblical World: Ancient Near Eastern Iconography and the Book of Psalms.* Translated by Timothy J. Hallett. New York: Seabury, 1978.

_____. "Kanaanäische Sühneriten auf ägyptischen Tempelreliefs," *VT* 25 (1975) 413–69.

_____. *Jahwe-Visionen und Siegelkunst. Eine neue Deutung der Majestätsschilderungen in Jes 6, Ez 1 und 10 und Sach 4.* SBS 84/85. Stuttgart: Katholisches Bibelwerk, 1977.

_____. "Symbolik des Fußes im Alten Testament und seiner Umwelt," *Orthopädische Praxis mit Traumatologie, Rheumatologie, physikalischer, physiotherapeutischer und balneologischer Therapie des Bewegungsapparates der Baden-Badener Reihe für ärztliche Fortbildung* 18/7 (1982) 530–38.

_____. *Deine Blicke sind Tauben. Zur Metaphorik des Hohen Liedes.* SBS 114/115. Stuttgart: Katholisches Bibelwerk, 1984.

_____. *Die Bibel mischt sich ein. Predigten und "Worte zum Sonntag."* Zürich, Einsiedeln, and Cologne: Benziger, 1984a.

_____. *The Song of Songs.* Translated by Frederick J. Gaiser. Minneapolis: Fortress, 1994.

_____. "Jahwe in der Rolle der Muttergottheit," *Orientierung* 53 (1989) 89–92.

_____. *Das Recht der Bilder gesehen zu werden. Drei Fallstudien zur Methode der Interpretation altorientalischer Bilder.* OBO 122. Fribourg: Universitätsverlag; Göttingen: Vandenhoeck & Ruprecht, 1992.

_____. *Studien zu den Stempelsiegeln aus Palästina/Israel.* Vol. 4. OBO 135. Fribourg: Universitätsverlag; Göttingen: Vandenhoeck & Ruprecht, 1994.

_____. "Sturmgott–Sonnengott–Einziger. Ein neuer Versuch, die Entstehung des judäischen Monotheismus historisch zu verstehen," *BiKi* 49 (1994a) 82–92.

_____. *Corpus der Stempelsiegel-Amulette aus Palästina/Israel. Von den Anfängen bis zur Perserzeit. Einleitung.* OBO Ser. Arch. 10. Fribourg: Universitätsverlag; Göttingen: Vandenhoeck & Ruprecht, 1995.

_____. *Die Welt der altorientalischen Bildsymbolik. Am Beispiel der Psalmen.* 5th ed. Göttingen: Vandenhoeck & Ruprecht, 1996.

Keel, Othmar, Hildi Keel-Leu, and Silvia Schroer, *Studien zu den Stempelsiegeln aus Palästina/Israel.* Vol. 2. Fribourg: Universitätsverlag; Göttingen: Vandenhoeck & Ruprecht, 1989.

Keel, Othmar, and Max Küchler. *Orte und Landschaften der Bibel: ein Handbuch und Studienreiseführer zum heiligen Land.* 5th ed. Zürich: Benziger; Göttingen: Vandenhoeck & Ruprecht, 1996.

Keel, Othmar, and Christoph Uehlinger. *Gods, Goddesses, and Images of God in Ancient Israel.* Translated by Allan W. Mahnke. Minneapolis: Fortress, 1996.

_____. *Altorientalische Miniaturkunst. Die ältesten visuellen Massenkommunikationsmittel.* 2nd ed. Fribourg: Universitätsverlag, 1996.

Kieffer, René, and Jan Bergman, eds., *La Main de Dieu. Die Hand Gottes.* WUNT 94. Tübingen: Mohr, 1997.

Kieffer, René. "La main du Père et du Fils dans le quatrième évangile," in Kieffer and Bergman, eds., *La Main de Dieu. Die Hand Gottes* (1997) 107–16 (bibliography!).

Kischkewitz, Hannelore, et al. *Nofret die Schöne. Die Frau im Alten Ägypten.* Hildesheim: Römer-und-Pelizaeus-Museum, 1985.

Kittel, Gerhard, and Gerhard Friedrich, eds. *Theological Dictionary of the New Testament.* Translated by Geoffrey W. Bromiley. 10 vols. Grand Rapids: Eerdmans, 1964–76.

Klinger, Cornelia. "Was ist und zu welchem Ende betreibt man feministische Philosophie?" in Lynn Blattmann, et al., eds., *Feministische Perspektiven in der Wissenschaft.* Zürcher Hochschulforum, vol. 21. Zürich: Zürcher Hochschulforum, 1993, 7–22.

Köhler, Ludwig. *Hebrew Man. Lectures delivered at the invitation of the University of Tübingen, December 1–16, 1952. With an appendix on justice in the gate.* Translated by Peter R. Ackroyd. London: S.C.M., 1956.

Kötting, Bernhard. "Fuß," *RAC* 8 (1972) 722–43.

Küchler, Max. "Die 'Füsse des Herrn" (Eus. DE 6,18). Spurensicherung des abwesenden Kyrios an Texten und Steinen als eine Aufgabe der historisch-kritischen Exegese," in idem and Christoph Uehlinger, eds., *Jerusalem. Texte, Bilder, Steine*. NTOA 6. Fribourg: Universitätsverlag; Göttingen: Vandenhoeck & Ruprecht, 1987, 11–36.

Landsberger, Benno, and Hayim Tadmor, "Fragments of Clay-liver Models," *IEJ* 14 (1964) 201–18.

Lepsius, Richard. *Denkmäler aus Ägypten und Äthiopien*. Berlin: Hertz, 1849–58.

Lévinas, Emmanuel. *Totality and Infinity. An Essay on Exteriority*. Translated by Alphonso Lingis. Pittsburgh: Duquesne University Press, 1969.

Libânio, João Batista. "Zur Entwicklung der Befreiungstheologie," in Raúl Fornet-Betancourt, ed., *Befreiungstheologie: Kritischer Rückblick und Perspektiven für die Zukunft 1: Bilanz der letzten 25 Jahre (1968–1993)*. Mainz: Mattias Grünewald, 1997, 31–61.

Lindemann, Gesa. "Zeichentheoretische Überlegungen zum Verhältnis von Körper und Leib," in Annette Barkhaus, M. Mayer, N. Roughley, and D. Thürnau, eds., *Identität–Leiblichkeit–Normativität. Neue Horizonte anthropologischen Denkens*. Frankfurt: Suhrkamp, 1996, 146–75.

Loud, Gordon. *The Megiddo Ivories*. Chicago: University of Chicago Press, 1939.

Macmurray, John. *The Clue to History*. London: S.C.M. Press, 1938.

Malul, Meir, "More on *pahad yishaq* (Genesis XXIV 42,53) and the oath by the thigh," *VT* 35 (1985) 192–200.

_____. "Touching the Sexual Organs as an Oath Ceremony in an Akkadian Letter," *VT* 37 (1987) 491–92.

Matthiae, Paolo, et al. *Ebla. Alle origini della civiltà urbana*. Milan: Electa, 1995.

Mittmann, Siegfried. "Das Symbol der Hand in der altorientalischen Ikonographie," in René Kieffer and Jan Bergman, eds., *La Main de Dieu. Die Hand Gottes* (1997) 19–48 (bibliography!).

_____. "Die Grabinschrift des Sängers Uriahu," *ZDPV* 97 (1981) 139–52.

Moret, Alexandre. *Du caractère religieux de la royautè pharaonique*. Annales du Musée Guimet 14. Paris: E. Leroux, 1902.

Müller-Winckler, Claudia. *Die ägyptischen Objekt-Amulette. Mit Publikation der Sammlung des Biblischen Instituts der Universität Freiburg, Schweiz, ehemals Sammlung Fouad S. Matouk*. Fribourg: Universitätsverlag; Göttingen: Vandenhoeck & Ruprecht, 1987.

Norin, Stig. "Die Hand Gottes im Alten Testament," in René Kieffer and Jan Bergman, eds., *La Main de Dieu. Die Hand Gottes* (1997) 49–64 (bibliography!).

North, Robert. "Brain and Nerve in the Biblical Outlook," *Biblica* 74 (1993) 577–97.

Ogushi, Motosuke, "Ist nur das Herz die Mitte des Menschen?" in Frank Crüsemann, Christof Hardmeier, and Rainer Kessler, eds., *Was ist der Mensch?* (1992) 42–47.

Orthmann, Winfried. *Der Alte Orient.* PKG 14. Berlin: Propyläen, 1975.

Philonenko, Marc. "Main gauche et Main droite de Dieu," in René Kieffer and Jan Bergman, eds., *La Main de Dieu. Die Hand Gottes* (1997) 135–40 (bibliography!).

Pidoux, Georges. *L'homme dans l'Ancien Testament.* Cahiers Théologiques 32. Neuchâtel: Delachaux & Niestlé, 1953.

Postman, Neil. *Amusing Ourselves to Death: Public Discourse in the Age of Show Business.* New York: Viking, 1985.

Praetorius, Ina. *Anthropologie und Frauenbild in der deutschsprachigen protestantischen Ethik seit 1949.* Gütersloh: Gerd Mohn, 1993.

Prigent, Pierre. "La main de Dieu dans l'iconographie du paléochristianisme," in René Kieffer and Jan Bergman, eds., *La Main de Dieu. Die Hand Gottes* (1997) 141–56 (bibliography!).

Pritchard, James B., ed. *Ancient Near Eastern Texts Relating to the Old Testament.* 3rd ed. with supplement. Princeton, N.J.: Princeton University Press, 1969.

Reindl, Joseph. *Das Angesicht Gottes im Sprachgebrauch des Alten Testaments.* Erfurter Theologische Studien 25. Leipzig: St. Benno Verlag, 1970.

Rohde, Erwin. *Psyche. The Cult of Souls and Belief in Immortality Among the Greeks.* London, Routledge and Kegan Paul, 1950.

Rosenstock-Huessy, Eugen. *Die Sprache des Menschengeschlechts. Eine leibhaftige Grammatik in vier Teilen.* 2 vols. Heidelberg: L. Schneider, 1963.

_____. *Speech and Reality.* Norwich, Vt.: Argo Books, 1970.

Rosenzweig, Franz. *The Star of Redemption.* Translated from the 2d ed. of 1930 by William W. Hallo. New York: Holt, Rinehart and Winston, 1971.

Rossiter, Evelyn, ed. *The Book of the Dead: Papyri of Ani, Hunefer, Anhai.* New York: Miller Graphics, 1979.

Rühlmann, G. "'Deine Feinde fallen unter deine Sohlen.' Bermerkungen zu einem altorientalischen Machtsymbol," *Wissenschaftliche Zeitschrift der Universität Halle* 20 (1971).

Russell, Letty M., and J. Shannon Clarkson, eds., *Dictionary of Feminist Theologies.* Louisville: Westminster/John Knox, 1996.

Schäfer, Heinrich. *Principles of Egyptian Art.* Edited, with an epilogue by Emma Brunner-Traut. Translated and edited, with an introduction by John Baines. Oxford: Clarendon Press, 1974.

Schenker, Adrian. "Die Tafel des Herzens," *VHN* 48 (1979) 236–50.

Schroer, Silvia. *In Israel gab es Bilder. Nachrichten von darstellender Kunst im Alten Testament.* OBO 74. Fribourg: Universitätsverlag; Göttingen: Vandenhoeck & Ruprecht, 1987.

_____. "Du sollst Dir kein Bildnis machen . . . oder: Welche Bilder verbietet das Bilderverbot?" in G. Miller and F. W. Niehl, eds., *Von Batseba – und andere Geschichten. Biblische Texte spannend ausgelegt.* Munich, 1996, 29–44.

Schroer, Silvia, and Othmar Keel. "Von den schmerzlichen Beziehungen zwischen Christentum, Judentum und kanaanäischer Religion," *Neue Wege* 88 (1994) 71–78.

Schroer, Silvia, and Thomas Staubli. "Saul, David und Jonatan eine Dreiecksgeschichte? Ein Beitrag zum Thema 'Homosexualität im Ersten Testament," *BiKi* 51 (1996) 15–22.

Schüngel-Straumann, Helen. *Die Frau am Anfang. Eva und die Folgen.* Freiburg: Herder, 1989.

_____. "God as Mother in Hosea 11," in Athalya Brenner, ed., *A Feminist Companion to the Latter Prophets.* The Feminist Companion to the Bible 8 (Sheffield: Sheffield Academic Press, 1995) 194–218, translated by Linda M. Maloney from "Gott als Mutter in Hosea 11," *ThQ* 166 (1986) 119–34.

_____. *Rûah bewegt die Welt. Gottes schöpferische Lebenskraft in der Krisenzeit des Exils.* SBS 151. Stuttgart: Katholisches Bibelwerk, 1992.

Schwertheim, Elmar. "Iupiter Dolichenus. Seine Denkmäler und seine Verehrung," in Maarten J. Vermaseren, ed., *Die Orientalischen Religionen im Römerreich.* Leiden: Brill, 1981, 193–212.

Sölle, Dorothee. *Verrückt nach licht: Gedichte.* Berlin: W. Fietkau, 1984.

Sourdive, Claude. *La main dans l'Egypte pharaonique. Recherches de morphologie structurale sur les objets égyptiens comportant une main.* Berne, Frankfurt, and New York: Peter Lang, 1984.

Stamm, J. Jakob. "Die Imago-Lehre von Karl Barth und die alttestamentliche Wissenschaft," in *Antwort. Karl Barth zum siebzigsten Geburtstag am 10 Mai 1956.* Zollikon-Zürich: Evangelischer Verlag, 1956, 84–98.

Staubli, Thomas. *Das Image der Nomaden im Alten Israel und in der Ikonographie seiner seßhaften Nachbarn.* OBO 107. Fribourg: Universitätsverlag; Göttingen: Vandenhoeck & Ruprecht, 1991.

Stendebach, Franz Josef. *Der Mensch, wie ihn Israel vor 3000 Jahren sah.* Stuttgart: Katholisches Bibelwerk, 1972.

Ströter-Bender, Jutta. *Die Muttergottes. Das Marienbild in der christlichen Kunst. Symbolik und Spiritualität.* Cologne: DuMont Buchverlag, 1992.

Trible, Phyllis. *God and the Rhetoric of Sexuality.* Overtures to Biblical Theology 2. Philadelphia: Fortress, 1978.

Uehlinger, Christoph. "Das Image der Großmächte. Vorderasiatische Herrschaftsikonographie und Altes Testament. Assyrer, Perser, Israel," *BiKi* 40 (1985) 165–72.

_____. "Eva als 'lebendiges Kunstwerk.' Traditionsgeschichtliches zu Gen 2,21-22(23.24) und 3,20," *BN* 43 (1988) 90–99.

_____. *Weltreich und "eine Rede." Eine neue Deutung der sogenannten Turmbauerzählung (Gen 11,1-9).* OBO 101. Fribourg: Universitätsverlag; Göttingen: Vandenhoeck & Ruprecht, 1990.

_____. "Israelite Aniconism in Context," *Biblica* 77 (1996) 540–49.

Verdan, Claude. *La Main – cet univers.* Denges: Editions du Verseau, 1994.

Watson, Wilfred G. E. "The Unnoticed Word Pair 'eye(s)' / / 'heart,'" *ZAW* 101 (1989) 398–408.

Weis, Adolf. *Die Madonna Platytera. Entwürf für ein Christentum als Bildoffenbarung anhand der Geschichte eines Madonnenthemas.* Königstein: Langewiesche, 1985.

Winter, Urs. *Frau und Göttin: exegetische und ikonographische Studien zum weiblichen Gottesbild im alten Israel und in dessen Umwelt.* OBO 53. Fribourg: Universitätsverlag; Göttingen: Vandenhoeck & Ruprecht, 1983.

Wolf, Walther. *Die Kunst Ägyptens. Gestalt und Geschichte.* Stuttgart: A. Kröner, 1957.

Wolff, Hans Walter. *Anthropology of the Old Testament.* Translated by Margaret Kohl. Philadelphia: Fortress, 1974.

Wörterbuch der Feministischen Theologie. Gütersloh: Gerd Mohn, 1991.

Yadin, Yigael, et al. *Hazor I.* Jerusalem: Magnes Press, Hebrew University, 1958.

Zenger, Erich. *A God of Vengeance? Understanding the Psalms of Divine Wrath.* Translated by Linda M. Maloney. Louisville: Westminster / John Knox, 1996.

_____. *Gottes bogen in den Wolken. Untersuchungen zu Komposition und Theologie der priesterschriftlichen Urgeschichte.* SBS 112. Stuttgart: Katholisches Bibelwerk, 1983.

Illustration Credits

Figure 1: Fotoarchiv Siegfried Kreuzer, Wuppertal.

Figure 2: Drawing by Hildi Keel-Leu in Othmar Keel, Hildi Keel-Leu, and Silvia Schroer, *Studien zu den Stempelsiegeln aus Palästina/Israel.* Vol. 2 (Fribourg: Universitätsverlag; Göttingen: Vandenhoeck & Ruprecht, 1989) 293, Figure 43.

Figure 3: Staatsgalerie Stuttgart, with the kind permission of Frau Duane Hanson.

Figure 4: Othmar Keel and Christoph Uehlinger, *Altorientalische Miniaturkunst. Die ältesten visuellen Massenkommunikationsmittel* (2nd ed. Fribourg: Universitätsverlag, 1996), Plate III.

Figure 5a: With the kind permission of Frau Emma Brunner-Traut.

Figure 5b: Drawing by Hildi Keel-Leu in Othmar Keel, *Symbolism of the Biblical World* 221, Figure 303.

Figure 6: Drawing by Ines Haselbach.

Figure 7: Drawing by Hildi Keel-Leu in Othmar Keel, *Symbolism of the Biblical World* 73, Figure 83.

Figure 8: Photo by Thomas Staubli.

Figure 9: Photo by Thomas Staubli. Biblisches Institut Fribourg (Switzerland).

Figures 10a-b: Photo by Thomas Staubli. Biblisches Institut Fribourg (Switzerland).

Figure 11: Othmar Keel and Christoph Uehlinger, *Altorientalische Miniaturkunst* (see Fig. 4) 107, Figure 139.

Figure 12: Druckerei St-Paul (Fribourg, Switzerland).

Figure 13: Drawing by Hildi Keel-Leu in Othmar Keel, *Symbolism of the Biblical World* 336, Figure 447.

Figure 14: Photoarchiv Biblisches Institut Fribourg, Switzerland.

Figure 15: Drawing by Ines Haselbach.

Figure 16: Othmar Keel, *Symbolism of the Biblical World* 66, Figure 72.

Figure 17: Photo by Thomas Staubli.

Figure 18: Benno Landsberger and Hayim Tadmor, "Fragments of Clay-liver Models," *IEJ* 14 (1964) 201–18, 4.

Figure 19: Drawing by Hildi Keel-Leu in Othmar Keel, *Symbolism of the Biblical World* 186, Figure 251.

Figure 20: Verlagsarchiv Langewiesche Nachf.

Figure 21: Verlagsarchiv Langewiesche Nachf.

Figure 22: Drawing by Ines Haselbach in Othmar Keel and Christoph Uehlinger, *Gods, Goddesses, and Images of God in Ancient Israel* (Minneapolis: Fortress, 1996) 75, Figure 82.

Figure 23: Drawing by Hildi Keel-Leu in Othmar Keel, Hildi Keel-Leu, and Silvia Schroer, *Studien zu den Stempelsiegeln aus Palästina/Israel.* Vol. 2 (Fribourg: Universitätsverlag; Göttingen: Vandenhoeck & Ruprecht, 1989) 47, Figure 16.

Figure 24: Drawing by Hildi Keel-Leu in Othmar Keel, *Symbolism of the Biblical World* 203, Figure 277a.

Figure 25: Photo by Richard Schmidt.

Figure 26: Othmar Keel and Christoph Uehlinger, *Altorientalische Miniaturkunst* (2nd ed.) 161.

Figure 27: Regional Museum of Idlib, Syria. Drawing by Thomas Staubli.

Figure 28: Fotoarchiv Jürgen Liepe, Berlin.

Figure 29: Museo Egizio di Torino (Turin, Italy).

Figure 30: Photo by Thomas Staubli.

Figure 31: Urs Winter, *Frau und Göttin: exegetische und ikonographische Studien zum weiblichen Gottesbild im alten Israel und in dessen Umwelt* (Fribourg: Universitätsverlag; Göttingen: Vandenhoeck & Ruprecht, 1983), Figure 308. Drawing by Zita Rüegg.

Figure 32: Photo by M. Amar and M. Greyevsky, courtesy of the Bible Lands Museum, Jerusalem.

Figure 33: With the kind permission of Erik Hornung.

Figure 34: Copyright 1979, Belser Verlag, Stuttgart.

Figure 35: Photo by Thomas Staubli. Biblisches Institute Fribourg (Switzerland).

Figure 36: Richard Lepsius, *Denkmäler aus Ägypten und Äthiopien* (Berlin: Hertz, 1849–1858).

Figure 37: Drawing by Hildi Keel-Leu in Othmar Keel, *Symbolism of the Biblical World* 319, Figure 428.

Figure 38: Museo Egizio di Torino.

Figure 39: Gordon Loud, *The Megiddo Ivories* (Chicago: University of Chicago Press, 1939).

Figure 40: Drawing by Hildi Keel-Leu in Othmar Keel, *Das Recht der Bilder gesehen zu werden. Drei Fallstudien zur Methode der Interpretation altorientalischer Bilder.* OBO 122 (Fribourg: Universitätsverlag; Göttingen: Vandenhoeck & Ruprecht, 1992) 48, Figure 3.

Figure 41: Copyright VG Bild-Kunst, Bonn, 1997.

Figure 42: Copyright Eli Jah. Photo by Thomas Staubli.

Figure 43: Copyright Michael Böhme.

Figure 44: Urs Winter, *Frau und Göttin* (see Fig. 31), Figure 301. Drawing by Zita Rüegg.

Figure 45: Photo by Thomas Staubli. Biblisches Institut Fribourg (Switzerland).

Figure 46: Hugo Gressmann, "Die Lade Jahwes und das Allerheiligste des Salomonischen Tempels" (1920), in Othmar Keel, *Jahwe-Visionen und Siegelkunst. Eine neue Deutung der Majestätsschilderungen in Jes 6, Ez 1 und 10 und Sach 4* (Stuttgart: Katholisches Bibelwerk, 1977) 270, Figure 194.

Figure 47: Photo by Thomas Staubli.

Figure 48: U.S. one-dollar bill, verso.

Figure 49: Iraq Museum, Baghdad. Drawing by Ines Haselbach.

Figures 50a-d: Photos by Richard Schmidt.

Figure 51: Bayerische Staatsbibliothek, Munich, Clm 15903, fol. 49v.

Figure 52: Photo by Thomas Staubli. Biblisches Institut Fribourg (Switzerland).

Figure 53: Giraudon, Paris.

Figure 54: Jüdisches Museum der Schweiz, Basel (Switzerland), Inv. Nr. JMS 975. Photo by Max Mathys.

Figure 55: Egyptian Museum, Cairo. Drawing by Ines Haselbach.

Figure 56: Drawing by Hildi Keel-Leu in Othmar Keel, Hildi Keel-Leu, and Silvia Schroer, *Studien zu den Stempelsiegeln aus Palästina/Israel.* Vol. 2 (See Fig. 2) 97, Figure 5.

Figure 57: Drawing by Othmar Keel, *The Song of Songs* (Minneapolis: Fortress, 1994) 42, Figure 3.

Figure 58: Drawing by Hildi Keel-Leu in Othmar Keel, *Symbolism of the Biblical World* 200, Figure 274.

Figure 59: British Museum.

Figure 60: Photo by Monika Zorn. Institut für Vor- und Frühgeschichte und Vorderasiatische Archäologie der Universität des Saarlandes, Saarbrücken, Germany.

Figure 61: Hugo Gressmann, ed., *Altorientalische Texte und Bilder zum Alten Testamente* (Tübingen: J.C.B. Mohr [Paul Siebeck], 1909).

Figure 62: Drawing by A. Aebischer in Othmar Keel, *Symbolism of the Biblical World* 96, Figure 123.

Figures 63a-b: Photo by Thomas Staubli. Biblisches Institute Fribourg (Switzerland).

Figure 64: Photo by Thomas Staubli.

Figure 65: Drawing by Siegfried Mittmann.

Figure 66: Drawing by Othmar Keel in idem, *Symbolism of the Biblical World* 321, Figure 431.

Figure 67: Drawing by Ines Haselbach in Othmar Keel, *Corpus der Stempelsiegel-Amulette aus Palästina/Israel. Von den Anfängen bis zur Perserzeit. Einleitung* (Fribourg: Universitätsverlag; Göttingen: Vandenhoeck & Ruprecht, 1995) 219, Figure 470.

Figure 68: Urs Winter, *Frau und Göttin,* Figure 366. Drawing by Zita Rüegg.

Figure 69: Ovid R. Sellers, *The Citadel of Beth-Zur: a preliminary report of the first excavation conducted by the Presbyterian Theological Seminary, Chicago, and the American School of Oriental Research, Jerusalem, in 1931 at Khirbat et Tubeiqa* (Philadelphia: Westminster, 1933).

Figure 70: Wolfram Nagel, *Altorientalisches Kunsthandwerk* (Berlin: De Gruyter, 1963).

Figure 71: Drawing by Hildi Keel-Leu in Othmar Keel, *Symbolism of the Biblical World* 263, Figure 353.

Figure 72: Drawing by Siegfried Mittmann.

Figure 73: Stephanie Boucher, *Bronzes romains figurés du Musée des beaux-arts de Lyon* (Lyon: en dépôt aux Éditions de Boccard, Paris, 1973).

Figure 74: Erwin R. Goodenough, *Jewish Symbols in the Greco-Roman Period.* 13 vols. Vol. XI/1 (New York: Pantheon, 1964).

Figure 75: Drawing by Hildi Keel-Leu in Othmar Keel, *Symbolism of the Biblical World* 287, Figure 389a.

Figure 76: Norman de Garis Davies, *The Temple of Hibis in El Khargeh Oasis* (New York: Metropolitan Museum of Art, 1953).

Figure 77a: Photo by Thomas Staubli. Biblisches Institut Fribourg (Switzerland).

Figure 77b: Photoarchiv Biblisches Institut Fribourg (Switzerland).

Figure 78: Photoarchiv Biblisches Institut Fribourg (Switzerland).

Figure 79: Photo by Thomas Hartmann. Archiv Jüdisches Museum der Schweiz, Basel (Switzerland), JMS 81.

Figure 80: Photo by Thomas Staubli.

Figure 81: Photographie Palphot, Herzlia, Israel.

Figure 82: Drawing by Zita Rüegg in Othmar Keel, *Das Recht der Bilder* 119, Figure 69.

Figure 83: Drawing by Hildi Keel-Leu in Othmar Keel, *Symbolism of the Biblical World* 210, Figure 288.

Figure 84: C. L. Ransom, "Late Egyptian Sarcophagus," *Metropolitan Museum of Art Bulletin* 9 (1914).

Figure 85: Photo by Silvia Schroer.

Figure 86: Westfälisches Landesmuseum für Kunst und Kulturgeschichte, Münster (Germany).

Figure 87: Silvia Schroer, 1987.

Figure 88: Photo by Thomas Staubli.

Figure 89: Bethlehem Mission Immensee.

Figure 90: With the kind permission of Professor Barthel Hrouda.

Figure 91: G. Rühlmann, "'Deine Feinde fallen unter deine Sohlen.' Bermerkungen zu einem altorientalischen Machtsymbol," *Wissenschaftliche Zeitschrift der Universität Halle* 20 (1971).

Figure 92: Drawing by Hildi Keel-Leu in Othmar Keel, *Symbolism of the Biblical World* 254, Figure 341 (detail).

Figure 93: Drawing by Hildi Keel-Leu in Othmar Keel, *Symbolism of the Biblical World* 241, Figure 327.

Figure 94: Drawing by Othmar Keel in idem, *Symbolism of the Biblical World* 59, Figure 60.

Figure 95: Photoarchiv Biblisches Institut Fribourg (Switzerland).

Figure 96: Photo by Thomas Staubli.

Figure 97: Michal Dayagi-Mendels, *Perfumes and Cosmetics in the Ancient World* (Jerusalem: Israel Museum, 1989).

Figure 98: Biblioteca Nationale Marciana; cf. Paul Huber, *Hiob–Dulder oder Rebell? Byzantinische Miniaturen zum Buch Hiob in Patmos, Rom, Venedig, Sinai, Jerusalem und Athos* (Düsseldorf: Patmos, 1986).

Figure 99: Photo by Thomas Staubli.

Figure 100: Photo by Thomas Staubli.

Figures 101a-b: Photos by Thomas Staubli.

Figure 102: Bernisches Historisches Museum, Bern (Switzerland). Photo by Stefan Rebsamen.

Figure 103: Urs Winter, *Frau und Göttin*, Figure 33. Drawing by Zita Rüegg.

Figure 104: Drawing by Hildi Keel-Leu in Othmar Keel, *Symbolism of the Biblical World* 76, Figure 88.

Figure 105: Bildarchiv Preußischer Kulturbesitz.

Figure 106: Friedrich Dürrenmatt, *Bilder und Zeichnungen* (Zürich: Diogenes, 1978).

Figure 107: Archaeological Museum of Amman. Drawing by Ines Haselbach.

Figure 108: Erwin R. Goodenough, *Jewish Symbols in the Greco-Roman Period.*

Figure 109: Bethlehem Mission Immensee.

Figure 110: With the kind permission of Klaus Staeck, Heidelberg (Germany).

Index of Scripture

The italicized page numbers refer to biblical passages quoted verbatim in the text. The page numbers followed by an asterisk [*] indicate references mentioned in the captions of illustrations.